Law, Society, Policy series

Series Editor: **Rosie Harding**,
University of Birmingham

Law, Society, Policy offers an outlet for high quality, socio-legal research monographs and edited collections with the potential for policy impact.

Also available in the series:

Unsettling Apologies:
Critical Writings on Apology from South Africa
Edited by **Melanie Judge** and **Dee Smythe**

Death, Family and the Law:
The Contemporary Inquest in Context
By **Edward Kirton-Darling**

Deprivation of Liberty in the Shadows of the Institution
By **Lucy Series**

Women, Precarious Work and Care:
The Failure of Family-friendly Rights
By **Emily Grabham**

Pandemic Legalities:
Legal Responses to COVID-19 – Justice and Social Responsibility
Edited by **Dave Cowan** and **Ann Mumford**

Forthcoming:

Polygamy, Policy and Postcolonialism in English Marriage Law:
A Critical Feminist Analysis
By **Zainab Batul Naqvi**

Egalitarian Digital Privacy:
Image Based Abuse and Beyond
By **Tsachi Keren-Paz**

Find out more at
bristoluniversitypress.co.uk/law-society-policy

Forthcoming:

Observing Justice:
Digital Transparency, Openness and Accountability in Criminal Courts
By **Judith Townend** and **Lucy Welsh**

Children's Voices, Family Disputes and Child-Inclusive Mediation:
The Right to Be Heard
By **Anne Barlow** and **Jan Ewing**

Adult Social Care Law and Policy:
Lessons from the Pandemic
By **Jean McHale** and **Laura Noszlopy**

Sex Worker Rights Activism and the Politics of Rights:
Within and against the Law
By **Katie Cruz**

International advisory board:

Find out more at

bristoluniversitypress.co.uk/law-society-policy

INTERSEX EMBODIMENT

Legal Frameworks beyond Identity and Disorder

Fae Garland and Mitchell Travis

BRISTOL
UNIVERSITY
PRESS

First published in Great Britain in 2023 by

Bristol University Press
University of Bristol
1–9 Old Park Hill
Bristol
BS2 8BB
UK
t: +44 (0)117 374 6645
e: bup-info@bristol.ac.uk

Details of international sales and distribution partners are available at bristoluniversitypress.co.uk

British Library Cataloguing in Publication Data
A catalogue record for this book is available from the British Library

ISBN 978-1-5292-1737-7 hardcover
ISBN 978-1-5292-1738-4 ePub
ISBN 978-1-5292-1739-1 ePdf

Cover design: Andrew Corbett
Front cover image: Shutterstock/Space-kraft
Bristol University Press uses environmentally responsible print partners.
Printed and bound in Great Britain by CPI Group (UK) Ltd, Croydon, CR0 4YY

FSC
www.fsc.org
MIX
Paper | Supporting responsible forestry
FSC® C013604

For Maggie, Arrietty, Arthur and Diggory

Contents

Series Editor's Preface

The Law, Society, Policy series publishes high-quality, socio-legal research monographs and edited collections with the potential for policy impact. Cutting across the traditional divides of legal scholarship, Law, Society, Policy offers an interdisciplinary, policy engaged approach to socio-legal research which explores law in its social and political contexts with a particular focus on the place of law in everyday life.

The series seeks to take an explicitly society-first view of socio-legal studies, with a focus on the ways that law shapes social life, and the constitutive nature of law and society. International in scope, engaging with domestic, international and global legal and regulatory frameworks, texts in the Law, Society, Policy series engage with the full range of socio-legal topics and themes.

List of Abbreviations

ACT	Australian Capital Territory
AIS	Androgen Insensitivity Syndrome
CAH	Congenital Adrenal Hyperplasia
CAIS	Complete Androgen Insensitivity Syndrome
DSD	disorders of sex development
FOI	freedom of information
GIGESC Act	Gender Identity, Gender Expression and Sex Characteristics Act 2015
IHRA	Intersex Human Rights Australia
ILGA-Europe	International Lesbian, Gay, Bi-Sexual, Transsexual and Intersex Association
ISNA	Intersex Society of North America
LGBT	Lesbian, Gay, Bisexual and Transgender
MDT	multidisciplinary team
NHS	National Health Service
OGR	optimal gender rearing
OII Australia	Organisation Intersex International Australia
PAIS	Partial Androgen Insensitivity Syndrome
SOGISC	Sexual Orientation, Gender Identity and Sex Characteristics
TLC	Transgender Lobby Coalition

Acknowledgements

This book represents a body of work that we have been thinking around, working on and talking about for nearly a decade. Consequently, we have a huge volume of people to thank. The short version is that we are extremely grateful to everyone who has contributed their thoughts, insights, warmth and generosity to this project. The long version we set out below.

Most importantly, we would like to thank every single intersex person and organization who has engaged with us and our academic pursuits. This book would not have been possible without those individuals who gave up their time to talk with us, educate us as well as take part in our empirical projects. We are also thankful to those individuals and activists who have dedicated their lives and careers towards the pursuit of social justice. Your work is inspirational and we owe much of our own personal and professional growth to you. Significantly, the changes that we have seen in law and policy across the globe (and on which the book is based) is largely attributable to your relentless hard work.

Second, we are also specifically grateful to Imogen Jones. In a work in progress session that Mitch was giving in early 2020 Imogen asked if the paper was 'really' about embodiment. Wondering if it was about embodiment and whether we could exemplify it through intersex led to the creation of this book. Which just goes to show how a question can get out of hand – particularly when you're trapped in the house during lockdown.

Third, we must thank the funders that gave us the grants to do this research in the first place. The Socio-Legal Studies Association (SLSA) generously gave us a research grant in 2014 on 'Exploring different legal constructions of intersex'. The SLSA has continued to be a generative space to present our research over the past decade and we encourage socio-legal scholars to become involved with this excellent charity. Similarly, we must thank the British Academy for their 2019 funding for the project 'Evaluating the Operation of Malta's Gender Identity, Gender Expression and Sex Characteristics Act 2015: To What Extent Has It Enhanced the Bodily Integrity of Intersex Infants?', which informs some of the data in Chapter 5.

Fourth, we have to thank the people who took time to read the draft versions of our chapters: Flora Renz, Jens Thielen, Kay Lalor, Craig

Newbery-Jones, Ed Horowicz, David Griffiths and Peter Hegarty. Their comments and perceptions were hugely useful for ensuring the quality of this work. If anything is incorrect, however, then it is quite frankly their fault.

Additionally, we would like to thank members of the Centre for Law and Social Justice at the University of Leeds and the Centre of Social Ethics and Policy at the University of Manchester. In particular, Margot Brazier, Bev Clough, Neil Cobb, Sarah Devaney, Chris Dietz, Simona Giordano, Jen Hendry, Amanda Keeling, Sam Lewis, Amrita Mukherjee, Craig Purshouse and Julie Wallbank have all given feedback on various forms of this project over the years. We would also like to give special mention to Annie Austin, who has sadly passed during the writing of this project but whose invaluable insights and wisdom continue to inform our work.

While this project was not related to our PhDs, it is hugely indebted to the support of our PhD supervisors Michael Thomson, Marie Fox, Anne Barlow and Liz Trinder. Michael generously read an earlier version of Chapter 1 while Anne read multiple grant drafts. All of you have given so much to supporting our careers, for which we are forever grateful.

We also have to thank our colleagues working in the interdisciplinary field of intersex studies including Pieter Cannoot, Morgan Carpenter, Daniela Crocetti, Georgiann Davis, David Griffiths, Charlotte Jones, Lih-Meh Liao, Surya Monro, Tanya Ni Mhuirthile and Sharon Preves, all of whom fill us with joy every time they speak.

At Bristol University Press we must thank Becky Taylor, Phylicia Ulibarri-Eglite, Freya Trand, Helen Davis and Emma Cook. Special thanks to Rosie Harding and the anonymous reviewer whose editorial skills ensured that the monograph flowed as a whole.

Finally, we would like to thank our parents, siblings, friends and families: Fayme, Nick, Arrietty, Diggory, Maggie and Arthur. If we hadn't been trapped with you in lockdown this book would have been finished 36.2 per cent quicker. Much love.

1

Introduction: Embodying Intersex

This book engages with intersex people to understand the choices they have and the impositions they face in predominantly Western societies. As part of this, the main question the book asks is 'What is intersex?' To answer this question, we rely heavily on the accounts of intersex people gathered from our own empirical research while also paying close attention to the ways in which differing forms of regulation construct, shape and stifle the possibilities and experiences of being intersex. As a result, this book investigates the conditions that frame our understanding of the body and that create the institutional conditions under which intersex bodies can emerge or are denied. In doing so, it is attentive to the ways in which institutions create norms that give value to certain types of body and devalue others. This interrogation leads to three further questions: How has the idea of intersex been mobilized? Who has utilized the idea of being intersex? And for what purposes?

The examples that we focus on highlight the ways in which intersex is often interpreted through narrow institutional frameworks. In this book, each chapter focuses on a different regulatory framework. Chapter 2 considers medical guidelines and the pathologization of intersex; Chapter 3 explores the use of third markers on official documentation to recognizing intersex embodiment as non-binary; Chapter 4 critically examines the way in which intersex is constructed as LGBT, particularly through the institutional inclusion of intersex within equality laws; Chapter 5 considers legal rights-based frameworks which have prohibited non-therapeutic medical interventions; and, finally, Chapter 6 examines intersex within the context of psychosocial care. Each of these frameworks have been selected as they are important examples of regulative and institutional control over intersex people which offer an attempt to help intersex people but in doing so create the terms and conditions that frame what intersex is and what it can be. Moreover, the book demonstrates the power of medicine in determining how intersex has been understood and the difficulties that other conceptualizations have had in challenging narratives of disorder.

Some of the alternative narratives have faced difficulties because of the lack of ontological resonance with intersex people, but others – that have been informed by the experiences of intersex people – have also faced resistance because they clash with medical understandings of the intersex body.

At its core, then, this book uncovers the different ways in which intersex has been constructed to better understand the intersex experience. Acknowledging the systems in which intersex people are imbricated and reliant upon helps to better understand their legal needs and requirements. Ultimately, the book aims to influence discussions as to what intersex 'is' to better accommodate intersex people into policy decisions, legislation and clinical and juridical decision making.

To examine the impact of these differing frameworks we draw upon interviews with intersex rights activists. As the book explores, often law and regulation fail to engage with the lived experience and testimony of intersex people. This results in frameworks which are at best ineffectual and at worst harmful for intersex embodied people. Our broader aim therefore is to recentre policy-based discussions around the voices of intersex people by reflecting on first-hand accounts of lived experiences within these frameworks. Importantly, we wish to resituate intersex within academic research so that academia takes account for its role in informing the shape of these regulatory frameworks (Monro et al, 2021). There is a real need for academics and research bodies to directly engage with, listen to and provide platforms for intersex voices (Monro et al, 2021). This may also provide a 'case study' to make a larger point regarding law, law-making and marginalized groups and the need for law and policy to be informed by the experiences of these groups.

Our views on intersex inclusion are largely informed by our experience of working with intersex people. The main empirical project, which forms the basis of much of our discussion, allowed for much self-reflection and personal, and professional, growth. It was funded by the Socio-Legal Studies' Small Grant scheme and, as Chapter 3 explores, our initial project sought to interview intersex people about the then recent developments in Germany and Australia relating to third gender markers and anti-discrimination legislation. However, some of the first participants we asked to interview rejected our request on the basis that we had failed to mention non-therapeutic medical interventions. Largely informed by misconceptions within academia, it transpired that we had little insight into the main issues affecting intersex communities: bodily integrity. It was only through engaging with individuals, listening and reflecting that we became aware of long-standing misunderstandings relating to intersex and we were able to reframe our research to be more inclusive of the topics intersex people wanted to discuss with us, and it enabled us to talk to intersex people about the developments in Malta in 2015. The latter part of this chapter sets out the methodology in detail.

During the course of our interviews, we developed a good rapport with our respondents and the research that came from the project was warmly received by many in the intersex community. It has proved to be an important tool in many intersex organizations' submissions to government. Building on this, we have continued to forge links with intersex communities. We are actively involved in several intersex organizations. We continue to attend conferences, workshops and gatherings on intersex issues. Through our work, we have developed many personal as well as professional relationships and we care about the issues that we are researching. While we do not, to our knowledge, have variations in sex characteristics ourselves, we feel capable of talking about the issues raised at least in the context of legal rights and regulation. That said, we do not talk *for* intersex communities but hope to continue to talk *with* them in the dialogue we have developed over the last decade. Our value to the intersex community has always been our knowledge of law and legal theory and the way our academic credentials and privilege have been able to open doors to policy makers, lawyers and, to a much more limited extent, healthcare professionals. In return, our work, and this particular project, is entirely indebted to the intersex people have who have taken their time and energy to speak with us and to (re-)educate us on what it means to be intersex.

The next part of this chapter highlights the different and contradictory definitions of intersex within which we situate our project. We then set out the theoretical lens of embodiment that we use to critically unpack these different frameworks. Finally, this chapter sets out the methodological and ethical details of the empirical projects that we draw upon to give insight into the lived experience of intersex embodied people.

Conceptualizing intersex

Before moving to conceptualize intersex more fully, it is first useful to consider some intersex variations in order to illustrate how intersex bodies develop. One intersex variation is Androgen Insensitivity Syndrome (AIS) which affects people with XY (typically male) chromosomes. People with AIS have a mutation in the AR gene that prevents them from processing androgen. Consequently, people with AIS develop female genitalia either fully (in the case of Complete Androgen Insensitivity Syndrome (CAIS)) or partially (in the case of Partial Androgen Insensitivity Syndrome (PAIS)). Despite the presence of female genitalia, people with AIS do not develop female reproductive organs such as a uterus or womb although they will develop breasts. Cases of PAIS are normally discovered during early childhood due to the presence of atypical genitalia. Cases of CAIS are usually discovered later in adolescence when the person does not menstruate. In both instances, individuals are typically raised as female. Congenital Adrenal

Hyperplasia (CAH) is another intersex variation. CAH affects the adrenal glands and the child's ability to produce cortisol. CAH can affect people with both XY and XX chromosomes. Children with salt-wasting CAH present a number of symptoms soon after birth, including heart rhythm abnormalities, dehydration and vomiting. Children will also have low levels of salt (hyponatraemia) and low levels of sugar (hypoglycaemia). These deficiencies can be fatal and so require immediate medical intervention. XX infants with CAH are also often born with atypical genitalia due to 'virilization' and this can lead to confusion as to sex. Typically, XX children with CAH are raised as girls. Another variation is Klinefelter Syndrome. This variation occurs where individuals have an extra X chromosome resulting in them being XXY. Many people with this variation do not realize that they have it although it can result in slow muscle growth, reduced facial and body hair, a small penis and testicles, enlarged breasts (gynaecomastia) and infertility. People with Klinefelter Syndrome are typically raised as boys.

We take the time to outline some of these variations as they highlight the interactions between chromosomal, hormonal, reproductive and genital conceptions of sex and their potential influence on social understandings of gender. These variations are all very different and require differing levels of medical and social support. These are also just a selection of the different intersex variations that exist – there are over 40 variations recognized internationally (Jones et al, 2016). A significant proportion of people are born with an intersex variation. The most commonly cited incidence rate is 1.7 per cent of all live births, an estimate made by Anne Fausto-Sterling and her research team (Fausto-Sterling, 2000; see also Blackless et al, 2000). Fausto-Sterling notes that this is an order of magnitude estimate taken from a wide variety of populations. This figure has been replicated in many academic and activist texts including the Council of Europe's *Human Rights and Intersex People: Issue Paper* (2015). Some scholars, like Sax, have criticized this figure for over inclusion, contesting the intersex status of genetic variations like Klinefelter Syndrome (XXY) and Turner Syndrome (X), and other variations including late-onset adrenal hyperplasia and vaginal agenisis (Sax, 2002). Excluding these variances, Sax estimated a lower figure of 0.018 per cent (Sax, 2002). A recent paper by Garland et al (2021), however, which conducted freedom of information (FOI) requests to all NHS trusts in England, estimated an incidence rate closer to 0.03 per cent based on referral rates of infants to multi-disciplinary teams specializing in intersex variations and treatment.[1] As Garland et al (2021) note, however, it is likely to be significantly more given that that only 75 per cent of NHS trusts responded to the question on incidence rates; healthcare typically uses an extremely narrow conceptualization of 'disorders of sex development'

[1] Although with some qualifiers that mean it could be as high as 0.05 per cent.

(DSD) leaving out variations like hypospadias (see below); and most intersex variations do not present themselves at birth and thus are likely not to have been captured by this FOI request.

The huge variety of intersex variations, the chances of them being undiscovered or 'invisiblized' by the medical profession and the lack of cultural awareness of intersex issues has meant that definitions of intersex are difficult. Moreover, intersex people themselves are divided (or sometimes ambivalent) about the terminologies that are relevant to them (Lundberg, Hegarty and Roen, 2018). Parents of children with intersex variations and children with intersex variations are more likely to prefer diagnostic and descriptive terminology when discussing their variations; however, they also note the need for different language needs in different situations (Lundberg, Hegarty and Roen, 2018). Intersex may be a more useful term than DSD or variation-specific terminology when attempting to achieve legal and political change (Lundberg, Hegarty and Roen, 2018). When using diagnostic and syndrome-specific descriptive terminology, intersex variations are difficult to extract from medical approaches and the treatments and practices that have been associated with such approaches depriving them of their political salience (Davis, 2015). Using the term intersex allows for a greater discussion of the social and cultural understandings that are associated with the term, including issues around sex and gender. Even when using the same term, however, the way that term is mobilized or understood can be variable. To illustrate this, we now outline three contrasting definitions of intersex taken from a community retreat, the European Parliament and a consensus statement of leading endocrinologists. We will then discuss some of the commonalities and difficulties raised by these statements.

In 2017, after a community retreat, leading figures in the international intersex community released a joint consensus statement known as the Darlington Statement. In that document, they answered the question 'What is intersex?' by noting that:

> Intersex people are born with physical or biological sex characteristics (such as sexual anatomy, reproductive organs, hormonal patterns and/ or chromosomal patterns) that are more diverse than stereotypical definitions for male or female bodies. For some people these traits are apparent prenatally or at birth, while for others they emerge later in life, often at puberty. … We recognise our diverse histories and use the word intersex inclusively, and acknowledging our right to self-determination. (Darlington Statement, 2017)

The first European Parliamentary Resolution on Intersex *Promoting the Human Rights of and Eliminating Discrimination against Intersex People* (Resolution 2191) defined intersex in 2017 as:

> people … born with biological sex characteristics that do not fit societal norms or medical definitions of what makes a person male or female. Sometimes a person's intersex status is detected at birth; sometimes it only becomes apparent later in life, notably during puberty. Despite the wide variety of situations concerned, the majority of intersex people are physically healthy. Only a few suffer from medical conditions that put their health at risk.

Contrastingly, the 'Consensus Statement on Management of Intersex Disorders', a document created in 2006 by leading endocrinologists who worked closely with intersex variances, noted that:

> Advances in identification of molecular genetic causes of abnormal sex with heightened awareness of ethical issues and patient advocacy concerns necessitate a re-examination of nomenclature. Terms such as intersex, pseudohermaphroditism, hermaphroditism, sex reversal, and gender based diagnostic labels are particularly controversial. These terms are perceived as potentially pejorative by patients, and can be confusing to practitioners and parents alike. The term 'disorders of sex development' (DSD) is proposed, as defined by congenital conditions in which development of chromosomal, gonadal, or anatomical sex is atypical. (Lee et al, 2006)[2]

Here we are presented with a number of differing conceptions of intersex. We take the time to quote these in full, as they present alternating accounts of what intersex *is* and what it *can be*. The struggles over who defines intersex cut to the very core of our arguments in this book. Terminology and definitions utilized by different institutions and actors are indicative of the ways in which intersex has been, and ought to be, regulated. These differing approaches are key to the arguments that we shall go on to outline in due course as they justify the ways in which institutional bodies have responded to intersex and enfolded it within their institutional practices.

---

[2] In turn, in the 2016 follow-up to the 2006 consensus statement 'Global Disorders of Sex Development Update since 2006: Perceptions, Approach and Care' this definition largely persisted: 'The broad term DSD, adopted at the Consensus Conference, has been generally accepted by many medical professionals but not universally by some patient and support groups. ... Positive aspects about having a term include providing for scientific accuracy within a biological and medical context, bona fide genetic disorders facilitate access to healthcare and insurance, an umbrella classification helps in generating comprehensive and integrated models of care, at the same time it avoids confusion by not overlapping with conditions such as transgender, gender dysphoria and homosexuality, and it provides a framework for knowledge accumulation and research funding' (Lee et al, 2016).

Before that, however, there are certain commonalities within the definitions that we shall now turn to.

All these definitions discuss the congenital nature of intersex. One shared aspect of intersex, therefore, is its innateness. Intersex people are born rather than made, and it is not a 'choice' one can make about their own body or an identity that one can develop. This is backed by references to 'chromosomes', 'hormonal differences', 'gonadal' development and reproductive parts that can include the aesthetic appearance of the genitals. All these biological markers are used to identify intersex as something material; a corporeal bodily experience that we can verify through technological advancement. Whereas in the past, these variances may have gone unnoticed, in contemporary times technology has given us greater tools to understand the complexity of sex characteristics.

As such, these biological markers are not used in isolation. All of them are discussed in reference to sex. In particular, intersex is understood as something that, in part, ruptures the sex binary in some way. The materiality of the intersex body leads it to exist between stereotypical definitions of male and female[3] or to 'mix'[4] the previously separate spheres of male and female. The medical definition similarly refers to 'atypical' or 'abnormal' sex. These variations are categorized as 'disorders' of sex development implying that these bodies are abnormal and in need of medical fixing. This commitment to the gender binary is prevalent in the definition of intersex given in the medical consensus statement. The medical profession notes the controversial nature of understanding intersex in terms of 'sex reversal, and gender based diagnostic labels'. For those involved in the creation of the consensus statement at least, the maintenance of the gender binary continues to have significant value. This has been confirmed in subsequent research interviewing medical professionals involved in the care of intersex people where 'anxieties about gender' continue to be a key reason for performing non-therapeutic medical interventions (Liao et al, 2019). Of course, these anxieties do not come from the child themselves, but from parents and medical professionals (Timmermans et al, 2019). While technology has given us the tools to identify variance in sex characteristics, the same technologies have been used to rigidly police the sex binary ensuring that intersex people are (surgically) allocated to the categories of male and female. Intersex, therefore, is imbricated in real and important ways within the sex binary. Medical interventions on intersex bodies, in addition, have formed an integral aspect of intersex campaigning over the last 30 years,

3 Intersex Human Rights Australia (2017) 'Darlington Statement' [online] https://ihra.org.au/darlington-statement/ [Accessed 13 September 2022].

4 Council of Europe (2017) *Promoting the Human Rights of and Eliminating Discrimination against Intersex People* (Resolution 2191) [online] www.assembly.coe.int/nw/xml/XRef/Xref-XML2HTML-en.asp?fileid=20057&lang=en [Accessed 13 September 2022].

making it difficult to separate *definitions* of intersex from the *challenges* they face – namely early non-consensual non-therapeutic medical interventions.

Another point of definitional agreement throughout the documents, and as we raised earlier, is that intersex (or DSD) is an umbrella term. Intersex is capable of housing a significant range of variations often based on medical understandings of disorder and diagnoses. Although these variations have their basis in medicine, the inclusion and exclusions of different groups has been (and remains) markedly political (Griffiths, 2018a). We will turn to these political contestations in due course, as the question of 'who is intersex' is dependent, to a large degree, on the political motivations of the institution or organization that is asking the question. By way of example though, hypospadias and cryptorchidism (one or more undescended testes) are not routinely understood as DSD unless the individual presents proximal (severe) hypospadias (where the urethra opening is at the bottom of the shaft or on the scrotum) and it is accompanied with cryptorchidism. Instead, hypospadias is more likely to be understood as a symptom, rather than a condition, or syndrome, per se. Accordingly, hypospadias is not always medicalized and, importantly, there is current evidence of disagreements among UK DSD clinicians as to whether and why they should be subject to medical intervention (Roen and Hegarty, 2018: 981). The 2006 international consensus statement notes however that if 'all congenital genital anomalies are considered, including cryptorchidism and hypospadias, the rate may be as high as 1:200 to 1:300' (Lee et al, 2016: 159). For many intersex groups, therefore, including hypospadias as an intersex trait is politically important, as its relative commonality in people assigned male vastly inflates the statistics for incidence rates of intersex throughout the population, giving their campaign work greater legitimacy. At the same time, excluding hypospadias from medical definitions of intersex continues the idea that intersex variations (and the surgeries that have been performed on them) are relatively rare occurrences. Who is included under the umbrella of intersex, therefore, is not apolitical.

To date, the medical profession has played the biggest role in defining what intersex is. Healthcare is important as it is both the initial and the primary vehicle through which intersex is understood and its meaning conveyed. The concept of intersex is thus anchored within this medicalized narrative both societally and on an individual level for the intersex person. Chapter 2 explores how, since at least the 19th century, medical professionals have played an important role in identifying, cataloguing and understanding the intersex experience. However, the governing logics of the medical profession have also dictated a need to 'cure' or 'fix' intersex people. While intersex variations are predominantly benign (Zillén et al, 2017: 42), the treatment paradigms for intersex have largely been informed through reference to salt-wasting CAH. As previously noted, this variation, if left untreated, can lead to the death of the child. As a result, intersex treatments have been understood through a lens of 'emergency' (Garland and Travis, 2020b). This approach has ensured that a range of variations which lead to the appearance of atypical internal and external reproductive organs are dealt with as medical emergencies. The appearance of this type of atypicality creates a 'social emergency' which, taken with the medical emergency, has legitimized medical practitioners performing aesthetic 'normalizing' interventions to ensure that the child is raised within the gender binary often before the child is old enough to consent (including but not limited to genitoplasties, gonadectomies, clitorectomies and labioplasties). The reality is that the emergency hormonal treatments used for life-threatening salt-wasting CAH are wholly separate from genital normalizing interventions (Garland et al, 2021). Thus, experiences of healthcare have been particularly problematic for many intersex people, who have long contended that such a medical framing "changes something which is a natural variation of humanity through to illness" (Respondent 7).

The efficacy of these medical interventions has been heavily questioned as these interventions directly lead to a range of negative consequences that we will outline in more detail in Chapters 2 and 5. As a result, intersex surgeries have been criticized by international civil society. Since 2009, there have been over 40 reprimands from UN Treaty bodies and a total of 23 states have been condemned for allowing unnecessary and non-consensual medical interventions to take place (Garland et al, 2022). In 2013, for example, the Special Rapporteur on torture and other cruel, inhuman or degrading treatment or punishment, Juan E. Méndez, conceptualized intersex surgeries as a form of torture and pushed for 'States to repeal any law allowing intrusive and irreversible treatments, including forced genital-normalizing surgery, involuntary sterilization, unethical experimentation, medical display ... when enforced or administered without the free and informed consent of the person concerned' (2013: 23).

While there are a number of commonalities, therefore, between the definitions outlined at the start of this section, the disagreements between them are profound. Although the Council of Europe claims that 'the majority of intersex people are physically healthy', many intersex people do have ongoing dependencies on the medical profession, including access to hormone treatment, monitoring for cancer risks and psychosocial care. That being said, some of the dependencies that intersex people face are *caused* by previous medical interventions (Liao, Tacconelli et al, 2010; Engberg et al, 2016; Schweizer et al, 2017). Removing an individual's gonads, for example, will result in the individual requiring life-long hormone replacement therapy. Healthcare, therefore, is a particularly fraught area within intersex studies particularly where it has attempted to place intersex solely within its own jurisdictional remit – outside the scope of legal regulation (Davis, 2015;

Garland and Travis, 2020a). Consequently, the consensus statement's shift away from intersex to DSD has been met with some suspicion. As the term intersex has increasingly gained legal and cultural recognition, it has achieved greater success in highlighting the damage that has been done to intersex people by medical professionals. Law, therefore, has been increasingly used in opposition to medicine in this field rather than as a complementary force where both are utilized for the benefit of intersex people.

Intersex activists have been prominent in highlighting these issues since the early 1990s.[5] Law and policy makers, however, have been slow to react with no meaningful legal change for intersex people in the West until 2013. As we will discuss in more detail in the next section and for the substantive chapters of the book, different jurisdictions have taken markedly different approaches to intersex each of which has a framing effect on what intersex is understood to be and how intersex people ought to be treated. These approaches include Germany's understanding of intersex as a 'third gender' since 2013 – where intersex was conceptualized as outside the gender binary until the 'true sex' could be determined. In Australia, since 2013, intersex has been included in federal law primarily through the use of anti-discrimination legislation. The intersex experience in Australia has primarily been understood by policy makers as an LGBT issue – downplaying the specific needs of intersex people. Finally, some jurisdictions have taken the step of prohibiting intersex surgeries through legislation. This was first seen in Malta in 2015, Portugal in 2018, Germany in 2021, and, as of 2022, Greece, with more jurisdictions likely to follow suit. These legislative responses send an important symbolic message to intersex people and their relationship with the medical profession. Nonetheless, these prohibitions have suffered from several problems in their practical effects, which we discuss in Chapter 5. Each of these different legislative responses to intersex tell us something important about how intersex is culturally and legally understood. However, for the most part they have yet to disrupt the dominance of the medical profession's paradigmatic construction of intersex. Before mapping out these chapters more fully, we now turn to the theoretical lens that informs this book.

Embodiment

These conceptual differences and discrepancies lead us to discuss how intersex people are embodied. Embodiment, for us, can be understood as the ways in which bodies are constructed through material, discursive and institutional frameworks. To this end, this book understands the term

[5] The Intersex Society of North America for example, started in 1993.

embodiment to encompass the material experience of the body and its relationships with both discourse and institutions. Michael Thomson has recently defined legal embodiment as 'the role that legal discourses and practices play, when we experience our embodiment at the intersection of discourses and institutional practices that are specific to time and place' (Thomson, 2022). Utilizing such a lens allows for an interrogation of the ways in which law, medicine, culture and society, conceive of, construct and create our bodies. This is particularly useful when analyzing the embodiment of those complicated traditional sex or gender categories as it highlights the difficulties in decoupling material experiences from their legal and medical contexts (Fox and Thomson, 2017; Travis, 2019). Moreover, such an analysis shows how crucial institutions have been in harming those deemed to be non-normative. Intersex people provide an important account of embodiment. How can we understand the experience of being intersex without reference to law or healthcare? What would intersex be if it had not been understood as a medical issue in need of 'fixing'? Or had been given greater legal or cultural value? How does the societal dominance of the gender binary influence the apparently 'neutral' and 'objective' lens of medicine?

In the legal and jurisprudential imagination, law is often constructed as disembodied (Naffine, 2003, 2009; Grear, 2006, 2007; Fineman, 2008, 2012, 2014 2017, 2020; Travis, 2014; Leiboff, 2015; Fox and Thomson, 2017; Dietz et al, 2020). As a result, law is primarily understood as an institution that is not dependent on bodies for meaning and that has little effect on bodies themselves. As Sean Mulcahy has noted: 'it would seem that legal scholars … are predisposed to conceiving of law as non-bodily' (Mulcahy, 2021: 126) and Mariett Leiboff has observed: 'We in law prefer to imagine that our bodies are surplus to the real task of our endeavours with word and thought' (Leiboff, 2015: 84). This book challenges this disembodied understanding of law in four respects. First, it recognizes that the body has a material presence. This corporeality is essential to understanding the corporeal effects that law (and other institutions) can have on individuals. Focusing on materiality, therefore, is an important aspect of any socially just approach to law or jurisprudence. Second, and relatedly, law is lived through the body. Legal meaning is derived from bodily encounters (Shaw, 2021) and is always contingent upon the body (Mulcahy, 2021). Third, and crucially for the purposes of this book, bodies can only be understood in relation to law (and other institutions such as healthcare). The meaning of bodies is always contextual and so law plays an important shaping effect in how bodies are recognized and produced (Thomson, 2007). Finally, these institutional constructions do not take place in a vacuum; bodies are also co-constituted through cultural and societal knowledges or practices of discourse. These can sometimes conflict with institutional constructions of the body but, for the most part, they do not. In combination, these four elements underscore what we would understand as legal embodiment.

We start with the premise, therefore, that the materiality of the body is important to the study of law. As Joshua Shaw notes, if we only study the discursive aspects of jurisprudence then 'This reifies law as disembodied and discursive, and neglects the complex ways through which law is produced in, and matters to social life' (Shaw, 2021: 86–7). This corporeal focus is essential for our consideration of intersex issues. The congenital nature of intersex variances requires careful attention in terms of shaping what intersex *is*. In addition, the nature of the physical and psychological harms that intersex people face prevents us from considering these issues in a purely abstract (or disembodied) manner. Our interviews and our subsequent relationships with the intersex community highlight the need for a focus on a distinctly *bodily* conception of law and social justice.

This understanding highlights that law is lived through the body. As Mulchay notes: 'law is deeply concerned with and embedded in the body as an embodied practice. The human body is a body of law. Law is inscribed and embedded in the body. It regulates bodily movements just as it is brought into practice through movement' (Mulcahy, 2021: 19–20). Bodies, as a consequence, are not just regulated by law but actually 'enact the lived experience of law' (Shaw, 2021: 73). Legal meaning, therefore, is created through the process of bodily interaction, with their environments and other bodies. As Shaw continues: 'legal meaning is made and remade through bodies coming together, combining and separating, and coming back together, through circulations of affect' (Shaw, 2021: 85). Law is, as a consequence, always contingent upon the body for its reproduction and maintenance. As Peter Goodrich notes: 'the law is staged through the body' (Goodrich, 2000: 242).

Perhaps more importantly than law's contingency on the body, however, is the shaping effect that law has on the body itself. Law does not simply 'categorize' different types of body but actively produces them. This construction of the body is one of the central premises of this book and will be outlined in more detail later in this section. For the time being, however, it is important to note that the body is always produced through institutional contexts. As Shaw notes: 'our bodies are always expressed in the specificity of place as bodies-in-ecologies, leaky and porous and fluid, affecting one another' (Shaw, 2020: 12). Similarly, as Michael Thomson has recently argued: 'Understanding and challenging the socio-political foundations of embodiment requires that the "natural" realm be subject to critical scrutiny, particularly in addressing how gender becomes naturalized within biological and biomedical discourses which then become embedded in law' (Thomson, 2022). Tanzil Chowdhury (2020), in his recent consideration of temporality, the legal subject and law, has urged us to consider how (criminal) legal judgments produce particular types of legal subject. Specifically, he highlights how judges' temporal framings have the power to consider the legal subject over the life course or offer a mere 'snap shot' of the individual. These temporal framings:

> produce the paradigmatic, deracinated, liberal legal subject by 'transcending' particular types of pasts that would otherwise render the situatedness and constituted nature of the legal subject visible. This is possible given the features of spatial temporality (divisible, uniform, juxtaposed and simultaneous) that enables the framing out and elision of these other types of pasts. (Chowdhury, 2020: 76–77)

For Chowdhury, then, law plays a vital element in the production of the body and the types of materiality that it renders intelligible. This applies not only to bodies but also to the acts that bodies perform. Institutions are a crucial locus for how acts are understood. As Sabrina Giliani writes: 'we cannot describe pain, injury, and death as properties of the body, any body, but rather as discursive-material enactments that arrange the body in relation to other bodies, matter, and ideas so that they become sense-able to the rest of us' (Giliani, 2020: 3). As she continues: 'Violence is not criminal at the moment it takes place, when one body connects with another. There is no inherent truth as to the lawfulness or unlawfulness of violence apart from the pronouncement of judges and juries' (Giliani, 2020: 11). These discussions of violence have important ramifications for our understandings of non-consensual non-therapeutic surgical interventions on the bodies of children. It is only the institutional coding of the medical profession (and the deference shown by law) that stops these practices from being understood as harmful (Thomson, 2007; Earp et al, 2017; Fox and Thomson, 2017; Fox et al, 2020; Garland and Travis, 2020a). Law constructs bodies, but also the ways in which harm to those bodies can be rendered authentic. Law's silence also has an important shaping effect on bodies.

Law is not the only institution that co-constitutes the body, however. The body is also co-produced through other institutions (such as healthcare: Dietz, 2018; Dietz et al, 2020; Garland and Travis, 2020a) as well as cultural and social understandings of the body. As Giliani notes: '"human" agency is deeply embedded within the environment in which bodies act, and those environments are themselves organised on the basis of prevailing ideas about the ways our bodies can and should act' (Giliani, 2021: 186). Moss and Dyck similarly highlight that the body 'consists of the context, discursive inscriptions, material inscriptions, the biological, and the physiological' (Moss and Dyck, 1999: 388–9). Likewise, Elizabeth Grosz outlines that we cannot think of the body outside of its historical, cultural and social context (Grosz, 1994). For intersex people, historical and cultural accounts of their bodies are often missing, fragmentary, invisiblized, exoticized or made spectacular. Tracing these accounts of the intersex body and situating intersex people within these histories is an important element of this book. Moreover, we hope that this book's engagement with the voices of intersex people provides space to challenge these histories, highlighting their contested and problematic nature from the perspectives of intersex people themselves. Nonetheless, as we shall outline, cultural and social discourse around intersex has framed the experience of intersex into particular legal directions. These various framings inform the way in which we have structured the book.

Chapter 2 starts by exploring how, since the 19th century, in the West intersex bodies have become inextricably imbricated within healthcare. The increasing pathologization throughout the 20th century and technological advancements gave medical professionals the ability to 'correct' intersex bodies in infancy. The result of such early 'correction' was to erase intersex at the cultural and institutional levels: while intersex had also been provided for in various laws as early as the 13th century, by the 19th century it had all but disappeared. This has meant that medicine has largely shaped understandings and responses to intersex, defining it in terms of disorder and surrounding treatment with shame and secrecy. However, even in legal systems where intersex is not explicitly mentioned, it is important to note that law's silence is not apolitical. Instead, it frames medical regulation as appropriate and, in some cases, inevitable. Where legal intervention has taken place, it has constructed the terms under which intersex can be understood – in some instances problematically framing out key questions raised by the intersex community themselves. Paternalistic attitudes, the young ages of the intersex people involved and a lack of longitudinal data collection have further contributed to healthcare's framing of intersex as a disorder in need of 'fixing'. As a result, healthcare has routinely used non-therapeutic surgical interventions to physically shape the intersex child's body to fit the gender binary. Medical responses to intersex have centred on attempts to erase intersex as a political space or an identity and instead focused on protecting the gender binary and heteronormative society. For the medical profession intersex is a disorder to be fixed.

Operating under a different lens, intersex communities, at least to begin with, found community and support within the LGBT community in part for shared experiences stemming from homophobia and transphobia. In the present, the ready inclusion of intersex within many LGBT organizations and policy approaches has met with wide ranging responses from the (divided) intersex communities. While some have expressed support for such inclusion and increased visibility, others have raised concerns about the ways in which funding has been taken away from intersex priorities and the concomitant concealing of intersex voices. More recently, some intersex organizations and activists have fundamental disagreements with being included in LGBT policy and spaces as they feel a distancing from LGBT concerns. For these organizations, this type of inclusion has led to a profound confusion about intersex framing it as a sexuality, or a choice. While we may take issue with such concerns, it is certainly true that intersex is often included within policy making under the auspices of LGBT issues, and this is explored in Chapters 3 and 4. This, in itself, has been a type of institutional and discursive framing that plays out in important ways in relation to issues around campaigns for the recognition of third genders and anti-discrimination. In many ways this backdrop has increased parental desire for their children to undergo non-therapeutic medical interventions as it means they might avoid their child being associated with LGBT issues (Carpenter, 2018). These discursive practices, therefore, have an important framing effect on what intersex is. Indeed, there is a duality in the way in which intersex embodiment is constructed as LGBT. On the one hand, an LGBT framing allows for a 'queer' reading of intersex embodiment that troubles institutions with their indeterminacy; on the other hand many readings of intersex embodiment as LGBT (particularly by the state) lens are in fact homonormative in nature.

Chapter 3 problematizes the contemporary ways in which third markers have been used to recognize intersex embodiment as synonymous with non-binary identity by law, academia and policy makers. While historically intersex was depicted as a place-holder for binary sex, the use of third markers has become the most prevalent way in which intersex has become recognized in non-medical realms and ultimately frames intersex as located outside binary conceptions of sex and gender. This epistemological shift from place-holder to non-binary has been heavily influenced by feminist and queer writings in this area, as well as the growing visibility and organization of the non-binary trans movement. In many jurisdictions, this non-binary conception of intersex has been cemented within law and policy for adults and children alike: Australia permits adult individuals to have third markers on identity documents such as passports, and jurisdictions like Chile and Germany have included third markers on birth certificates for children with indeterminate sex. Chapter 3 critically considers the lived impact of this non-binary framing and examines whether acknowledging intersex in this way has challenged the medical power imbalance that has dominated the 20th century. The chapter particularly focuses on Germany, which, in 2013, became the first European state to recognize third markers on birth certificates. Section 22 of the Gesetz zur Änderung personenstandsrechtlicher Vorschriften (Personenstandsrechts-Änderungsgesetz—PStRÄndG) 2013 states that 'If the child can be assigned to neither the female nor the male sex, then the child must be entered into the register of births without such a specification.' In Germany, third markers have been created to allow intersex infants and children to be understood as outside of the binary. While the legislation was originally envisioned as allowing parents and clinicians more time to fully understand the child's sex, in practice the opposite has occurred. In a study, Amnesty International found that parents were quicker and more likely to prioritize surgery in order to avoid children being placed into a third gender category (2017). Again, we perhaps see approaches that might be more suitable for the wider LGBT community (the disruption of the gender binary) failing to challenge the medical understanding of what intersex is and thus inadequately supporting the practical issues that intersex people face (Carpenter, 2018). Ultimately, we problematize the depiction of intersex embodiment as non-binary identity when followed through into policy development and legislation.

Legal responses to intersex have been slow to develop and diverse in their approaches. Intersex people have been included in equality law in a range of different countries in a variety of different ways. Australia, for example, has specific anti-discrimination legislation, which recognizes intersex status as a protected characteristic (alongside characteristics generally appertained/imputed to persons of intersex status). Australia's broad approach not only prohibits discrimination on the grounds of intersex status, but also on the grounds of characteristics generally imputed to intersex individuals.[6] This conceptualization may allow for a richer variety of possibilities in the formation and defence of legal identity without recourse to medical 'proof' of intersex status. Additionally, some Australian states have allowed birth certificates to omit sex where the sex of a child has been indeterminate,[7] and in 2003 Australia was the first country to allow 'X' markers on passports for intersex individuals. This was expanded in 2011 to include all those of indeterminate sex. Other jurisdictions have also attempted to include intersex under these types of legislative initiatives with mixed success – we outline these in Chapter 4. These approaches have a tendency to frame intersex embodiment as LGBT, thus justifying the state's placement of intersex issues within the pre-existing homonormative paradigm of LGBT issues. In Australia, for example, despite myriad contributions, petitions and commentaries to the contrary, the government failed to challenge the behaviours and practices of medical practitioners in this area. This was demonstrated in the 2016 case of *Re Carla* where, despite the introduction of Australia's federal anti-discrimination law in 2013, the Australian Family Court ruled that parents can consent to cosmetic genital surgery on their

6 Section 5C Sex Discrimination Act 1984.

7 This occurred in Victoria and New South Wales. For example, in *Norrie v NSW Registrar of Births, Deaths and Marriages* [2013] NSWCA 145 the High Court of New South Wales held that the registrar could record the sex of someone as 'non-specific' rather than 'male' or 'female'. Here, the court acknowledged that ' [n]ot all human beings can be classified by sex as either male or female'.

infant, even where it results in sterilization, without having to seek the court's approval.[8]

While non-binary and LGBT-based conceptualizations of intersex embodiment have allowed the medical profession to remain almost entirely unregulated, Chapter 5 sets out how some jurisdictions are introducing regulatory regimes which appear to directly challenge clinical practice. These jurisdictions therefore offer a new regulatory framework for intersex, premised on the notion of bodily integrity. Notably, in 2015, Malta took a different rights-based approach to intersex. Malta specifically outlaws unnecessary sex assignment treatment and surgery on intersex minors. Section 15 of the Gender Identity, Gender Expression and Sex Characteristics Act 2015 (GIGESC Act) prohibits sex reassignment surgery and surgical interventions on sex characteristics until the individual is able to make an informed choice. Section 15(2) recognizes there may be some exceptional circumstances whereby surgery takes place where a minor is unable to provide consent but states that 'medical intervention which is driven by social factors without the consent of the individual concerned will be in violation of this Act'. Additionally, Malta permits individuals to self-determine their own gender identity (without medical evidence);[9] extends its 'hate crime' legislation to incorporate sex characteristics and also sets out sex characteristics as a protected category within its anti-discrimination law.[10] After representatives of the Maltese government attended an international intersex conference where the use of testimony and experience was prominent, the government created legislation prohibiting the use of non-therapeutic medical interventions on intersex children. This approach has been influential with several other countries considering similar proposals.[11] This method is important, as it has placed the framing of intersex outside of simplistic medical and LGBT accounts. As a result, it offers the potential for significant new framings of what intersex is *and* what intersex can be. Unfortunately, and as we will discuss in Chapter 5, the reality of the intersex experience in Malta has not lived up to the promise of the 2015 legislation. This is predominantly due to an implementation gap where law is yet to

8 [2016] Fam CA 7. See Carpenter (2016) for a critique of the case.

9 Section 4 GIGESC allows individuals to change official records of their gender without any requiring medical evidence.

10 Section 4 GIGESC allows individuals to request change in first name and recorded gender to reflect self-determined gender. No medical evidence is necessary. Section 10(3) amends article 83B of the Maltese Criminal Code to include offences motivated on the basis of gender expression and sex characteristics. Section 14 GIGESC prohibits discrimination on the basis of sexual orientation, gender identity, gender expression and sex characteristics.

11 Iceland, Portugal and England and Wales have all cited this legislation as a possible outcome of reform proposals. Germany and Portugal have both introduced legislation which prohibits non-consensual surgeries on intersex children.

affect clinical practice and disrupt the disordered narrative. This serves as an important reminder of how resistant to change the medical framework is. For legal reform to be effective, the legal position must specifically engage with clinical thinking and, at present, the rhetoric of harm for intersex bodies is not reflected in the same way by clinicians. Consequently, the effects of legislative prohibition are limited. In important respects then, the institutional frameworks of Malta have been capable of lapsing back into medical and LGBT framings of intersex embodiment and are yet to deliver an alternative understanding of intersex. We also note, however, the dynamism of social change and highlight its ongoing and continuous nature rather than being a shift between two static points. State buy-in *after* law reform takes place is as important as that needed to introduce new legislation to disrupt medical embodiment.

Chapter 6 explores how psychosocial care within healthcare is an essential element of reframing intersex embodiment and care for intersex people away from paradigmatic medical narratives 'fixing' a 'disorder' and towards supporting a person. While some strands of psychosocial care have begun to step up to the task of ensuring that intersex people and their families are fully supported and empowered to make decisions, the bulk of psychological approaches in this area is rooted in the medical taxonomy of Chapter 2. As a result, biomedical accounts of intersex as a 'disorder' remain prominent in psychosocial provision, with care often been offered as an 'afterthought' or an 'emotional repository'. Such approaches fail to consider the transformative effect that psychosocial care can have on the intersex experience. Such care can offer support to ensure that intersex people and their families are equipped to deal with the *structural* challenges that they will face as a result of their intersex variations. This chapter thus looks to highlight promising examples of psychosocial care with the potential to ensure that intersex people and their families are able to flourish. These transformative approaches construct intersex as a contextual, situated and dependent individual in need of support in order to overcome the structural issues that they will be faced with. These insights are read alongside shifts in legal theory towards notions of 'embodied integrity' in order to outline a thicker conception of legal embodiment.

The embodiment of intersex people, therefore, encapsulates all these different institutional and discursive accounts. As a result, intersex people can find themselves being constituted completely differently in distinctive institutional contexts. The substantive chapters of the book, therefore, aim to outline and address some of these contexts in more detail. This will allow us to outline the diverse ways in which intersex people have been constructed and enables us to evaluate how capable these definitions are of protecting or empowering intersex people based on their needs and desires.

The empirical projects

As we highlighted at the start of the book, we believe that there is an absence of intersex voice within much of the writings and reflections on intersex needs and experiences. As Chapter 3 explores, academia is, in part, responsible for many of the misunderstandings that have problematically been translated into law and policy which is in significant need of redressing. We believe it is imperative that individuals writing about intersex engage with the intersex communities and make space for their voices (Monro et al, 2021). To offer real insight into the impact of law, policy and healthcare, our critique of these regimes is informed by empirical engagement with intersex rights activists. We stress, however, that our approach and our critique is not definitive. Neither author has a variation in sex characteristic that we are aware of, both are white, cis, heterosexual English-speaking academics located in the Global North: we are conscious of the privilege that we have that has enabled us to occupy this space and produce this work. Consequently, while this project offers some insight into these issues, it is important that the reader remains aware of our biases and our lack of lived experience as intersex: we do not speak for these communities. Our hope is that our project will shed some insight onto these issues and aid discussions that push for change in legal and healthcare systems.

The empirical work that we draw upon originates from two projects. The first project was a qualitative study funded by the SLSA that critically explored different legal responses designed to enhance intersex rights. Our methodology consisted of 17 semi-structured interviews with intersex rights activists between 2014 and 2016.[12] Given the sensitive nature of this topic, the authors ensured that the study complied with the SLSA's ethical guidelines.[13] The authors also asked individuals from two independent intersex organizations (one UK-based, the other US-based) to scrutinize the interview schedule and information sheets.

While the 'how many interviews' question is pervasive in qualitative research, we believe that, although this sample is small, it is nevertheless appropriate for the purposes of our study, providing rich insight into the comparative impact of different regulatory approaches towards

[12] Fourteen were interviewed by telephone, three submitted electronic email responses either because of resources or because they did not want to be interviewed. One telephone interview involved two of the respondents who wanted to be interviewed together. This term 'activists' also includes support groups and education workers. For a comprehensive explanation of the ways in which activism has developed in the intersex movement see Davis (2015), Dreger and Herndon (2009).

[13] For the Socio Legal Studies Association's Statement of Principles Guiding Empirical Research see www.slsa.ac.uk/images/slsadownloads/ethicalstatement/slsa%20ethics%20statement%20_final_%5B1%5D.pdf (accessed 9 June 2016).

intersex.[14] Our sample was never intended to be a statistical representation of the intersex population. Rather we sought to interview intersex rights activists who were actively campaigning for legal reform on international as well as national platforms. Their specific experience and expertise meant that these individuals would have a comprehensive understanding of global developments in intersex rights making it possible to discuss comparative regulatory approaches. Consequently, we purposively recruited our respondents by identifying individuals through intersex rights organizational websites and snowballing whereby we asked individuals for potential organizations/contacts to approach.[15] As a result, our sample comprises individuals from a range of states with differing regulatory approaches towards intersex embodiment (at the time of the study) including: non-responsive states like the UK, Denmark and Sweden, which entirely defer to the medical narrative of intersex embodiment; status-based states like Australia, Germany and recently the US, which equate intersex embodiment to non-binary or LGBT through a range of equality laws and third markers to encapsulate intersex; and holistic responses such as in Malta, Portugal and, most recently, Germany, which adopt a rights-based framework that actively attempts to distort the disordered narrative. The broad range of cultural, social and legal backgrounds meant that respondents were able to reflect broadly on their own national contexts and other approaches in different jurisdictions.

Given the size of the project, our choice of sampling and inevitable time and financial limitations, it is important to note that this project does not, and cannot, claim to offer a definitive truth on the lived experiences of intersex embodied people and their experiences of law. Notably, there are core voices which were absent from this project, particularly those from the Global South. While this exclusion was not conscious, it speaks to some of key attributes/privileges that the research required individuals to have to be able to participate in the project. Chiefly, all respondents had to speak English. Moreover, they needed to have access to certain resources such as time and technology, which inevitably limited many smaller groups and individuals from participating. As one organization responded to our request for an interview: "We have to decline giving telephone interviews; we have no employed staff and work with [their charity] on our spare time as best we can." Consequently, our respondents came from states with sufficient

---

14 Indeed, there is no 'minimum' threshold for viable qualitative research projects (Garland, 2014). See also Baker and Edward (2012).

15 While snowballing has its limitations, it is effective to find unattainable, or hard to reach populations making it particularly useful in the context of intersex (see, for example, Naderifar et al (2017)).

structures in place to facilitate discussions about law and legal reform. These states were 'welfarist' with strong civil societies, the concept of a 'rule of law' and which had 'moved from legal frameworks based on sexual "wrongs" to ones based on sexual rights' (Garland and Travis, 2018: n 92). This has inevitably influenced the data produced. Moreover, we view our interview data to be a co-constructed account of certain experiences of law. The data produced and presented here is therefore not an objective truth or fact nor is the 'interview' an impartial research instrument. Rather we share Talmy's (2011) belief that the interview is a social practice producing data which are 'representations or accounts' of certain realities, facts and experiences. As Holstein and Gubrium (1995: 70) note, the respondent 'not only holds facts and details of experience, but, in the very process of offering them up for response, constructively adds to, takes away from, and transforms [them]'. The active nature of the interview also means that we acknowledge the role that we, and our aforementioned privileges, have played in producing data. While semi-structured interviews allow for a certain degree of consistency among participants, questions have ultimately been devised by the researcher. Therefore, our epistemological, ontological and methodological premises – our interpretative framework (Guba, 1990) – has structured the interview process. Moreover, semi-structured interviews have flexibility for dialogue between researcher and respondent, each being able to ask further questions and make observations on the basis of the other's comments. Our interviews were interactive communications with intersex rights activists and thus the data produced were the product of working together. We also believe that this approach has significantly amounted to our personal and professional growth.

Our process of data analysis; how we interpret the data and ultimately decide what is and is not to be included; was similarly influenced by our positionality. To structure out approach, we used thematic analysis according to the six-step process outlined by Braun and Clarke (2006). This involved us familiarizing ourselves with the content of the anonymized transcriptions, generating initial codes, searching for themes, reviewing, defining and naming themes. Specifically, theoretical thematic analysis was used, generating themes by analysing the data through the lens of embodiment. Our analysis thus explored how far these differing types of legal governance framed the experience of being intersex and examined the individual's understanding of and relationship with law. The data for the purposes of this book have been organized around the differing ways in which intersex is embodied: medical embodiment; intersex embodiment as synonymous with non-binary; LBGT embodiment; holistic; and reframing intersex embodiment through psychosocial care. Consequently, this project is testimony to the researcher's influence on the production of qualitative knowledge. When we initially wrote up our findings for the SLSA back in 2018, we did not use the theme of embodiment to analyze the data. Rather, this book has allowed us to revisit our findings, reanalyze and rediscover important themes contained within the data. This also speaks to the importance of sharing raw data among academics where ethically appropriate. Not only does this reduce the pressure placed on individuals within a small community who are continually invited to interview, but alternative approaches and perspectives may bring to light important observations that could remain overlooked (Jones, 2022).

Our second project is ongoing. At the time of writing this book, the authors are in the middle of a project funded by the British Academy to explore the impact of Malta's GIGESC Act on the provision of healthcare for intersex people. This Act was passed *during* the data collection phase of our SLSA project, and was consistently referred to as a 'beacon of good practice' by our respondents. Consequently, we later sought funding to assess, seven years on, how effectively GIGESC had been at meeting the needs of the intersex community. To do so, we are conducting semi-structured interviews with intersex rights/gender policy experts from Malta, intersex individuals; parents/carers of intersex infants; and healthcare practitioners specializing in intersex variations and/or gender identity. Individuals are similarly being approached through websites/publication materials/workplace and contacted via email and also snowballing. This research complied with the British Academy's and University of Manchester's ethical guidelines (applying to its ethics committee) as well as complying with Malta's Health Ethics Committee.

At the time of completing this manuscript, we have interviewed four individuals as part of the British Academy project. Consequently, the sample produced is very small and thus there are limits to the claims we can make; we remain careful not to overgeneralize, particularly when we do not have the views of the intersex community. However, there is still inherent value in qualitative research with small samples especially as our respondents 'embody and represent meaningful experience-structure links' (Crouch and McKenzie, 2006: 493). The respondents interviewed all have knowledge regarding the impact and/or reception to Malta's GIGESC and thus their interviews provide deep insight into the (lack of) the Act. Such insight is of considerable importance for those considering similar reforms in other jurisdictions. We reiterate our caveat, however, that these interviews only produce representations or accounts of culturally and geographically specific experiences. Nevertheless, the data contains invaluable perception into the way in which GIGESC has been received and the relationship between legal reform and social change that underpins our reflections, particularly in Chapter 5. We identify our British Academy respondents as 'BA Respondent X' and SLSA respondents simply as 'Respondent X'. We have analyzed the British Academy data using theoretical thematic analysis (as set out above), specifically using ‘embodiment’ as our theoretical framing. Lastly, but most importantly, we forever remain indebted to these individuals who have taken the time to speak with us and shed some insight into the lived experience of intersex people. We hope the work is useful in achieving their goals and ambitions.

2

Medical Embodiment: Intersex as Disorder

Introduction

Accounts of legal embodiment are impoverished if they do not explore the ways in which other institutions contribute to our understanding of bodies. In the case of intersex embodiment, medicine is crucial for understanding how intersex people have been framed – indeed, and as we shall outline, medical accounts offer the paradigmatic account of intersex embodiment. Medicine investigates and explores the materiality of the body and presents its results as objective and value free. However, medicine's reporting back of this materiality is not neutral and is always, itself, immured in culture (Butler, 1993; Fausto-Sterling, 2000). Part of the importance of medicine's contribution to embodiment has been its ability to establish itself as the primary way through which we must understand the body. Medicine sets the discursive framing of the subject and constructs the parameters of laws engagement (Travis, 2015, 2019; Dietz, 2018; Garland and Travis, 2020a).

As noted in the previous chapter embodiment is a multifaceted concept. Nonetheless, the most prevalent construction of intersex embodiment is that of disorder. The medical profession has been instrumental in the determination of how intersex embodiment is understood and, consequently, how it ought to be managed. Most notably, this framing of intersex embodiment has presented intersex variations as in need of 'fixing' and accordingly justified the use of early non-therapeutic surgical and hormonal interventions before intersex people can meaningfully consent, delimiting the presence of law as unnecessary in this area. In recent years, an increasing number of intersex rights advocates and international bodies have sought to challenge this medical framing, contending that it unnecessarily and problematically pathologizes intersex people and their experiences. However, efforts have thus far been largely unsuccessful and, despite international condemnation from the UN (Garland et al, 2022), the disorder narrative of intersex embodiment prevails within contemporary medical practice and wider society. The power and influence of the medical profession has meant that their authority to determine what intersex *is* has, for the most part, gone legally and politically unchallenged.

This chapter examines what it means to understand intersex embodiment through a lens of disorder and how this view has developed over time. Given that our interviews focused on contemporary legal approaches post 2013, very few of our respondents from both our SLSA and British Academy projects reflected on the way in which medical approaches towards intersex embodiment developed over time. Consequently, we refer to our empirical findings at the end of the chapter to highlight the problematic nature of medical embodiment and the difficulties that activists have faced in challenging this narrative. Before this, however, we must first trace *how* medical embodiment has become the predominant construction of intersex. To begin with, this chapter explores how medicine became the dominant construction of intersex, most notably as medicine became professionalized during the latter half of the 19th century. While medical practitioners have always had an interest in understanding the 'phenomena' of intersex, changes in the authority of medical practitioners to understand the body and the technological advancements that allowed for such determinations resulted in the increasing trend of 'clinically treating' intersex individuals, chiefly adults. Throughout the first half of the 20th century, however, medical interventions on intersex infants and children became more commonplace and, after the work of John Money, part of the standard practice of treating, organizing and understanding children's bodies.

After setting out the medico-historical backdrop to medicine's jurisdictional claims over intersex, the chapter moves on to examine how medicine currently constructs intersex as a disorder. We set out how the term 'disorder' remains rooted in 19th-century heteronormative understandings of 'sex' and fears linked to deviance from normative expectations of behaviour. Here we also draw on contemporary research as well as our empirical work to demonstrate how the language of disorder reifies medical jurisdiction over intersex bodies and helps to depoliticize intersex issues. The use of the term disorder has been important for justifying non-therapeutic 'normalizing' surgeries on intersex children. Next, we turn to our empirical projects to set out how the medical framework has been problematized by intersex rights campaigners. All our respondents strongly objected to these non-consensual procedures and ranked challenging medical authority over the determination of what intersex *is* (and thus how intersex bodies ought to be treated) as a central goal for intersex activism. Finally, the chapter uses the empirical work to consider the different ways in which this medical framework is being challenged, but demonstrates just how entrenched medical embodiment of intersex is, making it difficult to instigate real change within medico-political spheres. Ultimately, this chapter outlines the medical embodiment of intersex, foregrounding later chapters that challenge or reify this approach through law.

How intersex became medically embodied

19th century: medical profession as the sole authority in determining sex

This section traces *how* medical embodiment has become the predominant construction of intersex. Prior to the professionalization of medicine in the 19th century, medical practitioners were not the sole authority in terms of determining an individual's sex (Daston and Park, 1985; Dreger, 1998; Greenberg, 2012; Mak, 2012; Sudai, 2021). Communal understandings of an individual's sex would have played an important part in determining their 'true sex' (Sudai, 2021). However, with the professionalization of medicine came a greater prestige on scientific determinations of sex along with the newfound power and authority of the medical professional (Foucault, 1980; Dreger, 1998). At this time, determination of sex as binary was becoming increasingly important as it had important implications for gender roles and status (Foucault, 1980; Dreger, 1998; Holmes, 2008a; Malatino, 2019). At least in the West, the idea of non-binary gender or a fluidity between the genders was unintelligible (Butler, 1993). Through determinations of sex, medical practitioners (and others) were concerned with the moral social fabric and notably the prevention of same-sex relationships (Foucault, 1980; Dreger, 1998; Holmes, 2008a; Malatino, 2019). Unlike modern understandings, distinctions between sex, gender and sexuality were not self-evident and were largely understood to be one and the same (Dreger, 1998: 10). Where sex was unclear, it was important to society that it was quickly and effectively resolved. This was paramount because the binary nature of sex was foundational to the ways in which status and roles were observed within the 19th century. Aspects of legal embodiment such as marriage, inheritance, guardianship, the holding of political office and the ability to bear witness were all determined by sex. Life opportunities available to people (particularly in terms of the gendered nature of work) were attributed through sex and thus individuals sought medical and legal assistance where their 'dubious' sex threatened their status and contingent 'rights' (Mak, 2012). Moreover, the policing of same-sex relations can be seen to be an overriding concern for medical practitioners of the time. As Holmes notes: 'The beginnings of separate definitions of heterosexuality and homosexuality hinged upon the development of politically motivated research especially committed to developing a theory of the incommensurability of two *opposite* sexes, male and female' (Holmes, 2008a: 35).

Against this gendered and heteronormative backdrop, the 19th century saw a concerted effort to 'identify, classify, and characterize' a whole range of sex and sexual variations (Foucault, 1980: xii). Indeed, Feder associates the modernization of Western European medicine in the late 19th century with 'measuring, classifying, and mastering knowledge of the human body and its functions, normal and aberrant' (Feder, 2014: 22). This focus on categorization occurred more or less simultaneously with the professionalization of medicine characterized by Greenwood as involving a systematic body of theory with the authority to define problems and their treatment; and community sanctions to admit and train its members (Greenwood, 1957). The process of professionalization increased the reputation and esteem of medicine and began to bring intersex identification and management under its sole jurisdiction (Garland and Travis, 2020a). Intersex specifically during this period is framed as 'managing a social menace' (Feder, 2014: 22; see also Dreger, 1998) and can perhaps be seen through a lens where clinical and moral understandings of (public) health were not so clearly distinct. Indeed, messages of 'health' were a key aspect of the professionalization project, ensuring the legitimacy and authority of medicine. Dreger notes that even the medical diagnostic criteria of the time were shaped by the challenges to understandings of gender and sexuality emanating from the perceived social threats of women's rights and homosexuality (Dreger, 1998: 166). These perceived social problems continued to be the key motivators in the medicalization of intersex and medicine was keen to establish itself as the sole solution to these issues. Indeed, two of our respondents suggested that the policing of intersex and its link to homosexuality was the result of claims made by homosexual individuals trying to evade homophobic persecution through access to legal protections which had been available to legally-termed 'hermaphrodites' until the late 19th century.[1]

> 'When the gay movement started out in Prussia in the second half of the 19th century, this sex or gender choice for hermaphrodites was still valid … Karl Heinrich Ulrichs was a jurist and he was persecuted because he was gay … He came up with this construction that gay people are actually hermaphrodites psychologically. Then for about 100 years this was the main argumentation of the gay movement. … if he would have been legally recognized as a hermaphrodite his troubles would have been over and he wouldn't even have them because he could have said, 'Okay, I'm a woman,' and then he could have gone on and married men. So from his perspective it might have been a reasonable argumentation but to the actual hermaphrodite he did a big disfavour. … This probably was the final nail in the coffin of the abolition of the gender choice for hermaphrodites because when even more groups come and want exceptions for themselves then the law.'

[1] Explored further in Chapter 3.

Nonetheless, prior to advancements in surgical practice and due to a lack of general knowledge about the comparative aesthetics of genitals, Feder notes that 'one would expect that the majority of cases of "genital ambiguity" … would not have caused particular consternation in a social climate where anatomical variation would be unremarkable and not regarded as the problem it would become in the middle of the [twentieth] century' (Feder, 2014: 22–3). It is only in the late 19th century with, as Dreger terms, the medical invention of sex, that intersex became depicted as a matter that could be clinically treated, categorized and fixed. While there is documented evidence of intersex surgeries taking place as early as the 11th century (Daston and Park, 1985), the late Victorian era is where surgeries to correct atypical genitalia started to become standard practice. Mak (2012) notes that development was attributable to two things: increasing access to intersex people and developments in technology. In the first half of this period, there remained a reluctance to involve doctors in these matters (Dreger, 1998). Towards the end of the 19th century a greater amount of intersex people contacted medical professionals. This was likely because of increasing trust and confidence in the legitimacy of the medical profession (Mak, 2012). This change shifted the regulation of sex (or perhaps more properly gender) from a social concern to a medical *diagnosis* – thus embodiment, at least for intersex people, was determined predominantly through medicine. This shift is similarly played out through in the way that these cases are reported in the literature – increasingly ignoring the way intersex people were socially perceived (Foucault, 1980; Mak, 2012). The reporting of these cases is important as biographical details about the intersex individual became seen as extraneous to the scientific pursuit of determining true sex. Categorization of intersex bodies was extracted from the social and cultural determinations that had been prevalent prior to medical professionalization (Sudai, 2021). Medical and scientific journals of the time were delineated from the popular periodicals of the time, which were often characterized by their sensationalist reporting styles (Newbery-Jones, 2018).

At the same time developments in technology such as anaesthetics meant that doctors could overcome shame (or pain) from medical examinations (Karkazis, 2008). Increasing contact between intersex people and the emerging medical profession, combined with an enhanced understanding of the urinogenital anatomy, meant that doctors were able to examine gonadal material under the microscope and were more frequently discovering intersex variations that were not visible to the external observer (Mak, 2012). Accordingly, the medical professional's 'scientific' conception of sex began to replace more common understandings of gender. The result was enhanced medical knowledge which led to a shift in focus between 1870 to 1915, from the genitals to the gonads as the primary method of establishing the 'true sex' of the intersex individual. This 'inner' aspect of the body concretized the medical professions expertise as it set itself apart from lay knowledge about genitals and subsequently justified its jurisdictional boundaries more fully – giving greater legitimacy to the claim that medicine be the sole authority through which intersex embodiment should be understood. This method continued to reify the idea that all individuals could be properly classified under a binary definition of sex (Foucault, 1980; Dreger, 1998) and thus ensured the continuance of binary determinations of sex prevalent prior to professionalization. In part, this conservative approach to sex may have reflected the precarity of the newly created medical profession in relation to other more established institutions such as law and religion. Nonetheless, the emergence of this gonadal method of classification was influenced by new developments in histology, embryology, evolutionary theory, and anatomy (Dreger, 1998: 29). As a result, diagnoses of 'true hermaphroditism', which were already incredibly rare, 'started to disappear because medical and scientific authorities cooperatively revised the criteria for this condition such that it became almost impossible by the end of the century for anybody to satisfy those guidelines' (Dreger, 1998: 138).

Moreover, rather than sit in a purely diagnostic capacity, medical professionals began to see an increase in individuals seeking them out to aesthetically correct their bodies in line with their lived sex rather than medically establish their 'true sex'. Medical jurisdiction therefore shifted from determining sex to also 'fixing' sex:

> All of a sudden many more hermaphrodites consulted doctors, not to have their sex diagnosed, but because they had a strong outspoken wish to have 'a growth' cut off or to be made 'apt' for marriage, to have a split urethra repaired, to straighten a curved down hypospadiac penis or to have breasts removed. … The request for, the offers of, and the actual performance of surgery or other treatments increased tremendously after 1900. Doctors therefore became entangled in decisions on hermaphrodites' sex assignments through surgery from 1900 onwards in a way they never had been before. … However, as soon as they became able to perform surgeries that helped hermaphrodites to look more like and function better as one or the other sex, they became directly responsible for irreversible decisions about their future social and legal sex. So, individual surgeons as well as the medical profession as a whole had to face new dilemmas from that time on. They had to contemplate whether, under which circumstances, or to what extent they wanted to meet their patient's wishes through surgery. (Mak, 2012: 171)

The implications of these surgical assignments were profound in changing the embodiment of intersex people within medicine where intersex people became *patients* in the clinical setting. Rather than now being designated as one sex or the other, intersex people could be 'fixed' into the sex determined by the physician. Prior to the 19th century, while surgeries were possible, they were not always offered by practitioners and many suggested 'other social solutions to establish hermaphrodites within normal dimorphic sex and gender paradigms' such as exile or buying appropriate clothing (Matta, 2005: 77). Writing in the US context, Matta notes that even when practitioners did recommend surgery, they could not legally force it and thus many intersex persons 'often shrugged off their uncommon bodies as harmless and went about their business as usual' (Matta, 2005: 77). However, the demand for surgery by intersex persons was growing and there are a number of historical accounts of patients and families pressuring doctors into performing surgeries (Dreger, 1998). This inevitably embroiled the medical profession into making irreversible decisions about the social and legal sex of a child. Clinicians had to reflect on when and how they would meet their patients and deal with the dilemma of the growing gap between enforcing the 'moral' gonadal determinants of sex and the everyday lived sex of the intersex person (Karkazis, 2008; Reis, 2019). Accordingly, medical practitioners began to develop their clinical practice in accordance with the desires of the patient. Doctors were also increasingly concerned with the psychological wellbeing of their patient, as much as their morality. As Mak states:

> They held that in cases in which a person had no doubts about her sex at all, it would dramatically shake her own sense of self and her orientation in the world if a physician would explain that an error in the initial sex assignment had taken place … but instead of forcing their patients to live according to a strict scientific gonadal criterion of sex ('true sex') – which they did not have the authority to do anyway – physicians were often much more pragmatic and strove for a properly functioning single sex: a less ambiguous looking sex. (Mak, 2012: 231–2)

Binary approaches to sex grounded in heteronormative understandings of sexuality were at the forefront of these approaches. During this period, however, the understandings of intersex as a 'disorder' that could be 'fixed' began to dominate the public consciousness controlling the narrative of intersex embodiment. This was linked in important ways to the professionalization of medicine that used the concept of intersex to show that medicine had more to offer than lay or folk understandings of sex. In order to do this, the medical profession likely inflated folk beliefs that intersex people were a 'third gender' or 'monster' (Foucault, 1980; Sharpe, 2009a; Sudai, 2021). Historical examinations of legal cases determining dubious sex highlight that these gender non-confirming individuals were almost invariably given a binary sex (Sudai, 2021). Nonetheless such claims strengthened the nascent medical profession's jurisdictional hold over intersex people and, by extension, binary understandings of sex and gender. Medical embodiment and the subsequent understandings of sex became central to establishing legal embodiment. These foundations were bolstered in the 20th century as entry standards and training were established by the medical profession ensuring that knowledge of intersex bodies was solely determined by the medical profession.

20th century: surgery as established practice

The background assumptions towards intersex and the change in the role of medical professionals informed the work of Hugh Hampton Young; a renowned surgeon at Johns Hopkins Hospital specializing in urology. In 1897, one year after beginning an internship at the hospital, he became head of 'genitourinary surgery'. In 1916, Young began publishing his work on the 'correction' of atypical genitals and established Johns Hopkins as 'the primary center for cases of so-called indeterminate sex' (Karkazis, 2008: 43). Motivated by the number of patients approaching him asking for surgical interventions (Young, 1937; Reis, 2019), over the course of his career Young pioneered a range of surgical 'normalizing' techniques that reshaped genitals developing the 'techniques that would mark the standard of care over the coming century' (Feder, 2014: 28). Young's approach to intersex variations continued the 'true sex' model that had dominated in previous centuries. Now, however, new developments in anaesthesia allowed medical professionals to take a much more interventionist approach to the regulation of the sex binary. This approach placed priority on the aesthetics of the body as male or female rather than the function and pleasure of the body. As his 1937 textbook *Genital Abnormalities: Hermaphroditism and Related Adrenal Diseases* notes, clitoral amputation was a routine response to cases of uncertain sex. Nonetheless this science was uncertain; there are medical accounts in Young's books of doctors determining 'true sex' for their patients *during* a surgery where they would remove healthy tissue or the decision being made after a vote was cast among medical staff (Reis, 2019). Accordingly, decisions relating to the affirmation of sex often happened without the individual's knowledge or fully-informed consent (Reis, 2019: 662). This, in part, was premised on medicine's claims to be establishing (rather than producing) true sex with the effect of giving medical accounts of embodiment a claim of 'naturality' rather than being socially constructed.

At the same time, however, Young expanded the range of indicators that had previously been used to establish sex by using personality and sexual desire as indicators of 'normal hormonal function' (Karkazis, 2008: 44).

Although Young's approach promised a focus on ascertaining 'true sex' through scientific method, it demonstrates a continuing reliance on gendered characteristics and sexuality. Importantly, sex was still understood to be binary and people could be placed in one category or another. Young's focus on hormones was enabled by a breakthrough in research by Frank R. Lillie in 1916 that allowed for an 'organized, generalized, theory of the possible role of hormones in the production of hermaphroditism' (Dreger, 1998: 73). Young's pioneering work on 'normalizing' surgeries bridges the gap between Victorian understandings of sex as binary and concerns about same-sex relationships and the emphasis on the psychological aspects of 'sex of rearing' that was to come. Binary sex, therefore, continued to influence understandings of the intersex body as disordered and the consequent management of these bodies. Social understandings of what was 'natural' played an important part in medical embodiment's claims to legitimacy over and above legal accounts. At this time, intersex people were increasingly seeking out medical professions based on their own beliefs about the gender binary and appropriate sex role. Medical professionals, therefore, were not the sole drivers of 'fixing' intersex people based on binary conceptions of sex.

From adults to children: refocusing medicine's regulatory gaze

As we have seen, the late 19th century saw the introduction of intersex adults into the clinical setting, whereby surgery became standard practice to 'treat' non-normative bodies. Yet, modern-day practice and the main concern regarding the medical regulation of intersex has been in relation to the early stage with which medical interventions are performed on the bodies of infants. The major shift in medical attention onto the intersex child can be traced throughout the 1930s, 1940s and 1950s so that, by the 1960s, medical interventions on intersex infants were standard practice. This was due to several medical and social developments including: the development of paediatric urology as a subspecialism in medicine; John Money's influential work on optimal gender rearing and the rise of psychology as a medical discipline more generally; global developments in regard to bioethics and informed consent of the adult patient; increasing survival rates of girls with salt-wasting CAH; and childhood as an increased temporal space protected by law and medicine.

Establishing erasure: 'normalizing' surgery on children

Lawson Wilkins joined Johns Hopkins as a urologist in 1936 – one year prior to the publication of Hugh Hampton Young's influential textbook. Wilkins quickly took issue with Young's practice of 'adrenalectomy' in the treatment of individuals with CAH. Instead, Wilkins developed the introduction of cortisone into his patients. Feder describes this 'enhanced ability to identify the disorder in affected infants together with the discovery of the drug that would make possible lifelong management of the disorder are rightly regarded as major advancements in paediatric medical care' (Feder, 2014: 27). The discovery of cortisol's effect on children with CAH increased the numbers of children with atypical genitalia surviving into adulthood (Piaggio, 2014). During his career, and primarily drawing on his successes working with CAH women, Wilkins developed an approach that was attentive to the wishes of the intersex individual. Drawing together new surgical and hormonal techniques with earlier understandings of sex 'The production of knowledge aimed now to settle the matter of doubtful sex by normalizing the bodies of those with atypical sex before they became the problem they had been taken to be in the previous period' (Feder, 2014: 30). These new pioneering techniques, as we will discuss further in the next section, began to introduce a shift in focus from consenting adults to younger children. As Davies explains: 'Surgically modifying genitalia for medically unnecessary reasons was possible only because doctors and parents believed that intersex infants could live normal lives if they were socialized in accordance with their surgically constructed sexes' (Davis, 2015: 56). Intersex embodiment understood through a medical lens, therefore, became increasingly concerned with its (early) erasure.

CAH differs from other intersex variations in several important respects. For one, the salt-wasting aspects associated with severe forms of CAH firmly place it more in the realms of a healthcare issue than other intersex variations, which usually manifest in ways that are medically benign. Nonetheless, Wilkins's work with CAH individuals has come to define intersex healthcare for all variations placing even medically benign variations under the umbrella of 'disorders'. Moreover, Wilkins's work cannot be seen as distinct from the work of Young but must be understood in conjunction with it. The patients with CAH who were part of Wilkins clinic were routinely subject to surgical interventions to their genitals and this approach to 'normalizing' surgery remains at the heart of medical approaches to intersex. As such, Wilkins and the broader team at Johns Hopkins are crucial in reinforcing intersex variations as 'disorders' and in maintaining earlier medical and societal legacies of sex as binary.

In the 1940s, in both the UK and the US, medical attention was increasingly turned to intersex children (Broster, 1953; Feder, 2014; Griffiths, 2018b). Following the Second World War paediatric urology began to concretize as a formal medical subspeciality (Griffiths, 2018b). In the UK, David Williams, often heralded as the 'father of paediatric urology', took a post at Great Ormond Street Hospital in the 1940s, coinciding with the establishment of the newly formed National Health Service (NHS). His reputation combined with the resources the NHS facilitated led to Great Ormond Street Hospital (GOSH) effectively becoming a central point for urology, and, importantly, paediatric urology. With the newfound hormonal treatments of CAH increasing the survival rates of XX infants with CAH 'surgical correction' of atypical genitalia became the central focus of medical practitioners (Piaggio, 2014).

Williams' concern for the lack of knowledge surrounding paediatric urology led him to write *The Urology of Childhood* (Higgins et al, 1951; Griffiths, 2018a). Drawing on the techniques pioneered by Young in his 1937 textbook *Genital Abnormalities: Hermaphroditism and Related Adrenal Diseases*, this book focussed specifically on childhood and contained detailed chapters on a number of distinct intersex variations (Griffiths, 2018a). This textbook focused more on the external genitalia than glands 'due to the disciplinary differences between urology and endocrinology' (Griffiths, 2018a: 485). Griffiths notes that while the adult context focused on issues relating to sexuality, in the context of the child the core issue was psychology; surgery was thus recommended to facilitate the psychological wellbeing of the child and there was considerable emphasis on enabling the child to ensure 'normal' functioning (Piaggio, 2014), including heteronormative sex (Fausto-Sterling, 2000), and for boys the ability to urinate standing up (Hegarty and Roen, 2018, Griffiths, 2021).[2] As Williams noted: "The guiding principle in the treatment of all this group of cases must be adaptation of the external appearance to the psychology of the child rather than to the histology of the gonad' (Higgins et al, 1951: 249; Griffiths, 2018a). Williams quickly followed this publication with another, 'The diagnosis of intersex', where he emphasized that surgeries should be performed sooner rather than later: 'Too often the decision is postponed to see which way the child will develop; the parents are left without guidance, and their natural anxiety is communicated to the child, who is thus in danger of becoming a psychological as well as a surgical problem (Williams, 1952). Nevertheless, there was some moral concern regarding this approach. For example, C.N. Armstrong, an endocrinologist working in the 1950s, was concerned that intersex variations destabilized the male/female binary and problematized the very definition of homosexuality, still at the time considered a social problem (Griffiths, 2018a). Accordingly, he questioned attempts to affirm social sex rather than ascertaining the 'true sex' of the individual (Griffiths, 2018a). Rather, he argued that clearer definitions of sex were needed in both medicine and the law and argued that this definition should be multifactoral – including gonads, 'nuclear sex', genitals, as well as social and psychological sex. The tension between Williams' approach and that of Armstrong highlights a disjuncture between

2 Surgery was recommended for children with hypospadias, where the uretha opening is not at the tip of the penis, for this very reason (Griffiths, 2018a, 2021).

approaches grounded in surgical alteration and determining the 'true sex' of the gonads. These differences highlight the disparities between the increasingly separate branches of urology and endocrinology. Armstrong's concern with the gonads was eventually rejected by the newly emerging science of karyotyping, which highlighted that genes determining sex did not necessarily coincide with gonads (Griffiths, 2018a, 2018b). Moreover, Williams' approach was grounded in a logic of 'fixing' rather than 'determining' sex in keeping with the medical embodiment approach that we have outlined. As a result, Williams' focus on surgery would have been much more favourable to concerned parents of the time – especially given the meteoric rise of psychology that was on the horizon.

The origins of current medical practice: optimal gender rearing

While the 1940s–1950s saw a sharpening of medical energies towards 'fixing' sex at birth and treating the intersex child, it was the work of John Money that paved the way to the current methods in which intersex people are medically embodied. As Respondent 7 stated: "John Money actually was the one that sealed the fate of millions of intersex children in the future and it's still going on." Money continued the psychological trajectory pointed towards by Williams in the 1940s and 1950s. In 1951, John Money joined Johns Hopkins as the first paediatric psychoendocrinologist bringing expertise in psychology to the emerging multidisciplinary team (though he was not a psychologist, surgeon or endocrinologist himself). In 1952, Money completed his PhD in Social Relations at the Harvard University entitled 'Hermaphroditism: An Inquiry into the Nature of a Human Paradox'. His contribution to the management of intersex variations has been described as 'singularly influential' (Morland, 2015: 69) as he introduced 'a systematic model of gender assignment and treatment for individuals with intersex conditions' (Karkazis, 2008: 47). Through his thesis and a series of subsequent publications Money outlined his initial conception of gender as well as his 'Optimal Gender Rearing Model'. This early work distinguished between sex as something biological and gender as something that is learnt through socialization (with a particular emphasis on rearing). Hampson (an early collaborator with Money) defined their understanding of gender as follows: 'a person's gender role and awareness is founded in what, from infancy onward, he learns, assimilates, and interprets about his sexual status from parents, siblings, playmates and others, and from the way he reads the signs of his own body' (Hampson, 1955: 265).[3] While in today's society such distinctions have

[3] Money later claimed he had authored this piece but allowed others to take the credit (Money, 2002).

become commonplace, at the time they were ground-breaking.[4] Bringing together new psychological approaches with Johns Hopkins pre-existing expertise in surgery and hormone management, Money reasoned that 'normalizing' the ambiguity of intersex genitals would allow them to form better social relationships (as it would relieve the anxieties of people coming into contact with the intersex person). To ensure the success of this gender assignment, Money insisted that 'age eighteen months was the temporal limit for deciding which gender a child would be raised, since during this period gender identity and role should be stabilized' (Meoded Danon, 2018: 91). The concept of a 'critical window' for interventions remains the basis for early surgical interventions performed on intersex infants despite a lack of systematic review (Mieszczak et al, 2009). While Money's approach is often considered 'ground-breaking', in reality, his work attempted to give the surgical interventions that were already occurring a veneer of psychological legitimacy. Similarly, it continued the construction of intersex embodiment as something that could be medically fixed, and thus erased as an identity.

In part of his research, Money found that most (though not all) intersex people accepted their sex of rearing. He concluded, therefore, that the social environment of the home was more important than physiological factors. As a result, Money's work decentred the previous emphasis placed on hormones and gonads (that were susceptible to changes during puberty) and cut short the newly emerging science of karyotyping (Money et al, 1955a: 284–5).[5] As Money wrote in conjunction with Hampson and Hampson: 'The sex of assignment and rearing is consistently and conspicuously a more reliable prognosticator of a hermaphrodite's gender role and orientation than is the chromosomal sex, the gonadal sex, the hormonal sex, the accessory internal reproductive morphology, or the ambiguous morphology of the external genitalia' (Money et al, 1957: 333). Despite the importance placed on psychology, Money still felt that surgical and hormonal interventions were important to support an intersex individual's assigned gender role. Indeed, this importance seems to stem from the idea that gender role was dictated by sexuality. As Malatino outlines: 'On account of this centrality of sexuality to gender role, we witness across Money's body of work … an intense focus on discerning the truth of a patient's sexuality, and a positing of that sexuality as absolutely integral to discovering the gendered inclinations of a given patient' (Malatino, 2019: 167).

4 Although the term 'gender' was also used by Blair Bell in 1914 as a more 'adaptable' understanding of social role than sex (Dreger ,1998: 166).

5 Although karyotyping would importantly extend the diagnostic reach of intersex into chromosomal variances such as Turners Syndrome and Klinefelter's Syndrome it did little to alter the clinical management of intersex variances (Griffiths, 2018a).

Although Money recognized that sex of rearing was not an absolute determinant of adult gender he continued to recommend 'normalizing' surgeries. As Karkazis notes: 'Such intervention was – and largely remains – aimed at enabling the individual to fit, more or less superficially, into the binary model of sex' (Karkazis, 2008: 31–2). Ultimately, however, Money and his team recommended surgery on the basis of the morphology of the genitals – and how easily they could they be reshaped (Morland, 2015: 74). Deception was recommended to other practitioners in order to convince parents of the 'true' sex of the child (Hegarty and Chase, 2000). Money and his team recommended that parents were told that the child's sex organs were 'unfinished' but could be finished through surgeries (Money, 1955; Dreger, 1998: 181; Griffiths, 2021). As Dreger notes: 'Because of this restitution narrative – in which sex has *temporarily* blurred – sex borders in intersex medical discourse continue to appear stable in all cases and at all times. A notion of "true sex" is discursively and publicly maintained in intersex cases, as is the one-body-one-sex rule founded so firmly in the nineteenth century' (Dreger, 1998: 185). Moreover, because of disparities in the available technology and skill required to make male genitalia this meant that a majority of intersex children were assigned to be female as it was considered 'easier' to make girls (Fausto-Sterling, 2000, Lee et al, 2006).

Money's approach grounded intersex issues as primarily occurring because of society but emphasized changing the individual to fit society rather than focussing on social or structural change. In keeping with the previous work produced by Johns Hopkins, Money's approach was committed to the sex binary and ensuring the heterosexuality of patients was an important outcome of 'successful surgery'. Despite engaging with new approaches in psychology and hormone management, locating the work of Money in its historical context highlights the *lack of change* within medical constructions of embodiment rather than a break from previous tradition. As Lesley Rogers and Joan Walsh write: 'While Money … and co-workers consider the social aspects of gender … they take for granted that there are two genders, that there are differences between them, and that fundamentally gender is a consequence of a biological blueprint for behaviour as well as physique' (Rogers and Walsh, 1982: 272). Similarly, Ruth Doell and Helen Longino highlight that, rather than being interactionist, Money's work is premised on the idea that the biological is the foundational aspect of gender (Doell and Longino, 1988). Money's work remains the starting point for much of the healthcare protocols for intersex health management (Karkazis, 2008: 48). We can see therefore that the framing of intersex embodiment through a lens of disorder was established through the creation of the medical profession and perfected by Young, Wilkins and Williams. John Money's work ensured the continuation of commitments to binary sex and heterosexuality, but now understood through a wider and more encompassing lens of psychological 'health'. Money's central contribution to this area was the emphasis on parents as sole guardians of the intersex child's gender stability and concomitant heterosexuality. This was crucial in shifting responsibility away from the medical professionals who had undertaken the (unnecessary) surgeries towards the parents. Despite gains with the treatment of salt-wasting CAH and the identification of Turners and Klinefelters (that complicated straightforward genetic division between the sexes) binary approaches to sex and heteronormativity continued to be the primary drivers for the medical management of intersex children's embodiment.

Although following the Second World War there was increased concern for patient autonomy in the context of adults,[6] Reis argues that the shift towards intersex children, which this section explores, "cloud[ed] the informed consent process" (2019, 667) as infants were unable to provide consent. As Reis writes:

> The Johns Hopkins protocols thus shifted the focus from adults who had a say in their own gender, as well as their own medical care, to infants, who did not. As we might imagine, it wasn't easy to persuade adults to switch from male to female or vice versa (non-binary gender was not an option at that time). Money's new strategy seemed like a godsend. (Reis, 2019: 668)

Questions regarding interventions on babies concerned gender identity and autonomy, not issues relating to consent and patient autonomy (Reis, 2009: 138; Reis, 2019: 665). This, for Reis, is the driving factor as to why intersex management has not benefited from 'the full force of bioethics' aspirational goals for the enhancement of patient care' (Reis, 2019: 659). Ultimately, these developments had profound institutional results on intersex people so that 'By the middle of the twentieth century, medical technology had "advanced" to a point where it could make bodies that had once been

[6] The development of psychology throughout the 1940 as a discipline in its own right placed an increasing emphasis on the needs and desires of the patient (Reis, 2019). This move towards patient-centred care attributes the shift towards 'a more a more humane approach that centred on patient autonomy' to international bioethical developments in the post-war era, most notably the Nuremberg Code, the Declaration of Geneva (Reis, 2019: 663). The Nuremberg Code 1947 set out a series of ethical principles relating to research that emphasized 'voluntary consent' particularly focusing on what would constitute informed consent. The Declaration of Geneva 1948 set out an International Code of Medical Ethics where doctors pledge to 'respect the autonomy and dignity of my patient' (Reis, 2019: 259). As a result of these developments, doctors began to adopt a more patient-centred approach towards their patients where they started to question their actions and consider the patient's psychological health. (Reis, 2019: 664).

objects of awe and astonishment disappear from view, all in the name of "correcting nature's mistakes"' (Fausto-Sterling, 2000: 37). In doing so, the medical profession reified the binary as a positivistic certainty while concealing the *cultural* discomfort that the uncertainty of intersex bodies produced. Now the medical profession was concerned with intervening as early as possible, with intersex embodiment being erased, made invisible or framed as disorder. In the next section we shall outline the 2006 Chicago Consensus Statement and highlight its conceptual grounding within and theoretical debt to the work of Money and his predecessors and the way it continues to frame intersex people through a medical embodiment approach.

From 'optimal gender rearing' to 'disorder of sex development treatment' model

As a result of Money's influential work, interventions on infants under 18 months became a central feature of the medical management of intersex and, by the 1960s, surgical intervention on infants was established practice (Reis, 2019). Despite severe ethical and methodological failings Money's work gained traction among the medical profession and beyond (we return to these issues in Chapter 6). In 2006, the participants of the International Consensus Conference on Intersex organized by the Lawson Wilkins Pediatric Endocrine Society and the European Society for Paediatric Endocrinology published the 'Consensus Statement on the Management of Intersex Disorders'. The Lawson Wilkins Pediatric Society is the largest paediatric society in North America, representing more than 1,000 paediatric endocrinologists. It was named in honour of the previously discussed Johns Hopkins-based endocrinologist Lawson Wilkins from its inception in 1972 until 2010, highlighting his importance and influence in the field of endocrinology. As Feder outlines: 'Wilkins had trained nearly every physician who in the 1960s would go on to become program directors of pediatric endocrinology: for this reason most pediatric endocrinologists practicing today … are "descended" from Wilkins' (Feder, 2014: 24). This in turn goes some way to highlighting the reach of the work of Wilkins and Money at Johns Hopkins.

The consensus statement introduced a number of important developments in the management of intersex care representing a shift from the 'optimal gender rearing' (OGR) model of treatment to a 'disorder of sex development' model (Clune-Taylor, 2019). Firstly, the document sought to alter terminology in this field from the dominant term 'intersex' to 'disorders of sex development' (DSDs) now to be defined as 'congenital conditions in which development of chromosomal, gonadal, or anatomic sex is atypical' (Lee et al, 2006: e488). Secondly, the statement placed emphasis on honesty between clinicians, parents and children rather than the secrecy that was previously mandated by John Money's research. The document also attempted to formalize the multidisciplinary teams necessary for the best practice regarding intersex healthcare. These built upon the interdisciplinary teams that had been practised by Johns Hopkins since the 1950s. Thirdly, it changed sex assignment recommendations for certain types of intersex variations (Clune-Taylor, 2019). Despite claims of it being a 'a quiet revolution in medicine' by one of the co-authors (Hughes, 2010: 160), the DSD model is not substantially different from the OGR model (Clune-Taylor, 2019). Key differences lie in its underpinning, however, while Money's model focused on 'a social-constructionist model of gender development, DSD is practically dominated by a biologically determinist model known as brain-organization theory, which holds that brains are "organized" into feminine or masculine patterns by prenatal hormone exposure' (Clune-Taylor, 2019: 693). This former theory has too been in receipt of extreme criticism on account of its adherence to the sex binary and its understanding that biology predetermines gender. Nonetheless, the shift in terminology reifies the place of intersex as primarily medically embodied and ensures that legal embodiment is seen through the lens of the medical.

The language of disorder

The term DSD quickly replaced intersex throughout the medical profession. One of the consensus statement authors noted that the change in terminology had been an 'enlightening advance' (Hughes, 2010: 161). The change in terminology was prompted in part by 'aspirations of distinguishing biological states from issues of identity' (Carpenter, 2018: 489). Such a move can be seen as part of a political strategy to distance intersex from its connections with LGBT (and the potential for negative medical connotations of 'conversion therapy').[7] This approach to the nature of intersex was considered to be more readily understandable to parents. While the term DSD was welcomed by some as an 'important break from the Victorian medicalization of bodies with atypical sex that saw in their anomalies not a risk to the health of those individuals but a threat to the social body' (Feder, 2014: 39), others were less accommodating. As Topp notes: 'Consensus supporters … ignore the stigmatizing effects of labeling someone as disordered and fail to acknowledge the gains made by intersex advocates while using the label intersex' (Topp, 2013: 181). Similarly, Davis notes that the change in nomenclature 'served as a perfect vehicle for medical professionals to reassert their authority and maintain their exclusive jurisdiction over intersex traits' (Davis, 2015: 70). Shifting the terminology used to discuss intersex people from 'intersex' to

[7] We explore the connection between intersex and LGBT in greater depth in Chapter 4.

'disordered' reifies the place of the medical professional in discovering and 'reordering' the disordered body while simultaneously moving responsibility away from the medical interventions (and categorizations) themselves. This approach to terminology continues to justify determinist and essentialist understandings of gender. As Davis continues:

> Medical professionals are trained to look at intersex through a biological rather than a social lens. A biological lens necessitates an essentialist view of gender to justify the medicalization of intersexuality and, more specifically, to justify the validity of the *disorder* of sex development diagnosis itself. Gender essentialism maintains that gender is – and should be – neatly correlated with a binary sex, and that the bodies of individuals who deviate from the pattern require modification for the sake of normalcy and consistency. (Davis, 2015: 72)

Clune-Taylor (2019) identifies that the recommendations for surgery proposed by the consensus statement are among the most conservative yet: 'Surgery should only be considered in cases of severe virilisation' (Lee et al, 2006: e491). However, building on the above point, the consensus statement failed to condemn non-therapeutic surgical interventions on the bodies of intersex children. Nor has it led to a reduction in the number of surgeries performed (Monro et al, 2017; Helms, 2018; Clune-Taylor, 2019). While some surgeons have listened to concerns (Ellens et al, 2017; Nokoff et al, 2017), Money's legacy continues to inform modern practice within contemporary guidelines (Lee et al, 2006), with one study finding that 78 per cent of practitioners prefer early surgery for virilized CAH infants before the age of two (Yankovic et al, 2013) or earlier (Clayton et al, 2002). Equivocally, the document notes that such practices relieve 'parental distress and improves attachment between the child and parents', but goes on to note that 'the systematic evidence for this belief is lacking' (Lee et al, 2006: e491). Nonetheless, recent interviews with medical professionals confirm that these beliefs persist (Liao et al, 2019). Despite this, the consensus statement fails to criticize non-therapeutic surgical interventions, and in fact foregrounds them in the section on surgical management. It did offer some different recommendations regarding surgery on 46 XX CAH infants, those 46 XY patients with a micro-penis (a penis less than 2.5 cm in length) and 46 XY patients with cloacal exstrophy. While Money's approach suggested these infants should be raised female due to the difficulty in constructing a penis capable of heteronormative intercourse (Creighton et al, 2012: 603; Clune-Taylor, 2019), the consensus statement suggested that they should be raised male and that medical practitioners should give more thought to other biological factors (Lee et al, 2016, 169; Clune-Taylor, 2019: 695) such as prenatal androgen levels.

Nevertheless, surgical concern within the consensus statement goes on to place emphasis on the function rather than the appearance of genitals, even when highlighting some element of risk: 'Because orgasmic function and erectile sensation may be disturbed by clitoral surgery, the surgical procedure should be anatomically based to preserve erectile function and the innervation of the clitoris. Emphasis is on functional outcome rather than a strictly cosmetic appearance' (Lee et al, 2006: e491). Later in the document, however, the consensus statement continues the tradition of emphasizing the 'ease' of feminizing surgery for individuals with hypospadias: 'The outcome in undermasculinized males with a phallus depends on the degree of hypospadias and the amount of erectile tissue. Feminizing genitoplasty as opposed to masculinizing genitoplasty requires less surgery to achieve an acceptable outcome and results in fewer urologic difficulties' (Lee et al, 2006: e496). We can see therefore, that while the consensus statement formalized a multidisciplinary approach to intersex health, it is grounded in an interventionist approach based on the sex binary. As Clune-Taylor notes therefore: 'DSD inherits from OGR both its aim and the empirically unjustified assumption that typical genitals are necessary for "normal" cisgendered development' (Clune-Taylor, 2019: 691).

The shift towards DSD was supported in a desire to base the classification of intersex variances in genetic science (Griffiths, 2018a: 126). However, as Griffiths notes, at the time of the consensus statement this science was not available and instead was very much promissory. As Griffiths writes, this hopeful understanding of science was 'built upon the expectation that, at some time in the future, improved genetic testing and increased genetic understandings will lead to clearer classification, quicker diagnosis and better treatments' (Griffiths, 2018a: 126). At present, however, this has not been the case. Indeed, the need for chromosomal variances such as Klinefelters Syndrome and Turners Sydrome to be classified as DSDs continues to be contested (Griffiths, 2018a).

In regard to gender and sexuality, however, there seem to have been some improvements. The consensus statement separates out gender identity, gender role and sexual orientation as follows:

> Psychosexual development is traditionally conceptualized as 3 components: 'gender identity' refers to a person's self-representation as male or female (with the caveat that some individuals may not identify exclusively with either); 'gender role' (sex-typical behaviors) describes the psychological characteristics that are sexually dimorphic within the general population, such as toy preferences and physical aggression; and 'sexual orientation' refers to the direction(s) of erotic interest (heterosexual, bisexual, homosexual) and includes behavior, fantasies, and attractions. (Lee et al, 2006: e489)

Sexual orientation is interpreted in a broader sense than had been previously understood within the field. Crucially, the consensus statement notes that, 'homosexual orientation (relative to sex of rearing) or strong cross-sex interest in an individual with DSD is not an indication of incorrect gender assignment' (Lee et al, 2006: e489). This is a vast improvement on previous medical practice and highlights a point of genuine divergence from 19th-century understandings of same-sex relations, intersex and morality. Underlining this point, the consensus statement outlines new outcomes for determining intersex health. These include: 'external and internal genital phenotype, physical health including fertility, sexual function, and social and psychosexual adjustment, mental health, quality of life, and social participation' (Lee et al, 2006: e493). Unfortunately, while it is acknowledged that individuals may not identify within the sex binary, this has not impacted upon the medical professions' decision making around non-therapeutic surgical intervention. As a result, this can be seen as a missed opportunity for the medical profession. Instead, intersex people remain 'invitations to diagnosis, and intersex people become experimental subjects on which the medical apparatus may machinate and elaborate its account of the constitution of sex difference in a way that all too often denies our autonomic capacities' (Malatino, 2019: 53). This stems from a governing logic within medicine that orients intersex embodiment through a lens of 'fixing' and thus erasure.

Challenges to the medical embodiment approach

Understanding intersex people through the lens of the medical embodiment approach facilitates and in some ways necessitates early surgical intervention. Nonetheless, the efficacy of the medical interventions and the consensus statement's unwillingness to condemn them outright has been heavily questioned. This next section draws upon the empirical SLSA project set out in Chapter 1. Despite not having any questions that specifically sought to examine themes relating to medical experiences *all* respondents were keen to emphasize the ways in which medicine regulated their experiences and that so far law had been unable to challenge this. Participants were eager to discuss the lived experience of 'disorder' and the effects of being understood through the jurisdiction of medicine. Respondents were hopeful, however, that law could be a powerful tool in challenging the dominance of medicine in dictating what intersex *was*. Moreover, participants highlighted the harms of being understood through the lens of 'disorder' (and the attempts to fix them that these demanded) as opposed to the harms of the variations themselves. As one respondent stated: "most intersex, at least I know, are very, very traumatized and suffer from physical and psychological harm of these genital surgeries during childhood" (Respondent 5).

Our respondents highlighted a number of inequalities arising out of the medical/individual power imbalance and the medical profession's construction of intersex as a disorder. Respondents took issue with the medical profession's understanding of intersex characteristics to be biological mistakes rather than 'natural variations'. The consequence of this mistaken categorization was that the medical interventions used to 'treat' these 'disorders' were considered inappropriate. Nearly all respondents framed cosmetic genital surgeries on children as having no real certifiable benefit and instead often contributing to long-term mental and physical health problems (Minto et al, 2003; Preves, 2003; Greenberg, 2012; Jones et al, 2016). Instead, our respondents highlighted how the surgeries (and medicine's response to intersex variations) have *caused* harm. Respondents criticized the lack of long-term follow-up studies that track the effect of such medical interventions and called for a stop to these practices and for more research to be collected (see also Creighton et al, 2001; Holmes, 2008a; Greenberg, 2012): "[T]here aren't enough studies that really track the longitudinal effect of intersex people who don't have their reproductive organs … I think that's what the medical community should actually invest in given that they're doing these surgeries, and in a way, it's leaving people out in the cold" (Respondent 15). Such criticisms are reflected in the growing evidence base which is demonstrating the range of negative consequences from surgery, including: reduced sexual sensitivity (Creighton et al, 2001; Minto et al, 2003; Crouch et al, 2008); sterilization (Creighton et al, 2014); vaginal stenosis (Wang and Poppas, 2017); being assigned to a gender with which the individual does not identify (Cohen-Kettenis, 2005); and reliance on artificial hormones (leading to conditions such as osteoporosis) (Mora et al, 1992; Rubin, 1998; Benetti-Pinto et al, 2002). Moreover, these surgical procedures remain experimental, so there is a likelihood of indirect negative consequences, including sepsis, infection, and multiple follow-up surgeries (Hegarty and Chase, 2000; Hughes et al, 2007; Wang and Poppas, 2017); it is not unusual for intersex people to have multiple non-consensual gender-normalizing surgeries on their genitals before they are able to engage with the decision-making process (Creighton et al, 2001). This then leads to more corrective surgery once the individual can consent – though this surgery is then presented as inevitable (Grabham, 2012). Framing intersex people through a lens of medical embodiment prevents these harms being seen as criminal (Giliani, 2020).

Surgery is not the only type of medical intervention that affects intersex people. Intersex people also report vaginal dilation (the stretching of the vaginal canal to accommodate a 'normal' penis) during childhood, either by parents, carers or healthcare professionals, as a deeply traumatic experience (Monro et al, 2017; Wang and Poppas, 2017; Orr and Watson, 2021). Hormone replacement regimes that do not relate to the gender with which the intersex person identifies can also be extremely problematic (Spurgas, 2009). The rarity of these variances mean that intersex people are also subject to a higher level of medical interest, which leads to medical photography and extra attention from junior medical professionals during 'rounds' (Creighton et al, 2002).

Not only were our respondents concerned that the early timing of these interventions meant children had little voice in these matters, but many respondents were concerned that individuals and/or their parents were not fully informed or consulted by the medical profession. This finding of a lack of informed consent is being increasingly supported by other literature (Jones et al, 2016: 106–9):

> 'When you are seven and you realize that your mother especially and also your father are very stressed, everybody is stressed and it has to do with your genitals, and then you consent out of wish to please or to take this stress away. Everybody knows that most children are doing things because they want to be accepted or liked or because they want to please their parents, and the doctors.' (Respondent 5)

Moreover, this medical approach has also been accompanied by a rhetoric of secrecy, leading to the erasure of intersex from mainstream discourse of which parents, as Respondent 7 put it, "become complicit in [erasure] innocently"; "Doctors largely dissuade intersex people from contacting intersex support and advocacy groups rather than encourage participation" (Respondent 2). Additionally, some individuals indicated that medical records were difficult to access or were often incomplete: "[it is very hard] to get this information that hospitals and medical professionals do not seem very willing to share it" (Respondent 8). All bar one participant stated that the fundamental concern of the intersex movement was therefore to prevent such unnecessary surgeries and, in doing so, directly challenge and override medical conceptions of intersex embodiment: "We need protection from irreversible, non-therapeutic medical intervention on intersex infants and children who cannot provide informed consent" (Respondent 2).

It is perhaps unsurprising then, that there have been numerous national and international challenges to this medical framework. Intersex activists since the 1990s have raised concerns about medical practice and the harmful consequences that this has produced (Davis, 2015). Consequently, the focus of the intersex movement has primarily been to stop non-therapeutic interventions happening without the individual's consent and in so doing shifting intersex embodiment from a medical framework to a legal framework. In 2013, at the third International Intersex Forum which was held in Malta, the international intersex community issued the 'Malta declaration' which set out the key priorities for the movement. First and foremost, on this list was the desire: 'To put an end to mutilating and normalizing practices such as genital surgeries, psychological and other medical treatments, including infanticide and selective abortion (on the grounds of intersex) in some parts of the world' (Malta Declaration, 2013).

Moreover, as a result of this widespread criticism, international bodies are beginning to take notice, defining such interventions as significant breaches of human rights. Accordingly, in the last decade, condemnation has come from international bodies such as the United Nations, the European Parliament, the Council of Europe Commissioner for Human Rights, the Special Rapporteur on Torture and Other Cruel, Inhuman or Degrading Treatment or Punishment, the UN Committee for the Rights of the Child, and the UN Committee for the Rights of Persons with Disabilities.[8] As the UN Special Rapporteur on Torture stated: 'genital-normalizing surgeries [performed] under the guise of "reparative therapies" … are rarely, if ever, medically necessary, lead to severe and life-long physical and mental pain and suffering and can amount to torture and ill-treatment' (Mendez, 2016: para 48). These bodies have condemned over 40 states, including the UK, for failing to protect intersex infants from these surgeries. So far, however, these supranational interventions have failed to effect medical practice (Garland et al, 2022). Nonetheless, and as the rest of the book makes clear, the medical conceptualization of intersex embodiment is becoming increasingly challenged by law.

Medical embodiment provides a very important backdrop to the ways in which legal embodiment is understood and produced (Fox and Thomson, 2017; Dietz, 2018; Thomson, 2022). Intersex embodiment is a particularly stark example of where our concepts about an issue or identity are produced directly from medicine and, indeed, many of the subsequent chapters are based around how far legal conceptualizations of intersex challenge or reproduce this medical framing. Nonetheless, there are myriad other examples of where medicine becomes the dominant lens through which bodies are conceptualized; some examples being trans embodiment (Sharpe, 2009b; Cowan, 2009; Latham, 2017; Dietz, 2018; Dietz and Pearce, 2020), disability (Keywood, 2010; Fox et al, 2020), pregnancy (Murphy, 1997; Naffine, 2003; Fox and Murphy, 2013), circumcision (Fox and Thomson, 2005, 2009, 2010, 2012; Earp et al, 2017;) and anorexia (Murphy, 1997; Keywood, 2000; Fox and Murphy, 2013). This list is, of course, non-exhaustive but highlights some of the spaces where medical conceptualizations of the body are either privileged over and above legal understandings of the body or where legal understandings are produced *through* medical framings. Part of the deference of law to medicine is

8 For an overview of these legal documents see Garland et al (2019) or Sudai (2017).

based around medical constructions still being understood as 'natural' and 'objective' rather than socially contingent (Butler, 1993; Fausto-Sterling, 2000; Thomson, 2022). As a result, much of the legal pushback, both at the UN and, as we shall explore in Chapter 5, in jurisdictions like Malta against aesthetic 'normalizing' interventions has stalled against medical frameworks that present atypical genitalia as 'unnatural' and the interventions as a return to the natural 'into the time of the (constructed) sex binary, where morphology fits social expectation. … Through these narratives, surgery is positioned as retrieval, cutting away unintended growth and refashioning developmental time-lines' (Grabham, 2012: 13). The construction of these surgeries as somehow natural and inevitable mean that the very real harms documented by intersex people fail to be seen as *legal* harms. The potential 'criminality' of the action is delimited on account of the legal silence around these issues (Giliani, 2020). Again, we will return to the interplay of medical and legal embodiment in the subsequent chapters.

The difficulties challenging medical embodiment

Despite these widespread criticisms, medical practice has not altered and surgeries on infants continue (Monro et al, 2017; Garland and Travis, 2020a, Garland et al, 2021). This is in part due to the strength of healthcare's jurisdictional claim over intersex (Garland and Travis, 2020a) which has now been largely unchallenged since the 19th century. Indeed, when the UK was challenged on this matter by the UN Committee on the Rights of the Child (CRC) in 2016, Flora Taylor Goldhill (then the Director for Children, Families and Communities, Department of Health) deferred responsibility for these matters stating that: "NHS England are responsible for specialised commissioning which covers this area. They wish to work with stakeholders to improve the services for these children and their families" (Taylor Goldhill 2016). This statement continues the reification of the medical construction of intersex that took hold in the 19th century. Such a deferral to medical authority has made it difficult for intersex activists to achieve meaningful change in terms of medical practice. Indeed, it was evident that our respondents felt unable to challenge the medical approaches to intersex embodiment and that their voices for the most part went unheard by the medical community: "it's unbelievable to me that clinicians do not want to hear from people, from a population who has been affected. How they insist that they have done the right thing when hundreds if not thousands of people are saying, 'No, you have not,' it's mindboggling" (Respondent 4). Many respondents felt that the intersex community lacked the resources to combat the dominance of the binary sex model perpetuated by the medical profession, which respondents stated was "very strong, very powerful, very well-funded" (Respondent 15). Comparatively, intersex activists, charities and organizations were unfunded, relying mostly on unpaid volunteers from a variety of backgrounds. One respondent could not take part in this project because "we have no employed staff and work on [the organization] in our spare time" (Respondent 10). Additionally, many individuals may not want to challenge the medical profession as they are reliant on the provision of medicine on account of their initial medical intervention:

> '[W]hen you have a child and then they do the castration when he's little and the parents really know when the child is after ten years we will need a doctor who gives us prescription for hormones. So there's also a dependency. They are dependent on the doctors and then they don't want to criticize them because there's some fear of reprisals in the background.' (Respondent 6)

This type of statement highlights the complexity of the embeddedness of the intersex person as they remain reliant upon the very institution they seek to alter. Consequently, respondents viewed law as an integral part of a broader strategy to challenge this power imbalance between medicine and intersex: "until doctors and clinicians are being sued and they feel it economically, I think that is going to have the biggest impact, that and then along with that education in the mainstream media" (Respondent 4). In the UK, there are some early signs of potential change in this area. The Government Equalities Office conducted a 'Call for Evidence on Variations of Sex Characteristics' in (2019) and the results from this are pending. The NHS Specialised Commissioning Group has proposed a clinical commissioning policy for gonadal and genital surgery for infants and children with differences in sex development, although this is still in development. In the US the Ann & Robert H. Lurie Children's Hospital and Boston Children's Hospital have pledged to stop performing some types of non-therapeutic surgeries on intersex children until the child can consent. This has been supported by American Academy of Family Physicians, the North American Society for Pediatric and Adolescent Gynecology, the Massachusetts Medical Society, and the Gay and Lesbian Medical Association (GLMA): Health Professionals Advancing LGBTQ Equality. However, gonadectomies, phalloplasties and surgeries on boys with hypospadias look set to continue, in part because medical professionals still understand these surgeries in terms of correcting a 'disorder'. Crucially, this is due to the consensus statement's decision to omit hypospadias from its remit except in some limited circumstances. As a result, hypospadias continues to hold a liminal space outside of disorders of sex development and intersex status that in turn shields medical professionals from the criticisms of these surgeries. The remainder of this book will examine the ways in which law constructs intersex embodiment and whether, ultimately, they represent a move away from the conceptualization of intersex and its framing through medical embodiment.

Conclusion

Since at least the 19th century, intersex embodied people have largely been absent from legal concern and instead have been constructed as a medical 'problem', forestalling questions of identity and legal protection. Consequently, intersex bodies have been regulated informally by the medical profession, which has constructed a biomedical narrative of intersex through a catalogue of sex development 'disorders' and 'diseases' that (despite their often benign medical nature) are portrayed as requiring medical intervention (Davis, 2015). As Malatino highlights: 'One can be intersex but only if it's a trait or disorder; one is always, despite being intersex, also irrevocably male or female – and it's the job of modern Western medical science to discern which of those one is' (Malatino, 2019: 53). This narrative has traditionally embedded these issues within the private sphere and outside of public concern and thus state responsibility. Since the early 20th century, intersex embodiment has been understood medically with a focus on 'normalizing' or 'fixing' these bodies through interventions to ensure they adhere to the sex binary. Surgeons routinely surgically alter children born with atypical genitalia, allocating them as male or female, which typically results in a lifetime of surgical treatments and hormonal dependency to maintain their allocated sex (Greenberg, 2012). These interventions are usually non-therapeutic, having no medical benefit and yet, as we have seen, can lead to life-long physical problems. Surgical interventions tend to occur soon after the child is born which, combined with the culture of secrecy that accompanies intersex variations, has led to an inability to frame intersex embodiment in terms of politics or law. Little is known about intersex outside the medical profession, and the shame and stigma attached to a 'disorders of sex development' label prevents families and individuals from speaking out. Indeed, many families go to great lengths to hide such a 'diagnosis' (Hegarty and Chase, 2000, Davis, 2015).

The construction of intersex as a disorder is not neutral – medical professionals are 'actively involved in the very production of the phenomena they represent' (Lachmund, 1998: 780). The notion of intersex as a disorder is 'freighted with meaning that is tied to a sense of self' (Karkazis and Feder, 2008: 2016). Moreover, framing intersex through medical embodiment constrains 'how parents view their affected children, how intersex people understand themselves, and how others not directly involved in medical settings – such as gender and legal scholars, historians, and media commentators – conceive of and theorize about gender, sex, and the body' (Reis, 2007: 536). The resistance to the term 'disorder' within our respondents was palpable. In contrast, those who have praised the success of DSD nomenclature are largely 'the same people who attended the conference. … The process has been insular and the praise, self-congratulatory' (Topp, 2013: 188).

Given law's role in determining who does and does not legitimately participate in society, its failure to recognize intersex people has had profound implications. Legal silence effectively legitimizes the medical account of intersex embodiment as a purely material concern, permits attempts to 'normalize' these bodies and enables their social or cultural erasure. Thus, law aligns itself with the biomedical discourse of intersex depicting such bodies as deviant or unruly and in need of taming (Travis, 2015: 182). In doing so, law reaffirms a binary understanding of sex (Dreger, 1998) and consequently places intersex individuals outside the scope of law; unable to participate in or to challenge the dominant biomedical narrative. Law's silence is therefore not neutral; rather it perpetuates the existence of a striking power imbalance between intersex people, their families and the medical profession (Garland and Travis, 2018). The history of the medical profession is tied to notions of binary sex which it reinforces and legitimizes (through the privileging of scientific knowledge) (Dreger, 1998) in order to maintain its own epistemic primacy. Treatment and diagnoses, therefore, must be understood through a general cultural, social and state acceptance of sex as binary. Within this context medical knowledge that reaffirms contemporary cultural norms is privileged over the lived experiences of individuals who do not conform to this binaristic model, who are routinely characterized as a very small, unrepresentative minority (Ahmed et al, 2016). Moreover, such an analysis is attentive to the pressures that medical professionals face from other institutions. The familial institution, for example, exerts considerable pressure on medical professionals to produce a 'normal' child in order to create certainty and stability for their own normative worldview (Timmermans et al, 2019). As a result, decision making in this field is a complex entanglement of cultural and social norms, scientific knowledge claims and medical pragmatism.

Against this background, at least for our respondents, law is often seen as a tool of empowerment, giving centrality to the voice, desires or best interests of the child (Bird, 2005). Law is capable of levelling the playing field and disrupting medical embodiment; and therefore the gradual legal recognition of intersex potentially indicates a shift in power and knowledge whereby intersex individuals can be framed in both medical and legal terms (Bird, 2005). Yet, as the rest of the book will explore, it is unclear how far, if at all, responses to intersex framed through legal embodiment are actually challenging this dominant medical narrative.

3

Non-Binary Embodiment: Intersex and Third-Gender Markers

Introduction

The last chapter traced the historical pathologization of intersex and how medicine came to dominate contemporary understandings and approaches to intersex embodiment. The result of this medical framing has not only been routine irreversible interventions performed on intersex children, but also the cultural and institutional disappearance of intersex as a concept. Medical erasure has worked to reify medical power/knowledge by making it extremely difficult for the intersex community to come together and challenge medical practice or to identify alternative conceptualizations of intersex embodiment. Accordingly, much activist work has centred on disrupting medical embodiment by raising awareness of intersex as the starting point to improve lived experiences and ultimately stop medical interventions on children.[1] This chapter traces the most prevalent way in which intersex embodiment has become recognized in non-medical realms – outside binary conceptions of sex and gender.

To begin with, the chapter traces the different ways in which institutions have recognized intersex embodiment as outside the binary. While some contemporary approaches have depicted intersex embodiment as synonymous with non-binary identity, historical institutional approaches viewed intersex embodiment as a childhood place-holder for the two-sex model. This often facilitated a more enlightened (although not unproblematic) approach to intersex embodiment than seen in modern discourse with themes of flexibility, deferability and, to some degree, individual lived experience and autonomy appearing within and informing legal frameworks.

[1] See, for example, Intersex Equality Rights UK recent campaign to increase the visibility of intersex in the LGBT Pride and Progress flags (Parsons, 2021) or Intersex UK's appearance in *The Independent* (Morrison, 2013).

The chapter then juxtaposes this to some present-day understandings of intersex embodiment which have placed intersex within a legal three-sex model. This epistemological shift from place-holder to non-binary has been heavily influenced by feminist and queer writings in this area as well as the growing visibility and organization of the non-binary trans movement. Discursively, this view has been reaffirmed by a number of high-profile news stories where intersex people have claimed that the state ought to legally recognize their sex as something other than male or female (Davidson, 2014; Associated Press in Denver, 2015; Anonymous, 2016; Jarvis, 2018; Bowcott, 2019). In many jurisdictions, this non-binary conception of intersex embodiment has been cemented within law and policy for adults and children alike: Australia permits adult individuals to have third markers on identity documents such as passports, and jurisdictions like Chile and Germany have included third markers on birth certificates for children with indeterminate sex. The US also announced a decision to introduce X markers on passports, with the first one being issued to intersex campaigner Dana Zzyym on 27 October 2021. This chapter critically considers the lived impact of this non-binary framing and examines whether acknowledging intersex embodiment in this way has challenged the medical power imbalance that has dominated the 20th century. Ultimately, we problematize the depiction of intersex embodiment as non-binary when followed through into policy development and legislation.

Intersex as a place-holder for binary sex

As set out in the last chapter, intersex embodiment has a long *medical* history of being placed within binary approaches to sex. In some *legal* traditions, however, intersex has been more commonly understood as outside the concepts of male and female. For some, this liminal space was a place-holder until the appropriate sex could be determined upon reaching the age of majority. Bracton wrote in 1260 that '[m]ankind may also be classified in another way: male, female, or hermaphrodite' and that '[a] hermaphrodite is classed with male or female according to the predominance of the sexual organs' (Bracton, 1968: 31), while in 1628 Lord Coke stated that 'an Hermaphrodite may purchase according to the sex which prevaileth' (Coke, 1628: XXXIII). These legal texts, almost 400 years apart, demonstrate a legal awareness of intersex embodiment framed as outside the sex and gender binary while also highlighting that legally they should properly be subsumed within the corpus of the binary when this can appropriately be determined. Legal embodiment, at least historically, has sought to reaffirm the gender binary. In contrast to contemporary approaches, these legal frameworks provided a degree of flexibility and autonomy to sex assignment by taking account of the lived gender experience of the individual. It is worth highlighting that sex was not formally and consistently registered on birth certificates at this time and so flexibility may well have arisen from a less rigid approach to legal requirements around recording of sex. However, at this time, conceptualizations of intersex did not challenge the 'natural' order of the binary and ultimately individuals had to conform to heteronormative expectations of binary gender roles.

Arguments for the recognition of a third gender across Europe have thus often been premised on the basis of their *pre-determinative* status. As discussed in the previous chapter, a 'true sex' would eventually be assigned. In 1840s France for example, there were calls to recognize the 'sexe douteux' or doubtful sex on birth registration documents (Loir, 1854: 1; Mak, 2005). These calls were premised on the basis of the avoidance of the 'sad results of errors' (Loir, 1854: 1). The sadness that stemmed from these errors, however, at least for Loir, arose from the potential for 'unnatural' and incongruous same-sex relationships. To combat these, Loir recommended legislative responses to protect individuals and society. Loir 'proposed three additions to the existing regulation. First, a physician should be present at all births to establish the sex of a newborn child. Second, doubtful sex should be indicated on birth certificates. Finally, all persons of doubtful sex should be physically examined before marriage' (Mak, 2005:199). This third gender, although indeterminate at birth, was understood as being properly determined by medical professionals once the child reached maturity. Thus, the gender binary is reaffirmed through science that can determine the 'truth' of sex (Fausto-Sterling, 2000). This early-proposed legal approach to intersex embodiment thus emphasized liminality and deferred decision making while also centering medical knowledge.

Similar provisions were suggested in Germany in the early 1900s where Hirschfeld made a proposal for the sex of children to be registered as undecided or doubtful in cases where midwives and doctors felt that the sex was unclear (Hirschfeld, 1906: 614; Mak, 2005: 204). Mak notes that in Germany there were a number of births recorded as '*zwitter*' (hermaphrodite) in the birth registry. In the cases Mak examined, however, these children died before maturity leaving the gender binary unproblematized. However, the debate in Germany offered a different perspective to that seen in France. While France had been concerned with the social and moral implications of those with indeterminate status, the debate that reigned in Germany centred on the harm that could be caused to the intersex individual themselves as a result of early sex assignment (Mak, 2012: 168). Many medical professionals argued that it simply was not possible to determine sex at such an early age and that accurate sex assignment required input from the individual themselves with some account of their 'psyche' (Mak, 2012: 168). Other practitioners were concerned about the social harm that would follow from designating an individual as 'indeterminate' (Mak, 2012) including ruptures to the 'naturalness' of sex as binary and the concomitant gender roles, sexualities and hierarchies (Dreger, 1998). On this basis Landau (1903) advised that sex assignment should be delayed until the onset of puberty (Mak, 2012). This proposed approach to legal embodiment prioritized autonomy and choice, ensuring that parents and the individual were able to choose for themselves at a later date (Wilhelm, 1909; Mak, 2012: 168).

These seemingly enlightened considerations of intersex lived experience and individual harms appear somewhat surprising given that many of these issues are largely absent from much of the contemporary debates on intersex. However, this German concern over the intersex individual is reflective of the historical recognition of intersex as a third sex for over 100 years in Prussian law, prior to the establishment of the German empire (von Wahl, 2019: 9). The General Prussian Code (ALR) of 1794 set out a series of provisions known as the 'hermaphrodite articles' (von Wahl, 2019):

> §19: When hermaphrodites are born, the parents shall decide which sex they should be raised as.
> §20: Such a person, after completing his eighteenth year, can choose which sex he wants to belong to.
> §21: His future rights are determined based on this decision.
> §22: If the rights of a third party are dependent on the sex of an ostensible hermaphrodite, then the former can petition for an examination by authorized experts.
> §23: The findings of the experts shall be decisive, even against the choice of the hermaphrodite and his parents.

These legal provisions reflect a similar understanding to England and Wales pre 20th century where intersex is depicted as a place-holder status; a temporary state that ended at adulthood rather than a permanent third marker (von Wahl, 2019: 10). Family autonomy is prioritized until the individual reaches 18 and, similar to the provisions within England, there is some degree of flexibility afforded to the individual with a greater account for choice and therefore their lived experience – they can choose their sex. However, under this model of legal embodiment the binary system of sex remained central to adulthood and therefore full legal citizenship. Nonetheless, even in this early legal model of embodiment we can see the overreaching power of the paradigmatic medical account of intersex embodiment who, per §23, could overrule the individual and their family. Some of our respondents from our SLSA empirical project were aware of these historical legal provisions in Prussia arguing that, comparatively, "how [intersex people] were treated was more enlightened than today. In the middle ages they were legally recognized. Every professor of law learned the first lesson in school, there are men, there are women and there are hermaphrodites" (Respondent 5).

However, the recognition that law had offered to intersex individuals was gone by the start of the 20th century, in part due to the pre-eminence of the medical account of embodiment. The Prussian provisions were not translated into the German empire's Civil Code 1900. Rather the new code recognized sex as a binary. In England, references to the hermaphrodite had all but disappeared from law by the end of the 19th century (Sharpe, 2009a: 125). This trend towards legal erasure and silence was largely the result of the developments in the field of medicine traced in Chapter 2. By fixing individuals into the sex binary, the need for such institutional recognition disappeared.[2] Intersex remained largely unrecognized by legal and political institutions in the Global North for over 100 years until Australia, in 2003, became the first jurisdiction in the West to allow for a third marker to be included on passports.[3] This new legal and political recognition, however, offers an interpretation of intersex where intersex is no longer depicted as a 'place-holder' status, but rather as a third sex. While the past ten years has seen a flurry of different jurisdictions begin to take account of intersex, in many jurisdictions such as England and Wales, there remains no legal acknowledgement of intersex. This chapter shall now examine instances where intersex embodiment has been conceptualized as non-binary through a 'third' gender lens and the problematic way in which this has influenced cultural and political debate.

Intersex as a third gender

Currently, one of the most powerful conceptualizations of intersex embodiment is that it is synonymous with the term non-binary. This contemporary framework is, in part, attributable to feminist and queer scholarship alongside the increasing cultural visibility of the non-binary trans movement (which we address in more detail in Chapter 4). While law and policy failed to recognize intersex for most of the 20th century, feminist and queer theorists began to write about intersex with increasing frequency (see, for example, Herdt, 1993; Turner, 1999; Tauchert, 2002; Benson, 2005; Bird, 2005; Knouse, 2005; Reilly, 2005; Morland, 2009; Holmes, 2008b, 2009; Bettcher, 2015; Rubin, 2017; Feder, 2021; Monro et al, 2021). Given feminism and queer theory's primary concern of unmasking inequalities on the basis of sex, gender and sexuality, such theoretical engagement with intersex has recognized potential in terms of unmasking

2 For more, see Chapter 2.

3 X markers on passports had actually been recognized much earlier, primarily for the quick processing of refugees following the Second World War. Australia, however, was the first jurisdiction to link these x markers to intersex embodiment.

the heteronormative underpinnings of medical interventions (Turner, 1999). However, much feminist scholarship has not focused on the harms produced by the medical profession, but instead used the phenomena of intersex to affirm social constructionist approaches towards sex and gender (see, for example, Koyama and Weasel, 2002, for criticisms of such academic appropriation). To understand the challenges that this has posed in terms of intersex embodiment and third-gender markers, it is first necessary to set out how and why scholarship became interested in intersex as an object of study.

Prior to the 1990s, anglophone first-wave and second-wave feminists argued that there was a nature/culture distinction between sex and gender: gender was culturally constructed, while sex was binary, natural and innate forming the basis for social expectations regarding gender roles. For some influential early second-wave feminists this work was directly influenced by the work of John Money (Oakley, 1972). In contrast, third-wave feminism began to challenge these binary and essentialist understandings of sex and gender. The most notable example of this can be found in Butler's *Gender Trouble: Feminism and the Subversion of Identity*, where Butler argues that sex is not an immutable characteristic but, as with gender, is a cultural construct (1993: 7): the social discourses that surround biology shape the very meaning of sex. Accordingly, Butler argued that there is no biologically 'true' essence of either man or woman (1993: 9). Moreover, there is no natural or inevitable relationship between sex and gender; sex does not form the basis for binary gender (1993: 9). Instead, gender is performed iteratively; it is something that people do rather than are. In depicting sex and gender as socially constructed, Butler's thesis widened the concept and potential of gender by destabilizing the binary models of sex and gender and the idea that a fundamental distinction can be drawn between men and women (1993: 10–12). In doing so, Butler paved the way for understanding that individuals can experience gendered identities that exist outside a binary system (1993).

Butler did not write about the intersex experience but instead drew on the experience of trans people and drag as examples of individuals subverting gendered identity norms. However, many scholars have used intersex to support a critique against socially imposed binary models of sex and gender. Turner, for example, writes how intersex exemplifies Butler's views as:

> Intersexed bodies can matter (i.e. can only exist socially) only if they can be made to fit within the dimorphic sex schema that follows from concepts of what male and female persons should look like and how they should act. Medical intervention is almost always deemed necessary in order to make the unruly intersexed body conform. (Turner, 1999, 459)

In doing so, these theorists have constructed a particular understanding of what it means to be intersex which has had consequences for the development of law and policy in this area. Significantly, many have sought to articulate intersex as a fully developed third gender – not merely as a temporary space of pre-assignment. A typical example of this line of thinking is expressed by Knouse who writes:

> The addition of a legitimate third sex category to our own social discourse-i.e., male, female, and intersex-would be a positive first step toward deconstruction of the male/female binary. … Recognition of intersex as an ontologically distinct sex category would liberate intersex individuals from the normalizing and constricting sex stereotypes that are currently imposed upon them, and would simultaneously begin a larger project of breaking down the sex stereotypes currently imposed upon males and females. Allowing sexual incongruities to exist among intersex individuals would presumably also assist in removing the stigma presently associated with other types of sexual incongruities, including those of gender variants, transgenders, lesbian, gay, bisexual, and transsexual individuals. (Knouse, 2005: 153)

This position is supported by several other theorists who see intersex as existing outside the gender binary. Benson for example, notes that 'children who are born intersexed … have no constitutional right to choose whether to remain intersexed or to become male or female' (Benson, 2005: 31). Such a position implies that intersex can itself be a fully-fledged gender category. She goes on to state that:

> As our society recognizes that the gender binary is simply a myth put into place to protect social mores … we will be more willing to recognize that there are other ways to live out one's life than to consistently be defined as man or woman. On that day, transgendered and intersexuals alike will truly know what it means to be free. (Benson, 2005: 63)

Again, the presence of a third gender here is invoked to, ultimately, undo gender, offering a greater level of freedom moving beyond binary models of identity and recognition. Of course, as Bettcher (2016) notes, not all feminist and queer scholars have depicted intersex in this third-sex model. For example, Herdt (1993) and Tauchert (2002) both argue that the embodied experience of being intersex cannot be accounted for by third-gender models. Tauchert instead argues for a more nuanced or 'fuzzy' account of gender that avoids a singular 'catch-all' category of those that do not fit into male or female categories. Rather they argue that there must be 'recognition of the interconnectedness of sexual embodiments … by centring on intersexed subjectivity as a new, and inclusive, normative ideal to which all embodied subjects conform to some degree' (Tauchert, 2002: 37).

Nevertheless, the extensive writing in this area has led to a body of 'academic knowledge' depicting intersex as non-binary. Moreover, some commentators have argued that there is a *need* to translate this third-gender model into law. Bird, for example, highlights the transformative possibility of recognizing intersex as a legal sex category in its own right but frames it as 'a tactic in a struggle' (Bird, 2005: 65). While acknowledging that such a tactic may have some (unexplored) downfalls she notes that 'one of the likely effects of the creation of a legal space for intersex would be the increasing social space for those who choose to occupy it' (Bird, 2005: 65). Likewise, Reilly criticizes the law's replication and rigid enforcement of the gender binary as a key issue facing intersex people. As she writes:

> the legal response to intersexuality is bound by wholesale acceptance of the deeply rooted assumption that sex identity is simple and binary - male or female. This acceptance, unquestioned and virtually invisible, has made the legal system an active enforcer of differentiation that operates inexorably to exclude intersexuals from basic protections of the law. (Reilly, 2005: 299–300)

Such an account acknowledges that the legal recognition of intersex status may empower in the long term; the creation of a legal space will increase the visibility of intersex individuals at the institutional and discursive levels. Bird, for example, argues that such legal acknowledgement of a non-binary account of intersex embodiment will not only create greater space for political negotiation, but it may create a social space for individuals to participate in if they so wish (2005: 67). This may in turn give individuals a legal platform to legitimately challenge the authority of the medical profession and fundamentally instigate broader social changes that redress substantive inequalities. Such academic calls have been echoed by high profile cases of intersex people presented in the mainstream media.[4] Dana

[4] One of the reviewers, Jens Thielsen, raised the point that using the term 'high-profile' might do some work to delegitimize the applicants in these cases and media stories by suggesting that they were lucky or privileged enough to have access to the courts, the media and other resources, whereas the majority of intersex people go unheard. In doing so we may inadvertently contribute to underemphasizing that the people involved in high-profile court cases and so on are also trans and intersex persons with a specific take on what social justice for them would look like: in this case, involving gender markers beyond the binary. Of course, we are trying to ensure that we take seriously the experience of being intersex from a range of perspectives. What is interesting though is that almost all news stories about intersex people revolve around third-gender markers. This may be because this is the most easily digestible understanding of what intersex *is* within popular

Zzyym, for example, made headlines internationally in 2015 when they sued the state of Colorado for the state's failure to provide a third-gender option on official state documentation (Associated Press in Denver, 2015). Similar cases have been brought forward by intersex people Alex Jürgen in Austria (Anonymous, 2016), Leonne Zeegers in the Netherlands (Jarvis, 2018), and non-binary activists Christie Elan-Cane in the UK (Bowcott, 2019), and Norrie in Australia (Davidson, 2014). At least for the intersex people involved in these cases, intersex embodiment should be understood as non-binary and is not merely a space prior to the determination of their 'true' gender that we saw in the historical institutional approaches towards intersex.

This understanding of intersex has had an important framing effect on the types of laws that have been introduced and, significantly, mark a very different conceptualization of intersex embodiment; intersex is not a liminal place-holder but rather a third option disrupting binary models of sex and gender. Australia's Department for Foreign Affairs and Trade recognizes a third marker on passports. New Zealand also allows 'X' on passports for those of 'indeterminate/unspecified' sex. However, there is no mention of 'intersex' and applicants are classified as 'transgender applicants'; thus it is questionable how far intersex individuals would be able to use this third marker.[5] Outside the West, Argentina, Bangladesh, India, Nepal, Pakistan, Taiwan and Uruguay all allow a third marker for its trans, intersex or third-gender individuals.[6]

Many of these non-binary approaches to legal embodiment focus on opt-in markers for adults – sometimes intersex only, sometimes for intersex as well as other non-binary identities. In this case, the marker tends to be optional, where the individual can *choose* to have a third marker rather than being compelled to do so on account of their intersex variation.[7] New Zealand, for example, allows individuals to select an 'X' on the passport without requiring changes to be made to birth certificates or citizenship records. The label of 'X' is not mandatory for the individual. Other jurisdictions, however, are using a third-sex model as a mandatory category for any infant born with indeterminate sex.

culture. So, a broader point would be not to lower the media coverage of intersex people seeking a third-gender marker but rather to amplify other experiences of being intersex.

5 See www.passports.govt.nz/transgender-applicants (last accessed 10 July 2018).

6 There is an important connection between colonialism and binary understandings of gender that we do not have space to discuss in depth. For more discussion see, for example, Herdt (1993).

7 The notion of 'choice' may of course be limited by gateway requirements. Germany, for example, has required individuals to provide medical evidence of an intersex variation in order to access third-gender markers. The key point here though is that the designation of 'X' is not mandatory.

Germany's Gesetz zur Änderung personenstandsrechtlicher Vorschriften (Personenstandsrechts-Änderungsgesetz – PStRÄndG) 2013 amended § 22 Abs 3: Personenstandsgesetz to state that '(3) If the child can be assigned to neither the female nor the male sex, then the child must be entered into the register of births without such a specification'. A recent decision by the Bundesverfassungsgericht went beyond this to highlight a need for the positive recognition of a third-gender option (Order of 10 October 2017 – 1 BvR 2019/16). The subsequent legislation in this area has limited this positive recognition to intersex people rather than a potentially broader category of non-binary people. Subsequently, the German government introduced the term 'diverse' to legislation, but limited this only to intersex people who could prove a variation of sex development through medical evidence. Here, the potential disruption of a non-binary account of legal embodiment to medical accounts of intersex embodiment is immediately subsumed within the power/knowledge of the medical profession.

While this account of intersex as a third gender or non-binary identity has had much influence on institutional understandings of intersex, there are two core themes that ultimately render this form of recognition as problematic, which this chapter now explores. The first is that legal embodiment that frames intersex through third-gender markers misrepresent the lived experiences of most intersex people. Typically, legal embodiment that focuses on a 'third marker' conceives intersex as a matter of 'recognizing' an intersex status rather than a matter of bodily integrity and thus lack substantive and effective legal protections. Second, it has further shaped intersex embodiment in a potentially negative way. Where the 'X' is mandatory *especially* for children, it can be harmful and actively undermine the campaign for bodily integrity and self-determination. To exemplify this point, we draw on the German experience which, perhaps ironically, had been introduced to 'ease the burden of the parents having to assign a gender to intersex children as quickly as possible … [and] as a signal to parents and their doctors that both the legal system and society accept the existence of intersex' (Helms, 2018: 373). In practice, however, the legislation had several problematic effects on intersex embodiment. We now address these two core concerns in turn, drawing on our empirical evidence.

Third markers as a misrepresentation of intersex embodiment

Using third markers as the core method through which intersex embodiment is recognized has the effect of depicting lived-experience as non-binary. Importantly, some of the intersex individuals who have contacted us since our study have identified as non-binary. This chapter does not reject the idea that some intersex people are non-binary but does highlight the difficulties of conceptualizing *all* intersex embodiment through a non-binary lens.

Nonetheless, the sex and gender binary is often reaffirmed by intersex embodied people (Garland and Travis, 2020c):

> 'The vast majority of people do not identify, intersex people, do not identity as gender queer or outside of the gender binary.' (Respondent 13)

> 'The grand majority of intersex people in the world, the grand majority meaning 80–90% of people, who are born intersex, who have a gender assigned to them at birth, either surgically or just with a pen and paper, are fine with the gender identities they were assigned with. They're fine. The grand majority …' (Respondent 4)

> 'The belief that intersex means bi-gendered, the belief that all intersex people have a neutered gender expression or identity … it's simply not true.' (Respondent 3)

This is in part because some individuals may not be aware of their intersex variation.[8] At the same time, the experiences of people who do receive a medical diagnosis remain under-researched. Studies that do focus on sex assignment have found that of most intersex individuals identify within the sex binary and this is true even where sex is atypical at birth and thus medically 'assigned' either at birth or in adulthood.[9] Moreover, findings also suggest that where intersex people are incorrectly assigned a sex at birth and later reassigned they typically do so within the male/female binary (although it must be noted that these may have been the only options available to respondents in the studies).[10] This finding is not itself determinative particularly given how overwhelmingly negative medical and societal reactions to the concept of a third gender have been. This following quotation, for example, comes from a prominent medical textbook on intersex issues from the late 1960s:

---

8 Intersex variations are not always apparent at birth: '[I]ntersex people are diagnosed visually, at birth, or via amniocentesis, by chromosome, and other blood tests. … Intersex differences may also be determined during infancy, at puberty, when attempting to conceive, or through random chance.' Consequently, some individuals may have a variation but may never become aware of this fact: The Australian Senate Community Affairs Committee Secretariat (2013: para 1.7).

9 Research conducted in Australia found that 75 per cent of 292 respondents with atypical sex characteristics applied either the male or female sex marker (Jones et al, 2016). Schweizer et al (2014) found that only 7 per cent of individuals with intersex variations chose gender roles other than male or female.

10 Cohen-Kettenis (2005) found between 39 and 64 per cent of children with certain intersex traits changed from their assigned gender. The change was typically to either a male/female gender role.

> [The] normal functioning of sex is vital to the survival of our race, essential to our full assimilation as individuals into society, and pervades every aspect of our lives. To visualize individuals who properly belong neither to one sex nor to the other is to imagine freaks, misfits, curiosities, rejected by society and condemned to a solitary existence of neglect and frustration. Few of these unfortunate people meet with tolerance and understanding from their fellows and fewer still find even limited acceptance in a small section of society: all are constantly confronted with reminders of their unhappy situation. (Dewhurst and Gordon, 1969: vii)

Thus, it is not true to say that all intersex embodied people happily fall within the male/female binary (Garland and Travis, 2020c). A number of studies have shown that significant minorities of individuals identify outside the binary in some form. Jones et al (2016) for example, identified that 19 per cent of 292 respondents with atypical sex characteristics selected an 'X'/ 'other' marker rather than m/f, and 6 per cent were undecided as to which marker they would use. Similarly, Schweizer et al (2014) found that 18 per cent of individuals were unsatisfied with their current gender allocation. Other studies indicate that a small minority of intersex embodied individuals experience distress as a result of their sex assignment on birth.[11] The point we stress here is simply that given that the majority of intersex embodied people identify as either male or female, the conceptual and legal conflation of intersex with a third gender (as we will shortly discuss in relation to Germany) is both inaccurate and unhelpful (Garland and Travis, 2020c). It incorrectly implies both that most intersex individuals will identify outside male and female (because of their experiences with their bodies) and at the same time that only intersex embodied persons will have a gender identity that stretches beyond male and female (Garland and Travis, 2018 2020c; Renz, 2020a). Framing intersex legal embodiment through a non-binary lens therefore does not reflect the lived realities of most intersex individuals. As Respondent 15 stated: "not all intersex people are queer but some queer people are intersex."

When asked to discuss reforms such as the ones in Australia and Germany, many of our respondents claimed that status-based approaches failed to tackle the day-to-day concerns of intersex people and there was a general sense that status-based reforms would be ineffectual in practice. While interviewees

[11] These figures vary between studies. For example, Furtado et al (2012) found that 8.5–20 per cent of intersex embodied individuals experienced some sort of distress in relation to their gender identity. In comparisons, Callens et al (2016) found that 3.3 per cent of individuals changed gender and experienced distress about their gender from childhood.

generally recognized the potential that third markers like 'X', 'O' or 'I' on official state documentation (such as passports or birth certificates) had in terms of challenging the sex binary (and thus an important development for non-binary trans people who wish to choose a non-gendered or third-gender marker) the majority believed third markers were not appropriate to address specific concerns raised by intersex people. Many stated third markers would be an ineffective lens through which to understand intersex embodiment, as most intersex individuals would not actually use 'X' on documents like passports: "It's not an intersex issue. Most intersex are not interested in this" (Respondent 5); "Most intersex people … either identify as being male or female and that is reflected on the passport" (Respondent 1). Moreover, some were concerned that understanding intersex embodiment solely through a third-marker lens would further distort narratives that stem from the intersex communities themselves. A third-sex approach would fail to recognize sex as a spectrum with an infinite combination of possibilities and simply lead to a tertiary system with rigid categories: "I oppose them as far as 'X' includes intersex. The use of 'X' for intersex establishes or reinforces a notion that intersex is not 'male' or 'female'. This is nonsense. Sex is a spectrum from male to female (or vice versa) and intersex is a blend of both" (Respondent 2). Most notably then, respondents emphasized that a third marker should not be compulsory for intersex embodied individuals; X "should not be predicated on having intersex anatomy" (Respondent 4). Rather, third markers should be available for any individual who wished to use one.[12]

The question then is *how* has law and policy as well as much of academia so extensively misrepresented the main issues relating to intersex as well as the multifaceted ways in which intersex individuals experience gender.[13] The answer appears simple: the absence of lived intersex testimony informing academic and political debate. Despite feminism's deconstructive potential, most feminist engagement with intersex has come under considerable scrutiny for using intersex as an object of study rather than engaging with intersex subjectivities and their actual lived experiences (Turner, 1999; Koyama and Weasel, 2002; Holmes, 2008a). Accordingly, many academics

12 This would fit the trend towards self-declaration in legal gender recognition for trans people (for example, Ireland, Norway and Malta) and additionally benefit non-binary identities. For a critique of self-declaration see Dietz, 2018.

13 It is important to note that this chapter is also not suggesting that *all* feminist and queer scholars have depicted intersex in this third-sex model. Moreover, commentators like Kessler (1990) and Fausto-Sterling (2000) extensively critiqued the medical approach towards intersex and drew attention to the need to focus on the bodily integrity of those individuals. There are also an increasing number of intersex scholars who are enhancing the debate in these areas and recentring academic debates around intersex lived experiences. For an overview of this see Monro et al (2021).

have failed to account for or misrepresented the major issues facing intersex people, namely early and non-consensual interventions performed by medical professionals (Charlebois, 2014) and our respondents were aware of this issue: "you academics talking about issues like this, but how do you really know what these people feel like?" (Respondent 7) In doing so, this means that a large body of academic work actively misrepresents the multifaceted ways in which intersex individuals experience gender. Academia carries its own power/knowledge where it creates norms once research is peer-reviewed and published. This body of accepted knowledge then informs the shape of subsequent research, appearing in literature reviews as well as teachings on university courses (Koyama and Weasel, 2002). In an environment such as higher education in the UK which actively seeks research to be 'impactful', that is research which has 'an effect on, change or benefit to the economy, society, culture, public policy or services, health, the environment or quality of life, beyond academia' (REF 2021, 2019: 68), there is real and proven danger that academic misrepresentations of intersex may then inform law and policy, having a very real-world impact on how intersex embodiment is understood. This may be one reason why so much recent legal and political recognition of intersex embodiment has focused on the third-gender model rather than matters relating to bodily integrity. Our respondents often noted the poor research that was available to policy makers:

> 'One of the key things that we do is, a lot of policy members don't have the understanding to be able to tell what's good data, from what's bad data, or good policy from bad policy.' (Respondent 16)

> 'I think that intersex people face is being forced to conform to gender norms that are employed by society and those gender norms and sex norms um like are actually also supported by this information gathering system that the government uses.' (Respondent 1)

Concern about research quality and abuse of power by academics is ongoing, with many intersex organizations finding that their voices are misrepresented in potentially agenda-setting research.[14] Such epistemological problems within research are hard to correct. Not only are intersex embodied people a hidden population making it hard to find research participants, but this historical academic misrepresentation has created an understandable and very real distrust between intersex individuals and academic researchers. Our respondents demonstrated a 'caution' about engaging with research projects 'on' intersex: "I

[14] See, for example, Intersex Greece (2021) https://intersexgreece.org.gr/en/2021/11/02/press-release-about-bring-in-research-project/ where Intersex Greece issued a press statement about misrepresentation in academic research.

do not engage with academics who want to 'use' intersex people and our experiences without any benefit to us" (Respondent 2). Ultimately, this makes it even it harder to gather much-needed accurate data to challenge medical power/knowledge and drive real change in medical practice.

Such issues were reflected in our empirical work. Our initial framing of the project from which this book mostly draws upon was originally entitled 'The possibility of being X: Lessons from Australia's Construction of Intersex'. It focused on intersex as non-binary and ultimately set out to establish the impact of reforms in Australia that allowed third markers on passports and amended anti-discrimination legislation. As we began to reach out to activists, a number drew attention to our problematic focus and were concerned that we were focusing too heavily on issues relating to third genders rather than bodily integrity. This led to some refusing to take part. We have since had consent from these individuals to use our email exchange as data for this project:

> After reading, and re-reading this request several times, I do not feel it appropriate to participate. May I ask how changing designations on passports assists people born intersex? (Respondent 9)

> By framing your argument around the gender marker you are missing the point. The key issues lie elsewhere - and those other issues are what needs to be reported. (Respondent 18)

> Conflation of the X gender marker with intersex misgenders the overwhelming majority of intersex people, and is a human rights abuse that denies their identities, bodies and histories. (Respondent 18)

It was not until we engaged with intersex rights activists that we realized how misplaced our initial project was, and accordingly reframed it (and retitled it) to make sure that it did not conflate issues regarding gender identity and third markers with that of the intersex community.

Yet, for the most part, in legal challenges seeking non-binary or third-gender status markers and more general campaigns for non-binary recognition cases, intersex is often utilized as a tool to validate the legal need for a third gender. This approach to non-binary accounts of intersex directly opposes the first historical account of non-binary sex as pre-determinative. Whereas the latter seeks to police and reaffirm the gender binary, the former seeks to subvert and, in some circumstances, destroy it. A potential problem with both, however, is how spaces of third gender are understood, determined and regulated. Not only do these effect understandings of intersex, but they also shape the lived experience of intersex and produce knowledge about what intersex is. Ultimately, as we will now explore in regards to Germany's experience of intersex embodiment and third-gender markers, such legislation may inadvertently strengthen medicine's ability to determine who falls into these legal categories, as well as the (surgical and medical) methods needed to avoid them (Carpenter, 2018). While third-gender markers seem appealing to expanding adult choices, these same options may seem very daunting to the parents and carers involved in the clinical decision making around intersex children and unintentionally reduce the autonomy of those children.

Mandatory third markers as harmful

Our respondents emphasized that conceptualizing intersex embodiment purely though a third-gender approach, particularly for children, were likely to be harmful in practice. This means that framing intersex embodiment in particular ways can have a profoundly negative impact on lived experiences. Chiefly, non-conformity with the sex binary is highly associated with shame and stigma (Garland and Travis, 2020c). Therefore, most intersex people actively avoid being depicted as non-normative for fear of social marginalization and ostracization. Consequently, they (and their parents) *want* to be seen as 'normal' and view social acceptance to be intrinsically linked with conformity to the sex binary (Garland and Travis, 2020c). The use of a third marker would be counterproductive to this goal, potentially exposing information that they wish to remain unobserved (Garland and Travis, 2018): "They don't want to stick out. If they had the possibility they wouldn't use this opportunity to put an X instead of F or M. … Most intersex people I know, they are really afraid that somebody knows that they are intersex, even in the family" (Respondent 5). Rather than enhancing lived experiences, automatic third marker could actually be harmful and othering. Garland and Travis (2020c) note that it would further serve to 'other' intersex individuals, presenting intersex embodiment as a deviant or lesser sex, and thus ostracizing individuals at both cultural and institutional levels:

> 'The moment you start putting Os and Xs on there, it's like aren't you stigmatizing a group? Are you empowering them? Are you giving them more freedom or are you taking freedom away? … If I had an "X" on … my passport, I would not feel happier I think. I would not feel like I had more freedom.' (Respondent 13)

Such concerns have been played out in the German approach to intersex children despite the central justification behind the legislation being to protect intersex infants (Garland and Travis, 2020c). Concerns about the medical interventions performed on intersex infants had been politically debated in Germany following the mid-1990s. Since 1996, in Germany there have been four parliamentary inquiries into intersex and one motion.

In addition, in 2002 Michel Reiter started legal proceedings against the civil registry office for their refusal to register him as '*zwittrig*' (hermaphroditic), intrasexual or intersexual (FamRZ 2002, 955, 955). While the court acknowledged the long-term effects of hormonal and surgical management of intersex people they decided that every person is, ultimately, male or female. In 2006 the German Equal Treatment Law introduced limited protections for intersex people through an extension of the category of 'sexual identity' to 'homosexuals, bisexuals, transsexuals and intersexuals alike' (Kolbe, 2009: 152).

In 2012, following increasing pressure from intersex activists, the German Ethics Council, having been commissioned by the federal government, gave an opinion on the situation of intersex people in Germany. The opinion followed several discussion forums and hearings in 2010 and 2011, as well as an online public consultation phase. In their press release, the Ethics Council recommended that:

> Irreversible medical sex assignment measures in persons of ambiguous gender infringe the right to physical integrity, to preservation of sexual and gender identity, to an open future and often also to procreative freedom. The decision concerned is personal. The Ethics Council therefore recommends that it should always be taken solely by the individual concerned. In the case of a minor, such measures should be adopted only after thorough consideration of all their advantages, disadvantages and long-term consequences and for irrefutable reasons of child welfare. This is at any rate the case if the measure concerned serves to avert a serious concrete risk to the life or physical health of the affected individual. (Deutscher Ethikrat, 2012a: 1)[15]

They go on to note that:

> The Ethics Council also believes that personal rights and the right to equality of treatment are unjustifiably infringed if persons whose physical constitution is such that they cannot be categorized as belonging to the female or male sex are compelled to register in one of these categories. Provision should be made for such persons to register not only as 'female' or 'male' but also as 'other', or for no entry to be made until they have decided for themselves. ... Future decisions on legislation should be based on a consideration of whether it is still necessary for a person's sex to be registered at all. (Deutscher Ethikrat, 2012a: 1)

15 These materials were originally published in both German and English.

In the opinion itself they state that:

> The German Ethics Council takes the view that personal rights and the right to equality of treatment are unjustifiably infringed if persons whose physical constitution is such that they cannot be categorized as belonging to either the *female* or the *male* sex are compelled by law to be designated in one of these categories in the civil register. ... Provision should be made for persons whose sex cannot be unambiguously determined to register not only as 'female' or 'male' but also as 'other'. (Deutscher Ethikrat, 2012b: 166–7)

Despite the Ethics Council taking a strong stance on non-therapeutic medical interventions, only the recommendations on third markers on birth certificates were taken forward by the German government.

Prior to 2013, in Germany, the birth of a child had to be reported to the civil registry office within one week (§ 18 PStG), stating the names of the child and the parents, the sex of the child and the time of birth. Registration was only declaratory, however, and could be corrected.[16] As stated previously the Gesetz zur Änderung personenstandsrechtlicher Vorschriften (Personenstandsrechts-Änderungsgesetz – PStRÄndG) 2013 amended, § 22 Abs 3 Personenstandsgesetz so that: '(3) If the child can be assigned to neither the female nor the male sex, then the child must be entered into the register of births without such a specification.' The legislation was introduced to 'ease the burden of the parents having to assign a gender to intersex children as quickly as possible … [and] as a signal to parents and their doctors that both the legal system and society accept the existence of intersex' (Helms, 2018: 373). Crucially then, this legislation had been introduced to *improve* intersex lived experience and avoid medical interventions from occurring so early, and much of the discussion reflected some of the 19th-century concerns about introducing a third space on birth certificates. In practice, however, this legal framing of intersex embodiment had a number of problematic effects. First, the power to determine sex was largely left to medical doctors, ensuring that parents turned to surgical interventions more quickly in order to prevent their child being placed into this category (Travis, 2015; Amnesty International, 2017). Second, the wording of the legislation appeared to make the decision of whether a child should be recorded without gender as mandatory through the use of the term 'must'. Helms, however, describes this as a 'misconception' and is contravention of the 'intent and purpose of the provision, as well as the will of the legislature' (Helms, 2018: 372). Where the gender has not been

[16] OLG Zweibrucken 15.1.2003, *StAZ* 2003, 171, 172.

recorded parents can give this information to the civil registry office at a later date (§27(3) PStG). This information is dependent, however, on medical evidence (again reaffirming the medical approach to intersex embodiment).

Our empirical study reflected these concerns. Our interviews were carried out between 2014 and 2016 and therefore in the early years after this piece of legislation was introduced. None of our respondents were German although some did live in Germany at the time. Despite this, there was a lot of awareness of the legal developments in that jurisdiction. Notwithstanding the recency of the introduction of this legislation, our respondents were concerned that viewing intersex embodiment through the lens of a legal third marker would increase the likelihood of unnecessary medical interventions being carried out. Many respondents were highly critical of the approach adopted in Germany. While some respondents felt the ability to leave birth certificates blank where children were of indeterminable sex would alleviate the time pressures placed on parents, potentially preventing them from making hasty and irreversible decisions, many respondents were concerned that a blank or third marker on birth certificates would actually increase the chance of medical interventions:

> 'Allowing a birth certificate to be filed with an indeterminate marker would give parents time and doctors time to come to rational decisions and that that would discourage surgery. There's been various fears about it, including fears that doctors will say, "Well, I must … if you don't let me do surgery, I have to mark unknown on the birth certificate," or that parents or doctors will rush the surgery to avoid that unknown marker. We haven't seen yet how it plays out.' (Respondent 14)

This is because individuals and parents may go to extreme lengths to keep their/their child's intersex variance secret (Davis, 2015), severing contact with friends or family or even 'mov[ing] to another town and not [telling] anybody where they went' (Hegarty and Chase, 2000: 128). Indeed, understanding intersex embodiment through the frame of non-binary could drive parents towards gender-normalizing medical interventions and certainly in the German context this has been the effect (Travis, 2015; Amnesty International, 2017). The evidence produced since the introduction of this law has demonstrated a very small number of people who have been entered into the civil registry without a gender. The Federal Ministry of the Interior (Bundesinnenministerium) surveyed the use of the law during its first two years of enactment.[17] They found that during this period only 12 people had had no sex recorded. In roughly half of those cases, another gender

[17] BT-Drucks 18/7310, p 3.

was submitted within two months of the initial declaration suggesting that medical interventions and fundamental decisions about gender pathways had been made in an extremely short space of time. Althoff records that only 4 per cent of intersex children were recorded as outside male or female (2018: 395). This perhaps reflects the pressure from doctors who 'advise parents to choose a gender for their child "as a working assumption" in order to facilitate their integration into our society's binary gender order' (Helms, 2018: 374). Germany's approach to legal embodiment may therefore be implicitly pressurizing parents to place their children into the sex binary to avoid their child being categorized as outside the categories of male and female.

Framing intersex embodiment as non-binary may actually strengthen medical embodiment rather than disrupt it, as decision-making by the medical profession and parents are still underpinned by heteronormativity and binary assumptions. Therefore Laws that position intersex children as non-binary may infringe upon bodily autonomy, encouraging parents to agree to normalizing surgeries '– thus, handing more power to healthcare professionals' (Carpenter, 2018). This raises an interesting concern about the practical limits of a push against the gender binary. Even if intersex proves academic writings that binary sex is a social construct, there are consequences (or at least perceived consequences) for failing to conform to that social norm (Garland and Travis, 2020c). Children should not be at the forefront of such challenges: "If people were forced to fit into any box just because of their biology I would think that would be a case for further discrimination or stigmatization down the line" (Respondent 1); "parents will even more readily sign the consent form for compulsory medical treatment" (Respondent 5).

Interestingly, this view was taken into account by the German Ethics Council. As they note:

> However, since some people feel neither male nor female and also do not consider themselves to be living in a third sex, the designation of a third sex cannot take account of the needs of all those concerned, so that the problem would only be shifted elsewhere. … Again, new categories might contribute to the consolidation of old categories, so that the recognition of a third sex might lead not to acceptance by society but might even – and more probably – result in more extensive exclusion and stigmatization. (Deutscher Ethikrat, 2012a: 132–3)

Althoff also speculates, however, that it may reflect 'a lack of knowledge of the new regulations for medical professional groups, a lack of implementation in forms and IT systems (birth announcements), and also uncertainty as to when the medical conditions for a blank gender entry are met' (2018: 395).

The small figure, however, also included some adults who retrospectively recorded their gender as neither male nor female. Presumably for these adults, being outside the categories of male and female constituted a valid category in and of itself. In addition, the rate of non-therapeutic 'normalizing' surgeries performed between 2004 and 2014 remains unchanged (Althoff, 2018: 409), highlighting that the recognition of a third gender does not necessarily link to a decrease in these medical practices (Kloppel, 2016).[18]

Since the data collection from our empirical project, there have, however, been some attempts by Germany to improve this area of law. One of the chief criticisms of the Act was that initially the legislation understood intersex people as outside the gender binary but only in the negative sense that a sex was not assigned to them; indeterminant sex was 'recorded' by leaving the sex blank. Intersex embodiment was constructed in terms of not being male and female rather than in positive terms of what it is (or could be). In 2017, this was challenged in the German Constitutional Court for increasing the likelihood of medical interventions. In 2017 the German Constitutional Court (BVerfG) made a ruling on German birth registers (*1 BvR 2019/16 (2017)*) that the 2013 Gesetz zur Änderung personenstandsrechtlicher Vorschriften (Personenstandsrechts-Änderungsgesetz— PStRÄndG) established a 'negative' recognition of non-binary individuals, as the blank gender marker constituted a form of gender-based discrimination.[19] The complainant, Vanja, represented by the campaign group Die Dritte Option ('the third option'), outlined that the 2013 law pressurized parents to accept non-therapeutic medical and surgical interventions in order to secure a (male or female) registration rather than the blank space of non-registration. The BVerfG found in favour of the complainant, noting that that 'the current birth/gender registration system violated the right to the free development of a person's identity as encompassed in Article 2 of Germany's Basic Law. Having one's gender identity accurately recognised in law is therefore a fundamental right that the government needs to accommodate' (Renz, 2020a: 156). As Theilen notes, such a stance acknowledges that 'the availability of non-binary gender options within civil status law becomes a matter of visibility and of symbolic recognition … a step towards empowering those outside the gender binary by disrupting its self- evidence' (Theilen, 2020: 108). Further, the court found that the blank space designation:

18 Although it is perhaps worth noting that the introduction of the third gender has not neccessarily made things worse.

19 The BVerfG, had previously outlined the right to determine one's own gender identity within the context of binary gender options. In 2008 the court gave recognition to a constitutional 'right to recognition of one's self-determined gender identity' ('*Recht auf Anerkennung der selbstbestimmten geschlechtlichen Identität*') (*1 BvL 10/05 (2008)*). See, further, Dunne and Mulder (2018) and Renz (2020a).

> retains the exclusively binary model of gender and creates the impression that the legal recognition of an additional gender identity is not an option, with the entry of a legal gender instead being merely unsettled, unresolved, or forgotten about. This does not constitute recognition of the applicant's own experience of gender.[20]

As a result, the BVerfG determined that the German government had two potential options that needed to be implemented by 31 December 2018: provide a 'positive' third-gender option, such as 'inter' or 'diverse', or the removal of gender on birth certificates for all citizens. While the case was brought by an intersex person, the case was supported by an organization made up of both intersex and non-binary trans people. In addressing the specific concerns of the intersex applicant, the court utilized some narrow phrasings in both the operative parts of the judgment and in some parts of the justification. Nonetheless, the substance of the justification and other parts of the phrasing draw on the BVerfG's long-standing and relatively expansive case-law on trans rights, enabling the judgment to be progressive for both intersex people and non-binary individuals.[21]

In giving its reasoning the BVerfG interpreted gender as a crucial and inherent element in the creation of personality, a component that has 'outstanding significance' at an individual and societal level.[22] Given that the right to a free development of personality is constitutionally protected under German law the government are obligated to safeguard the expression of gender identity and ensure that people are supported in their gender expression. In the judgment the blank space of the 2013 legislation was understood as an inherent violation of this principle, particularly in the way it othered those included within it as being 'non-recordable' or without gender.

In December 2018 the German government responded to the BVerfG decision, through the creation of a new section, § 45b, to the Personenstandsgesetz (Personal Status Law).[23] This revision enables people to alter their legal sex/gender to a third-gender status of 'diverse'. However,

[20] German Federal Constitutional Court, Decision of 10 October 2017, Translation from Thielen (2020).

[21] On this potential ambiguity of the scope of the judgment, see also Dunne and Mulder (2018).

[22] 1 BvR 2019/16 paras 38–9.

[23] An alternative law was drafted by the left-wing party Die Linke, which suggested a 'more thorough and expansive reform of civil status law (e.g. broader scope of the third option, more flexibility in its designation, possibility of repeated change of legal gender, lack of medical gatekeeping) but also of other areas of law (e.g., most importantly, a prohibition of non-consensual surgeries performed on intersex infants; but also issues such as health care for trans persons and non-discrimination measures)' (Theilen 2020: 103).

this marker has been limited only to intersex people capable of providing medical evidence proving their variation in sex characteristics.[24] Positively, the amendment changes the 2013 law from a mandatory category to a more recognizably opt-in model (Theilen, 2020), responding to criticisms that had been made of the previous law (Travis, 2015). However, the government has implemented a very narrow interpretation of the BVerfG decision. In doing so the government have been keen to link the third gender to a biological understanding of sex. Consequently, as Renz notes, the amendment,

> problematically equates intersex conditions with gender diversity [and] … while some intersex people may wish to be recognised outside the female/male dichotomy, (e.g. the claimant in the BVerfG decision) … many individuals do not. This means that overall this new provision serves to maintain the outsider status of non-binary people while only bringing some intersex people inside the ambit of legal recognition. (Renz, 2020a: 158)

Theilen similarly notes:

> even intersex persons can only access these options if they are willing to submit medical certificates or, in some cases, an affidavit which likewise retains the focus on medical conditions and thus an element of gatekeeping and pathologisation; … the designation as '*divers*' remains the only option besides the blank space, with no possibility of further specification to accord with the diversity of self-identified signifiers among trans and intersex persons; and … the new law, like its predecessor, restricts itself too narrowly to one issue among many in civil status law, as well as leaving aside pressing issues in other areas of law such as the prohibition of non-consensual surgeries on intersex infants. (2020: 104)

Given the fear, secrecy and shame that drives many parents towards surgical interventions, this amendment to German Law, while symbolically significant, is unlikely to undo the harmful effects that the 2013 Act introduced. As with Australian anti-discrimination legislation (which will be discussed in Chapter 4) the victory here might be seen as largely symbolic and in terms of the state recognition of intersex embodiment. Kolbe noted: 'The establishment of a third sex would delegitimize the medicalization of intersexual bodies' (Kolbe, 2009: 164). However, the

[24] Bundesministerium des Innern, für Bau und Heimat. 2018. Entwurf eines Gesetzes zur Änderung der in das Geburtenregister einzutragenden Angaben. Berlin.

reality is that in Germany this has not been the case; the rates of surgeries have not decreased as a result and placing a third option on birth certificates has therefore not been enough to disrupt medical power/knowledge (Carpenter, 2018). Germany has since introduced its Law on the Protection of Children with Variants of Gender Development (2021), which expressly prohibits medical interventions that are unnecessary. While this piece of legislation is not without flaws (as we discuss in Chapter 5) (for example it has no penalties in place for the breach of this law), it represents a big step forwards in terms of the state engaging with intersex concerns. It also further, highlights the importance and efficacy of piecemeal and symbolic legislation over time.

Conclusion

Legal embodiment is produced through law's understanding of (and effect upon) bodies. In jurisdictions where intersex is understood through a non-binary lens a version of intersex is created that challenges paradigmatic medical understandings of intersex embodiment. Rather than a 'true' binary sex being 'discovered' sex and gender are culturally and epistemologically positioned as much more liminal. This potentially allows for more ontological opportunities for intersex people to identify with. In many ways, therefore, legal embodiment that is produced through a non-binary lens weakens the hold that medicine has over defining intersex – not least because both claim to engage with the materiality of the intersex body. Indeed, non-binary constructions perhaps do a better job of making sense of intersex people's chromosomal, hormonal and aesthetic make-up.

However, at the same time, law's production of non-binary subjects has done little to rupture the cultural value that is placed on the gender binary. While legal embodiment has created the possibility for non-binary legal subjects, the familial institution (a key factor in socialization) has quickly stepped in to reject this type of embodiment. In order to entrench children's position *within* the gender binary, parents have been quick to reaffirm medicine as their preferred method for constructing and interpreting their child's embodiment (Carpenter, 2018; Timmermans et al, 2019).

As a result, we can see the ways in which cultural and institutional understandings of intersex embodiment as non-binary are problematic when they are followed through into policy development and legislation. In part, this is because while some intersex people identify as non-binary the majority of our respondents were happy to define as male or female. Perhaps more importantly, policy and legislation that understand intersex embodiment solely or even primarily as non-binary has unintentionally strengthened medical power over intersex people and their placement within the sex binary (Carpenter, 2018). This may be because, while there has been a push for the recognition of a third gender, the nature of that third gender is itself contested. For medical doctors and many parents the third gender remains a pre-determinative space that comes before the appropriate assignment into the gender binary. In contrast, for many adults, the third gender is an identity that allows for freedom, acceptance and recognition. Ironically, however, the growing acceptance of the latter leads to an increase in power to the former. The recognition of a third gender, therefore, may lead to the consolidation of the gender binary. As Renz notes:

> In this process of providing a stable and legally intelligible and recognisable category, there also seems to be a concurrent process of implicitly stabilising and reifying the other two sex/gender categories. It is notable that the new German category 'divers' seems to suggest that while this new third option may contain a multitude of different identities, the other two are conversely limited to two clear identities with no room for diversity of genders. … This is of course not to suggest that having access to a third gender marker is not both practically and symbolically meaningful to people, but it nevertheless raises the question of whether this third category mainly serves to channel gender non-conformity away from the two pre-existing categories rather than offering a wider challenge to the legal categorisation of sex/gender as a whole. (Renz, 2020a: 162)

The German experience has highlighted many of the problems in this area when non-binary accounts of intersex embodiment become semantically (and legally) synonymous. Such legislative and policy approaches risk failing to give broader recognition to those that need them while misrecognizing many intersex people. As Theilen remarks: 'it clearly teaches us that attempting to use the law for emancipatory purposes is a risky endeavour, and it constitutes a stark reminder that legal gender recognition which truly challenges the gender binary without immediately reinstating static and coherentist notions of gender has yet to be achieved' (Theilen, 2020: 117). Similarly, as Holmes notes: '*recognition* of third sexes and third genders is not equal to *valuing* the presence of those who were neither male nor female, and often hinges on the explicit devaluation of women' (Holmes, 2004: 1). Clearly, the German approach to intersex has been undermined by the semantic linkage of intersex with non-binary and yet the newly introduced Law on the Protection of Children with Variants of Gender Development (2021) might see a move from superficial recognition towards a much more purposive approach focused on engagement, participation and voice in regards to intersex issues.

Unsurprisingly, then, most intersex rights activists do not advocate an intersex-specific third-gender marker for children and have serious concerns over the implications of such a legal device.[25] Intersex people were largely open to the idea of third-gender recognition for adults, but only on an opt-in (non-mandatory basis). Third-gender markers for children were seen to not only 'other' intersex individuals by constructing them in a manner that is entirely unsuited to their experiences, but also as pressurizing parents and medical practitioners into performing the very sorts of gender-normalizing surgeries that the community is seeking to prohibit by depicting intersex embodiment as non-binary. Most respondents believed that sex/gender markers should be entirely removed from official documents like birth certificates and passports,[26] not just for those who are intersex:

> 'Any sort of third category on a birth certificate can, in fact, be dangerous … because it may warrant medically unnecessary intervention, so parents may authorize such procedures in order to prevent their child from being placed into any third category. To me, the bigger issue is why do we need those categories at all?' (Respondent 13)

While respondents felt society was not ready to move away from sex/gender markers entirely, some respondents called for greater fluidity on birth certificates so children could amend the birth certificate if they wanted to. Participants noted that this alone, however, would not do enough to challenge the medical profession's continued use of non-therapeutic interventions. Certainly, participants were wary of paternalism, stigma and surveillance in their rejection of third-gender markers. Moreover, these types of legislation highlight the dangers of focusing on formal rather than substantive equality. State constructions of intersex as a third sex through legislation fail to take into account the wishes and desires of the intersex community, the majority of which define as male or female. Nonetheless, the most important consequence of the introduction of a third gender has been the concomitant strengthening of medical power and its continued regulation of the gender binary (Carpenter, 2018). This is in direct contrast to scholars like Kolbe who thought: 'The creation of a registration possibility like … "intersexual" would provide a legal basis for understanding intersexuality not as a disease or a malformation but as a valid sex category. … Furthermore, the creation of a third sex would make the punishability of surgical interference obvious' (Kolbe, 2009: 164). Such a view has been criticized by Morgan Carpenter, who notes that:

---

[25] However, most respondents welcomed a third-gender marker for all those who wished to use it. Their main concern was that a third-gender marker should not be used automatically for those with intersex variations.

[26] For an interesting discussion on this point see Cooper and Renz (2016).

> an assumed consequential relationship between non-binary classifications and an end to 'normalizing' medical interventions lacks evidence. Third sex models of intersex assume homogeneity in identity and fail to explain how new classifications interact with medical practices. Indeed, new classifications for infants and children have been opposed by intersex-led organizations in Australia and Europe, for adding to pressure promoting medical interventions in order to avoid perceived uncertainty and public disclosure. ... [Such analysis] homogenizes and naturalizes intersex bodies as 'others,' assuming that a natural and singular identity realized by intersex people is necessarily non-binary. (Carpenter, 2018: 491–2)

Legal approaches to intersex embodiment that are framed through non-binary accounts are therefore supported by some on the grounds of adult choices based on the unique experiences of the intersex body and the ontological choices that this enables. Problematically though, such arguments have a tendency to hand more power back to medical accounts of embodiment which attempt to eradicate differences and ambiguities in order to uphold the gender binary. In the Chapter 4 we trace similarities between the semantic, social and political linkages between legal embodiment that frame intersex through non-binary accounts and understandings of legal embodiment that frame intersex as LGBT, notably using a homonormative lens.

4

LGBT Embodiment: Queerness, Homonormativity and Anti-Discrimination Law

Introduction

In Chapter 3, we set out the problematic ways in which states frame intersex embodiment through a non-binary lens. This form of recognition *mis*recognizes many intersex people, constructing intersex in a way that is often unsuited to their lived experience. As we found from our interviews, many intersex people identify strongly within the gender binary and do not feel comfortable with the idea that intersex is synonymous with non-binary. As a result, third markers are an ineffective mechanism through which to disrupt medical embodiment and potentially harmful state response when used as a solitary or mandatory way of recognizing intersex persons. Our respondents felt that was particularly the case for children as this was more likely to encourage parents to undergo non-therapeutic medical interventions in order to avoid their child being determined as outside of the gender binary (Carpenter, 2018).

This chapter introduces a third way in which intersex embodiment is constructed – where intersex bodies are constructed as 'LGBT'. This LGBT framing applies regardless of the sexual or gender identification of the intersex person. Consequently, while intersex people might not necessarily agree with this framing on an individual level, through discursive and institutional positioning intersex people are understood through a lens of LGBT (Garland and Travis, 2020c). This framing of intersex embodiment as LGBT is constructed through (and produces much of) the stigma that intersex people face. As noted in Chapter 2, this stigma has roots within homophobia but, more recently, also shares similarities with transphobia. The stigmatization of LGBT embodiment plays out in a number of different ways for intersex people in the way in which they manage and experience their bodies and identities. Firstly, it contributes to the medical management and framing of intersex embodiment. As we identified in Chapter 2 much of the rationale for medical interventions on intersex people stemmed from an institutional desire to police same-sex relations relationships (Foucault, 1980; Dreger, 1998; Holmes, 2008a; Malatino, 2019). Early calls to medicalize the determination of sex were done explicitly to prevent 'unnatural' relations (Loir, 1854: 1). Loir suggested that same-sex relationships could be prevented, at least in part, by policing intersex people through the registration of indeterminate sex on birth certificates, medicalizing sex registration and the physical examination of intersex people before marriage (Loir, 1854; Mak, 2005). The very premise of 'fixing' intersex people was, therefore, based on the societal homophobia inherent to heteronormativity. This idea of 'fixing', however, does not address the social and cultural issues that intersex people face – instead focussing on fitting the individual into society.

Depending on the institutions (and cultural understandings) involved, this LGBT framing can then be subdivided into two separate approaches: queer and homonormative. These approaches can have very different impacts on the ways in which intersex people manage and experience their bodies and identities. In this chapter we begin with an examination into the ways in which understanding intersex embodiment through an LGBT lens has at different points categorized intersex embodiment as queer (where the destabilizing potential of intersex people in regards to institutions is foregrounded) or homonormative (where gaining access to heteronormative institutions is prioritized at the expense of challenging the medical institution). While we address the potential that LGBT brings for 'queer' readings of intersex embodiment that trouble institutions with their bodily indeterminacy, we outline that many institutional readings of intersex embodiment through this lens are in fact homonormative. Homonormativity refers to the potential for LGBT activism and policy development to be assimilative and reflect broader heteronormative goals (Duggan, 2002). Homonormativity is the cooption of the LGBT movements by those with capital (often cisnormative gay men) and the twisting of the movement towards their desires (for example the push for gay marriage rather than trans healthcare) (Warner, 1991; Barker, 2012).

After setting out this queer/homonormative dichotomy in LGBT embodiment, we demonstrate how the homonormative lens through which the state understands LGBT embodiment logically results in the use of equality laws for intersex, most commonly anti-discrimination law. While this has some potential for intersex-embodied persons, particularly as equality laws can facilitate access to certain public institutions and resources, their homonormative qualities inevitably mean that anti-discrimination legislation is ill equipped to distort medical embodiment. To demonstrate this point, we use Australia's Sex Discrimination Amendment (Sexual Orientation, Gender Identity and Intersex Status) Act (Cth) 2013 as a case study. In this example, even though significant attempts were made to understand intersex issues as distinct from LGBT concerns or, as 'gender identity' resulting in more inclusive terminology being used within the Act, the initial framing of intersex embodiment through an LGBT lens restricted the reach and scope of the legislation and the subsequent effect on the lives of intersex people. Moreover, it perpetuates misunderstandings of intersex where policy makers and legislators understand intersex as primarily, or even exclusively, through an LGBT lens, allowing for homonormative presentations of intersex people rather than focussing on their lived experiences and concerns. Importantly, we discuss that framing intersex embodiment through an LGBT lens may have increased parental desire for their children to undergo non-therapeutic medical interventions as it means they might avoid their child being constructed within the 'adult' sphere of LGBT 'sexuality' (itself premised on the homophobia inherent to heteronormativity). Ultimately, while inclusion within anti-discrimination law has had some symbolic importance it has had limited positive impact for intersex people, and, indeed, may have further reinforced the dominance of the medical embodiment paradigm. This reductionism, however, is not the fault of LGBT activism. Rather it is the inevitable result of the institutional structures that exist, constrain, and shape the terms of 'politically legitimate' social activism.

Intersex and LGBT embodiment

The queer and disruptive potential of LGBT

Intersex bodies produce an institutional 'queering effect' that problematizes structures premised on a binary sex model (Garland and Travis, 2020c). In the past, these have included marriage, political office and employment (Dreger, 1998; Mak, 2005) but could also be extended to sport (Greenhow and Weinert, 2019; Patel, 2021) and other spaces of sex segregation (Renz, 2020b). Holmes outlines a queer reading of intersex embodiment as the collapsing of sex/gender distinctions (2009) that enable the challenging of heteronormativity. Similarly, Malatino conceptualizes queer embodiment as 'bodies that don't cohere according to cis-centric, sexually dimorphic, ableist conceptions of somatic normalcy' (Malatino, 2019: 2). Roen makes the point that the term queer can be used 'to imagine spaces where difference may be embraced and celebrated, rather than needing to be erased' (Roen, 2009: 35).

Rather than preventing an LGBT framing, medical approaches have been subject to the criticism that they may be *producing* the type of queer embodiment that they are seeking to erase (Roen, 2009). As Roen writes:

> Would surgical removal of potentially shaming body parts facilitate embodied becoming? Or does it reinforce the shameful feeling of being different? Does the shame lie in the body part that is cut away – is the shame thrown out with the surgical waste – or does that shame

> reside in the embodied subject who bears the knowledge that s/he is different? (Roen, 2009: 34)

Medical embodiment thus helps to co-produce and reify the queer embodiment that we wish to discuss in this chapter. The historical origins of contemporary medical embodiment reveal underpinning homophobic assumptions around intersex people. Such an approach encourages intersex people to understand their differences as a problem and minimizes opportunities to celebrate difference (Roen, 2009: 35). Indeed, the stigma associated with queerness encourages many intersex people to reject this framing of intersex embodiment.

The homophobia (and transphobia) that intersex people have faced have encouraged others to seek connections and alliances with the broader LGBT community. This can be traced to the political and community spaces in which intersex activists found allies during their establishment in the 1990s and in some cases continue to occupy. Intersex people's perceived destabilization of the sex and gender binary was seen as socially and politically important to a range of LGBT organizations, queer theorists and feminist activists (Butler, 1993; Fausto-Sterling, 2000; Greenberg, 2012; Davis, 2015; Morland, 2015; Preves, 2005). Moreover, intersex groups and LGBT groups had "overlapping concerns … to do with the binary ideologies around sex, gender and sexuality" (Respondent 13) and thus had "parallel struggles that required similar strategies to fight cultural and institutional norms hostile to LGBT embodiment" (Garland and Travis, 2020c: 170):

> 'When I am talking about on a trans and intersex platform … of course there are differences, but the commonality is like bodily autonomy, that people get to choose what they want to do with their bodies.' (Respondent 15)

> 'The root of our [parallel] problems comes from homophobia and transphobia and you can say non-binary phobia.' (Respondent 4)

Accordingly, as Sharon Preves writes, the intersex movement built upon the successes of 'earlier activists, such as those in [LGBT] movement … [providing] an expanded level of social tolerance for those with nonbinary genders and a plurality of sexualities, ultimately paving the way for intersex movement to take shape' (Preves, 2005: 205). Cheryl Chase, widely regarded as being a pioneer of intersex activism, outlines that the strategies adopted by the early movement paralleled those adopted by trans activists. Pamphlets, media advertisements, internet presence and retreats all mirrored the successes that had been garnered in the broader LGBT community (Preves, 2005; Chase, 2017). Additionally, the support network of the newly established

Intersex Society of North America (ISNA) predominantly consisted of LGBT activists (Chase, 2017). As Chase writes:

> Transgender and lesbian/gay groups have been supportive of intersex political activism largely because they see similarities in the medicalization of these various forms of identities as a form of social control and (especially for transsexuals) empathize with our struggle to assert agency within a medical discourse that works to efface the ability to exercise informed consent about what happens to one's own body. (Chase, 2017: 399)

As a community, the LGBT movement had also allowed intersex people a 'space' in which to participate: "It's giving intersex voices. It has centralized intersex voices. … definitely the queer community has really given intersex people, intersex activists a platform in which to address these sort of human rights violations" (Respondent 15). The emergence of intersex activism, therefore, is inextricably tied to its framing as a type of queer LGBT embodiment through earlier LGBT organizations, community and political protest. Some of the largest and most successful intersex groups, such as ISNA's public association with LGBT groups, has helped to solidify in the public consciousness the idea that intersex correctly falls under the LGBT umbrella and solidifies its status as queer. The similar (homophobic) pressures faced by these groups means that there have been many instances where intersex has been included within the parameters of LGBT organizations.

There are strategic advantages to building alliances and finding points of common ground with other marginalized groups, particularly through inclusion within queer and LGBT groups (Garland and Travis, 2020c). Specifically, these groups provide intersex activists with a platform to "raise the profile of intersex people and simultaneously use collective action to precipitate social and legal change" (Garland Travis, 2020c: 171). Such strategies have had direct impact in terms of instigating legal reform across multiple jurisdictions. One example stems from Malta's ground-breaking legislation, which we discuss in Chapter 5, prohibiting gender -normalizing surgeries and discrimination on the basis of sex characteristics, can be traced back to an intersex conference funded by ILGA-Europe (International Lesbian, Gay, Bi-Sexual, Transsexual and Intersex Association). This event is a direct example of how LGBT organizations can provide a space for dialogue between intersex activists and Maltese policy makers. In the UK, in 2020 the LGBT consortium helped a new intersex group, Intersex Equality Rights UK, with the processes of constitution writing – enabling it to access its community interest company status. There is clearly a case for LGBT alliances in order to access the funding necessary to achieve social and legislative change in line with the broader intersex community's goals (Garland and Travis, 2020c): "the LGBTI alliance is really useful to us because it's really our only source of funding" (Respondent 1). Such alliances are an integral strategy for many intersex activists to ensure that intersex falls inside rather than outside law's protective sphere. They help politicize intersex, giving visibility, platforms and access to resources that are of fundamental importance in terms of instigating social change – albeit while continuing to frame intersex embodiment through an LGBT lens.

This framing of intersex embodiment has cemented its alignment with LGBT issues in the third sector, in policy and in legislation. Within academia, queer theory has been a useful stepping stone for considering the structural disadvantages that intersex people face, often drawing parallels with other LGBT groups (Butler, 1993; Fausto-Sterling, 2000; Greenberg, 2012; Davis, 2015; Morland, 2015).

LGBT embodiment, homonormativity and assimilation

While politically many of our respondents were happy to be aligned with the LGBT community, significant issues were raised about the potential for the coopting of intersex into LGBT groups and government policies that would then misrepresent or downplay intersex issues through the *homonormativity* present within those groups (Warner, 1991, 1999; Cohen, 1997). This is an important criticism as these vital early community support systems have also had a significant framing effect on the way in which intersex embodiment itself is politically and socially understood. This has had the effect of framing intersex legislation and policy through a lens of homonormative embodiment. However, rather than being the indeterminate and celebratory queer space envisioned above (Holmes, 2008a; Roen, 2009; Malatino, 2019), this lens understands intersex as inherently LGBT and primarily through the assimilative political agenda of understanding LGBT people as 'just like' heterosexual people (Warner, 1991, 1999; Cohen, 1997; Barker, 2012).

This production of homonormative embodiment is problematic. As these alliances have developed into law and policy, the particular valences of homophobia that intersex people face have often been lost. A number of policy makers have understood the problems that intersex people face to be similar to other members of the wider LGBT community. Because all these groups suffer from homophobia, some policy makers have mistakenly assumed that the remedies for this homophobia must be the same for intersex people as for other groups. This coupled with the homonormativity of the LGBT movement (Warner, 1991, 1999; Cohen, 1997; Duggan, 2002; Barker, 2012) has meant that in practice anti-discrimination and equality law has been seen by the state as a useful solution to the problems that intersex people face. Mainstream LGBT politics has predominantly focused on accessing rather than destabilizing 'conservative heteronormative institutions' (Duggan, 2002: 190) such as domestic privacy and the free market (Duggan, 2003; Vitulli, 2010). The close alignment between the political mainstream and neoliberalism (Duggan, 2002; Santos, 2013) has meant that discriminatory barriers, which prevent full entry to these (heteronormative) institutions, are posited as the primary concern of the movement. The result is that anti-discrimination legislation and other equality-based provisions become the primary vehicle through which to respond to mainstream LGBT political activism (Garland and Travis, 2020c) significantly reducing the destabilizing potential of queer embodiment. Accordingly, by aligning with the political mainstream, intersex as we will see becomes subsumed within a narrative of homonormative embodiment.

This approach – at the discursive and institutional level – shifts intersex away from the radical potential of queer embodiment and assimilates it within heteronormative expectations. Culturally and institutionally under this framework, intersex is understood through a prism of LGBT rights that prioritizes assimilation into a heteronormative society. Ultimately, this can have an effect on the materiality of intersex people – with modifications of genital atypicality being understood through a lens of heteronormative expectations. This can lead to a failure to challenge the surgeries involved in favour of a perceived aesthetic and social normality, As such, we use the term 'homonormative embodiment' to engage with some of the discursive, institutional and material conditions that frame intersex people.

These homonormative effects are potentially counterproductive given that, as Vitulli explains writing in the US context, through anti-discrimination provisions individuals 'are ultimately depoliticized – they assume that discrimination is aberrant, individual acts and not normative in U.S. society and state – and are about inclusion in the U.S. state in a way that reinforces and legitimizes current structural inequalities' (2010: 158). Moreover, such responses privilege LGBT individuals who replicate (and are assimilated into) heteronormative practices while simultaneously marginalizing other queer bodies and acts (Ng, 2013: 170). Thus the assimilation of intersex into the political mainstream may further entrench normative ideas relating to the sex and gender resulting in the invisibilization of medical power/knowledge and greater 'policing and reiterative performance of these sex/gender boundaries' (Vitulli, 2010; Garland and Travis, 2020c).

Consequently, our respondents' concern that intersex was being coopted and lost within LGBT groups and community spaces becomes an unsurprising phenomena given that, within the political mainstream, the LGBT movement is often presented as singular and experiences as universal (Vitulli, 2010). At the time of writing many organizations identify themselves as LGBTI,[1] and at a policy level intersex is often included under the auspices of LGBT issues.[2] The Scottish government, for example, in 2018, 'added intersex equality to its approach to sexual orientation and gender identity equality and now uses the acronym LGBTI to support the inclusion of intersex people in Scotland' (Scottish Government, 2018: 1). Similarly, England and Wales have included intersex issues within their LGBT Survey (Government Equalities Office, 2018b). This approach has been replicated by the Dutch government (Government of the Netherlands, 2018) and at a supranational level with the Council of Europe highlighting its commitment to 'Human rights of lesbian, gay, bisexual, transgender and intersex people (LGBTI)' (Commissioner for Human Rights, 2021). The inclusion of intersex in these terms highlights a homonormative approach to intersex embodiment where intersex issues are downplayed in favour of the wider group. Our respondents highlighted that this created a political misunderstanding whereby the particularities of intersex were understood through a homonormative framework of embodiment: in part, our respondents thought that anti-discrimination-based legislative responses were becoming more common, as adding intersex to existing trans or sex-based discrimination law was seen as an 'easy' quick-fix option. This 'addition' was sometimes attributed to the misrepresentation of intersex issues by LGBT groups that purported to talk on behalf of intersex people. Some respondents believed the misplaced direction of the legislative response was also due to policy makers' lack of understanding and interest in issues faced by intersex individuals again linked to the production of intersex through homonormative understandings of embodiment: "For the politicians and so on, it's easy to do this registration stuff because they can say, 'We have done something for the intersex. What's the problem?'" (Respondent 5).

This conflation with LGBT is unsurprising given that adopting the strategies and drawing analogies with other groups that are historically protected is a necessary strategy in a system where equality is constructed as anti-discrimination (Fineman, 2008, 2010, 2012, 2014). LGBT social movements have in recent years predominantly focused on liberation and

---

[1] Some examples are the Equality Network in Scotland (www.equality-network.org/our-work/community-development/), the International Lesbian, Gay, Bisexual, Trans And Intersex Association (https://ilga.org) and the LGBTI Health Alliance in Australia (https://lgbtihealth.org.au/lgbti/). This approach has been replicated by organizations with broader remits such as Amnesty International (www.amnesty.org/en/what-we-do/discrimination/lgbt-rights/), the Organisation for Economic Co-operation and Development (www.oecd.org/social/lgbti.html) and the UN Refugee Agency (www.unhcr.org/uk/lgbti-people-56a7a9164.html).

[2] At the international level some groups prefer the term or SOGISC (Sexual Orientation, Gender Identity and Sex Characteristics) mirroring changes in human rights law.

equal rights of which equality laws form an integral strategy (Warner, 1999; Barker, 2012).[3] Fineman, Fraser and others have emphasized that such an anti-discrimination approach can create competition between would-be allies in the search for social justice (Fraser, 2003; Fineman, 2008, 2010). Groups have to compete for resources and can be hostile to those who attempt to draw analogies, as they may view the tactic as 'diluting' their protection through 'lesser claims' (Fineman, 2010). As Respondent 5 noted, "There is increasingly money available but it always goes for discrimination and LGBT issues. In our experience the intersex groups who define themselves as LGBT they get the funding, but groups like us who want a change in the medical practice we get shunned" (Respondent 5). While our participants recognized that there are strategic advantages in including 'I' to facilitate collective action, there are notable concerns that doing so will further entrench policy makers' tendency to view intersex embodiment through homonormative accounts of embodiment. As we reflect elsewhere, this was because, where intersex had been included within LGBT groups, their real needs in fact remained 'outside' the remit of these organizations (Garland and Travis, 2020c: 176). The priorities of these LGBT organizations were in fact fundamentally different from those held by the intersex communities. The consequence of this was to not only fail to understand the primary needs of intersex people, but also to "misrepresent intersex-specific issues as relating to identity rather than bodily autonomy" (Garland and Travis 2020c: 176). Some respondents felt that this was a product of organizations only including the 'I' to increase their chances of funding "When an LGBT charity says, 'We help LGBTI people,' ... they have no concept of what [intersex] is, or how to help them; it looks really good, and definitely looks good to funders" (Respondent 3). Others were concerned that some individuals and organizations were misusing the word 'intersex' and thus perpetuating the misrepresentation and conflation of intersex issues with non-binary and trans issues, again hinting at a lack of engagement with intersex people:

> 'So there's a lot of preconceptions still around, and there's also a lot of trans people who say, "Actually, we're intersex, because we have intersex brains."' (Respondent 5)

> 'And some trans people will make that ... they will say, "I was socially assigned the wrong sex at birth." But that is what the definition of transgender is so that can be an extra dignitary hurdle if intersex people

[3] Although many early LGBT cases were framed in terms of autonomy/privacy – much closer to the frame that intersex activists are now considering. See for example Johnson (2010).

have to actually say or have their doctor say they're transgender when they're not.' (Respondent 7)

'You'll often read stuff by trans folk that uses intersex as a means of justifying the existence of trans people, but without going beyond that.' (Respondent 16)

However, this does not represent mal-intent, but rather reflects the way in which institutional structures shape social activism and strategy. There are a limited amount of grants available which typically come from charitable trusts, foundations and statutory grants who will also set the eligibility criteria and deadlines. A landscape fraught with a dearth of funding opportunities and resources, the lack of experience that those applying for grants may have, and the time pressures of grant deadlines all contribute to the empty inclusion of 'I' within organizational structures. Our respondents were keen to stress that this was also not representative of all LGBT allies: "I mean, there are also some very good, strong trans allies as well, who are amazing, and we're glad to work with. So, I mean, we can't make generalizations about the trans community" (Respondent 16). Nevertheless, such instances make it harder to distil a distinct intersex narrative and can distort discussions at a policy level in a way that presents discrimination as the primary issue that intersex people face. As a result, we note that the inclusion of intersex within dominant policy frameworks creates much welcomed and necessary recognition, but that they can also have powerful masking effects. To demonstrate this, in the next section we outline the potential for anti-discrimination laws but also their inherently problematic nature for ensuring substantive equality.

The disruptive potential of anti-discrimination law

Over the past 20 years, a growing number of states have included intersex in various ways within their anti-discrimination law. Australia,[4] for example, has specific anti-discrimination legislation, which recognizes intersex status as a protected characteristic (alongside characteristics generally appertained/ imputed to persons of intersex status). South Africa[5] and Jersey[6] have specific anti-discrimination legislation that includes 'intersex' within the protected

4 Sex Discrimination Amendment (Sexual Orientation, Gender Identity and Intersex Status) Act (Cth) 2013.

5 Section 16, Judicial Matters Amendment Act 2005 amended the Promotion of Equality and Prevention of Unfair Discrimination Act (2000) so that section 1 now includes intersex within the protected characteristic of sex.

6 The Discrimination (Sex and Related Characteristics) (Jersey) Regulations 2015 amended the Discrimination (Jersey) Law 2013 to include intersex within the definition of sex.

characteristic of 'sex'; Finland[7] includes 'gender features of the body' within the protected characteristics of 'gender identity and gender expression' and Greece and Bosnia-Herzegovina[8] prohibit discrimination and hate crimes made on the basis of 'sex characteristics'. Scotland offers more limited recognition, not within anti-discrimination law[9] but through an extension of 'hate crime' legislation where intersex is classified under 'transgender identity'.[10] Although the exact purpose of anti-discrimination laws and the way they are enforced will vary from jurisdiction to jurisdiction, this inclusion is significant given that these laws typically share the normative goal of enhancing wellbeing by 'ameliorating abiding, pervasive, and substantial relative group disadvantage' (Graham, 2019: 666). Hate crime law attempts to eliminate violence motivated by bias or prejudice while the fundamental purpose of anti-discrimination law is to remove 'any significant advantage gap between a protected group and its cogent groups' (Khaitan, 2015: 121). Khaitan identifies the three basic goods that anti-discrimination law seeks to protect as being freedom from interference (or negative freedom), access to valuable opportunities, and an appropriate level of self-respect (Khaitan, 2015). The fact that anti-discrimination law carries with it these basic social protections meant that some of our respondents were very positive about using it as a vehicle for empowering intersex individuals and its transformative potential in terms of the day-to-day reality of intersex embodied people:

> 'Many people feel the need to lie in their place of work … they might have to see doctors to deal with the ramifications of what has been done to them, for example to access hormone replacement therapy if they've faced some sort of sterilization and often these treatments are only accessible through specialists facilitating the need to travel to see medical professionals. … For someone who doesn't have any protections in place, it doesn't feel like something you can safely share in your workplace whereas if the community knows that ok, this is protected, even if I mention it or say something that people piece together, then my job security is safe. Then that's sort of a different reality to be surviving in.' (Respondent 8)

---

7 Section 3(5) laki miesten ja naisten välisestä tasa-arvosta/lag om jämställdhet mellan kvinnor och män, Act no 609/1986, Finland's Gender Equality Act was amended in 2015 to extend protections to intersex individuals.

8 Article 2 Law on the Prohibition of Discrimination 2009 was amended in July 2016.

9 Scotland's anti-discrimination law is governed by the Equality Act 2010, which does not recognize intersex as a protected characteristic. This Act also covers England and Wales.

10 Section 2, Offences (Aggravation by Prejudice) (Scotland) Act 2009. Rather problematically, however, intersexuality falls under the definition of 'transgender identity' under section 8(a).

Yet, in most anti-discrimination laws there is not an unfettered right of non-discrimination. Rather the individual has to demonstrate that they fall within a protected ground or characteristic. Most jurisdictions refer to 'sex', 'gender' or 'gender identity' within their legislation, but it is unlikely that such provisions will extend to intersex without specific inclusion. For example, in the UK, sex is a protected ground under section 11 of the Equality Act 2010 but section 11(a) qualifies that this 'is a reference … to a man or to a woman'[11] effectively excluding intersex as a specific ground from its remit. Where sex and/or gender is not written in such binary terms within equality law, there may be potential to include intersex; however this will largely depend on the way in which the law is interpreted and applied within the legal system: the legal system has to be willing to interpret discrimination against intersex as discrimination against sex/gender/gender identity. Given the dominance of the sex/gender binary, inclusion is questionable and such uncertainty effectively renders the individual in an uncomfortable legal limbo and unlikely to risk the fallout of non-inclusion. For some of our respondents therefore, omission from equality law was highly problematic given the discrimination intersex individuals face:

> 'But then we sort of say, hang on a minute, where's intersex? And it's not as if people can turn round and say, Well, they don't need protecting because they are fine. No, they are not. I mean, it's an absolute scandal. … Discrimination against intersex people begins at birth.' (Respondent 7)

> '[Anti-discrimination law is] very useful; obviously discrimination does happen as intersex people have been incredibly marginalized so much so that they have been socially erased in a lot of, from society, and that sort or stigma self acceptance and anything that would protect that situation for the future secrecy.' (Respondent 1)

The significance of exclusion is more profound than accessing protections. The list of 'included' characteristics that are afforded protection implies that those differences are natural and immutable (Greenfell, 2003: 51). Accordingly, exclusion serves to disempower and, as Young states: 'constructs as deviant those whose attributes differ from the group-specific attributes implicitly presumed in the norm' (Young, 1990: 169). Medical interventions to affirm sex are therein implicitly justified through such exclusion. Consequently, visibility,

---

11 Although the Equality Acy does not define sex, section 212 qualifies that man means a male of any age and woman means female of any age inferring a biological rather than social constructionist approach to sex (Cabrielli, 2020, 423). Accordingly, gender reassignment is a separate characteristic within the act under section 7.

as much as protection, was a vital reasoning for needing such inclusion: "just having the government seal of approval saying, 'These people exist and should not be treated badly,' is so important because it is the invisibility and stigma of being intersex which is so much of what drives these human rights violations" (Respondent 14). Our participants thus demonstrated a desire to move beyond formal equality law and into engagement with substantive equality or human rights frameworks.[12] While our participants were critical of the effects that constructing intersex embodiment through an LGBT lens can create in policy and law, the desire to address broader structural issues has also been considered in queer and LGBT work (Butler, 1993; Cohen, 1997; Warner, 1999; Fausto-Sterling, 2000; Greenberg, 2012; Davis, 2015; Morland, 2015; Malatino, 2019). A key issue, therefore, in creating an effective and inclusive equality policy for intersex people hinges around framing.

Anti-discrimination law and assimilation

While inclusion within anti-discrimination laws offers opportunities, throughout our interviews it was clear that legislative framing is integrally linked to success or, more accurately, failure. Those few respondents who were advocating inclusion were very cautious about the way in which intersex should be framed, and were concerned about the assimilative nature of law based on LGBT activism, which could overlook specific intersex issues.

> 'If there is a real commitment to anti-discrimination, that is inclusive of intersex folks. ... I think it's one thing to have a law, but what is the implementation? What is the practice? And how does it empower people? ... Intersex, how is intersex defined in the law? ... I think there is some worry among intersex activists. ... I think it offers possibilities, (but) I think those gaps can also increase vulnerability.' (Respondent 15)

> 'But if you're intending to provide specific protection for intersex people that isn't exactly what you're doing for transgender people, it's important how you define that group of people and the purpose of the law.' (Respondent 14)

> 'I'm somewhat wary, not about changing the law, but how it is changed and also how it is presented to the public.' (Respondent 7)

[12] Rights frameworks have yet to pick up much traction with intersex issues, particularly at a domestic level. Similarly on the international plane rights frameworks have struggled to impact the day-to-day lives of intersex people (Garland et al, 2022). Nonetheless, there is a case currently under consideration in the European Court of Human Rights (*M v France* https://hudoc.echr.coe.int/fre#{%22itemid%22:[%22001-205290%22]}).

Respondents were aware that language can limit who is actually able to access such protections. For example, and as explored in Chapter 3, just adding 'intersex' into legislation under the ground of sex in addition to male or female would effectively equate intersex with non-binary. Similarly adding intersex under the umbrella of gender identity or gender expression as in Finland[13] or indeed under 'transgender identity' as in Scotland, conflates intersex embodiment with trans embodiment.[14] Even the use of the term 'intersex' as a standalone ground is inherently exclusionary given that many individuals do not define themselves as 'intersex' (Garland and Travis, 2018). It also ignores the impact of secrecy and shame that individuals experience: individuals must demonstrate that they qualify as intersex under the legislation, which effectively requires 'outing' their intersex status. Evidently, the way in which intersex is included within anti-discrimination law needs to be attentive to lived experience and offer broad protections not based on an intersex 'status'. Accordingly, jurisdictions like Malta, which prohibits discrimination on the basis of sex characteristics rather than 'intersex', offer a better opportunity to limit discrimination on the basis of biological variations rather than status.

> 'I think just on the basis of that legislation being on the basis of intersex status is a bit problematic because status is usually something you are awarded or given in some way um so first you must obtain this intersex status before you can really be protected whereas a basis of sex characteristics would protect all intersex people and really if you think about it, it would protect non intersex people as well.' (Respondent 8)

> 'I mean, I think it is … if we are covered on antidiscrimination legislation on the ground of sex characteristics then I think that works. Yes, I think that would be … that's what we are aiming for.' (Respondent 4)

At the time of our empirical research, many jurisdictions engaging with intersex had adopted an intersex status model of anti-discrimination and unsurprisingly nearly all our respondents were very dismissive of the equality laws currently in place. Since then, a growing number of states introducing anti-discrimination laws have advanced protections based on sex characteristics.[15] While this is considerable progress, it still does not tackle the more pressing concern among

---

13 Section 3(5) laki miesten ja naisten välisestä tasa-arvosta/lag om jämställdhet mellan kvinnor och män, Act no 609/1986, Finland's Gender Equality Act was amended in 2015 to extend protections to intersex individuals.

14 Section 2 of the Offences (Aggravation by Prejudice) (Scotland) Act 2009. Rather problematically, however, intersexuality falls under the definition of 'transgender identity' under section 8(a).

15 Albania, Serbia, Netherlands, Belgium, to name just a few.

respondents: that this type of legislation quite simply does not address intersex needs and that anti-discrimination laws (even well-written ones) represent a superficial form of state response born largely out of a homonormative view of LGBT embodiment – one linked to neoliberal subjectivities. As Respondent 14 noted: "Isn't it discrimination to do risky, unproven surgeries on one population when you wouldn't ever consider doing something so risky and so unproven on any other population?" (Respondent 14). Such a response highlights the narrow ways in which questions of discrimination can be framed, which we will discuss further in the next section.

The dangers of the homonormative lens: anti-discrimination law as legal misdirection

> 'When I look at this I see new attributes protecting people on grounds of intersex status, and gender identity, and sexual orientation. Protection for intersex people, blah, blah blah … Recognition of intersex as a biological basis. Exemptions applicable to intersex. No sport exemptions. Removal of religious … blah, blah, blah. And then there's a lot about employment law. So I'm looking at this and I'm thinking … it almost doesn't mean anything.' (Respondent 3)

As aforementioned, most anti-discrimination law deals with the provision of public services or goods and the labour force. Anti-discrimination law does not by design challenge, interfere with or even recognize the medical jurisdiction over intersex bodies: "[The] adoption of anti-discrimination legislation in Australia has made not the slightest difference to the human rights abuses intersex people face in that country" (Respondent 9). Individuals were concerned that such anti-discrimination law would have limited legal effect in practice (it was not commonplace for intersex individuals to experience discrimination in the workplace on a day-to-day basis on account of their intersex status) and consequently ignored the real material experiences of intersex individuals:

> 'This is lip service. This protects no one … I don't know of any intersex people who've been discriminated against in the workplace because they're intersex people … if I don't see the terms bodily autonomy, or the right to self-determination in anyone's statement of, "We enacted this or that," all I see is people unable to protect themselves continuing to be unable to protect themselves.' (Respondent 3)

These concerns are also linked to broader issues regarding the limitations of anti-discrimination law. Many scholars have criticized anti-discrimination laws for being inappropriately designed to achieve substantive equality as they do not tackle broader issues of social inequalities. Ashley describes the use of anti-discrimination law in the context of trans rights as 'surface-level management of ostensive ills which fail by themselves to address the underlying roots of those ills' (Ashley, 2018: 25). Accordingly, even if anti-discrimination law is more broadly framed, it will 'fail to alter the underlying societal norms giving rise to harassment, discrimination, and violence' (Ashley, 2018: 28). In this context, anti-discrimination law fails to address the structural and institutional homophobia that intersex people face and may instead perpetuate them, reifying the binary of sex; it presumes a desire to 'enter' institutions that are inherently heteronormative in nature. Yet, the medical interventions are premised upon the framing of intersex embodiment as LGBT and the desire to avoid such a framing by both medical professionals and parents. Indeed, the Australian ruling in *Re Carla (Medical Procedure)* (2016) emphasizes this point. In this case, despite the introduction of a specific intersex status through Australia's federal anti-discrimination law in 2013, the Australian Family Court ruled that parents can consent to cosmetic genital surgery on their infant, even where it results in sterilization, without having to seek the court's approval.[16] Underlying discriminatory norms relating to sex, gender and the body were not challenged by Australia's anti-discrimination provisions despite, as this chapter goes on to discuss, the lengthy engagement it had with the intersex community. Indeed, the law can work to reify these norms rather than addressing them. Such inability to instigate systemic change has led commentators like Vipond to describe anti-discrimination law as 'a band-aid solution under the guise of equality' (Vipond, 2015: 19). This is evident in the intersex context where some respondents accused states of merely playing 'lip-service' to the needs of the intersex community rather than offering effective reforms. Respondents emphasized more generally that law needed to "have teeth" to the intersex community's needs or it would be "a waste of time" (Respondent 7), raising questions over whether anti-discrimination law framed through a general lens of LGBT embodiment alone will have any meaningful impact in practice. In Australia, activism has thus had to continue, and it is only now 10 years on from Australia's federal anti-discrimination law that states are considering the introduction of specific reforms designed to challenge medical embodiment. These reforms, notably, are not prefaced on an LGBT framing but rather on prohibiting unnecessary medical interventions.

Not only is anti-discrimination law ill-equipped to redress the dominance of the medical embodiment paradigm but, in most cases, states were not introducing anything alongside anti-discrimination law to do so. While

16 *Carla (Medical Procedure)* [2016] Fam CA 7 (20 January 2016). See Carpenter (2016) for a critique of the case.

over 15 states have included intersex in some form within their anti-discrimination law, only three states at the time of writing have gone beyond notions of formal equality and introduced legislation that targets medical interventions on intersex infants.[17] Consequently, anti-discrimination law represents a misdirected legal reform that fails to fully understand the real issues faced by intersex embodied people. The worrying implication is that at a policy level this could depoliticize the major issue within the movement by rendering states unlikely to challenge dominant medical framings of intersex embodiment as 'disordered'. Respondents were concerned that by effectively entrenching this limited understanding of intersex within law, such legislation may continue to perpetuate and reinforce narrow understandings of equality that presume that discrimination is the only barrier to achieving equality (Collins, 2003; Fineman, 2008, 2010; Fredman, 2016). The danger is that policy makers and society may then believe that the matter has been rectified and many respondents were concerned that this would actually strengthen the hold of medical narratives of embodiment by silencing the voices that challenged the medical regulation of intersex bodies: "it's used to silence discussions about IGM" (Respondent 6) (see also Carpenter, 2018). In the next section, we consider Australia's Sex Discrimination Amendment (Sexual Orientation, Gender Identity and Intersex Status) Act (Cth) 2013 as an active case study of these concerns. This law is an example of policy development and legislation that, despite the efforts of activists, still framed intersex through a lens of homonormativity. While we have traced the effects of anti-discrimination in terms of intersex embodiment, understanding *how* intersex becomes included into the corpus of anti-discrimination law is paramount to ensure that any progress in anti-discrimination law does not come at the expense of undermining the political attempts of activists to disrupt the medical framing of intersex embodiment.

(Mis)framing intersex embodiment as (homonormative) LGBT embodiment in law and policy: Australia's Sex Discrimination Act 2013

Australia's Sex Discrimination Amendment (Sexual Orientation, Gender Identity and Intersex Status) Act (Cth) 2013 was a significant landmark in terms of intersex rights in the West, as it was the first piece of Western legislation to introduce protections based on a specific intersex status into law. However, before examining this Act, it is first important to examine the context in which it was introduced to understand how an LGBT framing dominated understandings of intersex embodiment in this area.

[17] Malta, Portugal, Greece and Germany have introduced legislation that prohibits medical interventions on children.

The background: conflating intersex with trans

As a federal system, Australia's anti-discrimination framework includes both federal (commonwealth) legislation and state legislation working in parallel to one another. Prior to the introduction of the 2013 Federal Act, commonwealth anti-discrimination legislation was narrowly cast and there were no protections available for intersex people at a federal level. However, from the mid-1990s, a handful of states and territories began introducing anti-discrimination provisions that incorporated intersex individual's although inclusion was not consistent across Australia. Morgan Carpenter notes that the introduction of these state/territory level reforms pre-dated intersex activism in Australia.[18] Rather, they were the product of trans activism which significantly affected the way in which intersex was framed. Socio-political narratives of the time generally considered intersex to be a subdivision of transgender where individuals were born with 'indeterminate sex characteristics' and this framing was adopted by state legislators (Easten, 2003:1; see also Australian Civil Liberties Union, 2001). For example, in 1996 New South Wales passed the Transgender (Anti-discrimination and Other Acts Amendment) Act 1996. This Act introduced prohibitions against transgender discrimination into Part 3 of the Anti-Discrimination Act 1977 (NSW) (Australian Civil Liberties Union, 2001). Hooley notes that the shape and wording of the Act was largely the result of the trans pressure groups Transgender Lobby Coalition (TLC) and the Transsexual Action Group stating that 'The TLC sought to legitimise the term transgender, as inclusive of a range of identity options' (Hooley, 2006: 80). While the Act did not specifically mention intersex, section 38 defined a transgender person as one who:

(a) identifies as a member of the opposite sex by living, or seeking to live, as a member of the opposite sex; or
(b) has identified as a member of the opposite sex by living as a member of the opposite sex; or
(c) being of indeterminate sex, identifies as a member of a particular sex, by living as a member of that sex.

Section 38(c) therefore makes implicit provision for intersex persons, but misframes intersex through its focus on gender identity. Other states and territories began to introduce similar anti-discrimination provisions with increasingly specific reference to intersex, but defining intersex under the heading of 'gender identity'. In 2002, Queensland's Discrimination Law Amendment Act 2002 inserted the ground of 'gender identity' into its

[18] Email exchange with authors.

Anti-Discrimination Act 1991. The explanatory notes that accompanied the Act explained that this inclusion was 'to protect people of transgender identity and intersex people from discrimination and bring Queensland into line with other Australian States and Territories' (Easten, 2003: 5).[19] Section 4 accordingly defined gender identity to mean that the person:

(a) identifies, or has identified, as a member of the opposite sex by living or seeking to live as a member of that sex; or
(b) is of indeterminate sex and seeks to live as a member of a particular sex.

Consequently, by the time federal anti-discrimination reform was under discussion, there was a strong legal narrative at state level that framed intersex as an indeterminate gender identity (Australian Government, 2011: 22) with little to no engagement from intersex people. While these pieces of legislation were in many ways progressive in their attempt to include intersex, they were inherently problematic not only for the way in which they defined intersex, but also for representing intersex issues as related to status-based discrimination rather than bodily integrity. This misframing of intersex was attributed by our respondents to the way in which intersex had been understood through a general lens of LGBT embodiment:

> 'Intersex activists in Australia have been also fighting another thing, in terms – intersex is seen as a gender identity, and that's a result of – there was a court case by a trans person who claimed that they were intersex as well and that intersex is a gender identity. So that is creating lots of problems.' (Respondent 17)

> 'In Australia, and what's happened in ACT is an example of that, where essentially, there is a trans organization that frames itself as a trans and intersex organization – so, the government there actually doesn't really understand what intersex is … I'm sure they perceive intersex as some kind of transgender identity, rather than what it actually is.' (Respondent 16)

> 'In Australia also issues during the time that this was being worked on the issue of some trans people claiming to be intersex and sort of shifting the focus on issues that were perhaps more related to trans issues.' (Respondent 8)

Inclusion within these Acts, Carpenter posits, was an attempt to include non-binary gender identities rather than for the benefit of intersex persons.[20]

19 See also the Discrimination Law Amendment Bill 2002 (Qld), Explanatory Notes, p 5.
20 Email exchange with authors.

Similar to our findings in the Chapter 3, Australia has a long history of depicting intersex as non-binary. *In The Marriage of C and D (falsely known as C)*,[21] the Family Court of Australia annulled the marriage on the basis that the man had an intersex variation. Justice Sewell stated that marriage was between one man and woman and "since the respondent was a combination of both, a marriage in the true sense could not have taken place and did not exist" (528).[22] Such thinking was present in *Norrie v NSW Registrar of Births, Deaths and Marriages*[23] where the respondent applied to register their sex as non-specific under section 32A of the Births, Deaths and Marriages Registration Act. Their application was rejected as the Registrar stated that a person could only be registered as male or female. Norrie began legal proceedings in 2010 and eventually the case went up to the High Court of Australia, which stated in 2014 that it was possible to interpret the Act in a way that incorporated gender 'ambiguities'. As Carpenter (2014) notes, problematically during the case Norrie used the term 'intersex' as their preferred synonym of 'non-binary' stating at [39]:

> '39. … "Non-specific" is suitable, but "intersex" is another possible description … there is no reason to confine it to congenital intersexuality and current and proposed legislative definitions of that expression do not so confine it. Indeed, the mythological origins of the word "hermaphrodite" relate to a person who acquired that status as an adult.'

Commenting on this case, Carpenter states: 'The conflation of intersex status with an intermediate gender identity reveals a very narrow and unrealistic vision of who intersex people are. It's also damaging: it reinforces notions that intersex people who identify as male or female are not valid or considered suspect' (Carpenter, 2014: 1). While the High Court ultimately did not share Norrie's use of intersex as a gender identity, using the term non-specific gender instead, *Norrie* demonstrates the extent to which conflation occurs between gender identity and intersex:

> 'That's the *Norrie* case. That attracted lots of media attention, which was really a backlash for intersex people who really don't have many resources to be there. So, yes, this conflation of gender identity and intersex status has been also problematic on that front.' (Respondent 17)

21 (1979) FLC 90–636.
22 For more on this case, see Carpenter, 2012.
23 [2014] HCA 11.

> 'I think there is some worry among intersex activists and some advocates that if intersex were actually a legal, social category, then anyone can identify as intersex that doesn't identify as male or female.' (Respondent 15)

The introduction of intersex into federal anti-discrimination law

It was against this backdrop that discussions began about federal anti-discrimination law reform. in 2011, a year after Norrie's legal proceedings were underway, the Australian Labor government began to consider the need for reform and consolidation of their existing anti-discrimination law. Led by a 'Better Regulation Ministerial Partnership' between the Attorney-General and the Minister for Finance and Deregulation and falling under the purview of Australia's Human Rights Framework the initial consultation document looked to 'consolidate existing Commonwealth anti-discrimination legislation into a single, comprehensive law' (Australian Government, 2011: 6). Also falling under the remit of the project, was the government's need to deliver on its election manifesto promise 'to introduce new prohibitions on discrimination on the basis of sexual orientation and gender identity' (Australian Government, 2011: 6). Unsurprisingly, intersex embodiment was understood through a lens of LGBT in the consultation document, noting that they were to be defined as 'people born of indeterminate sex … who identify as male or female' (Australian Government, 2011: 22). The document relied upon a definition of intersex that had been generated by the Australian Capital Territory's federal legislation, the Legislation Act 2001 (ACT), which defined an intersex person as 'a person who, because of a genetic condition, was born with reproductive organs or sex chromosomes that are not exclusively male or female'. The discussion paper also invited comments from interested stakeholders. All submissions were then made publicly available on the Attorney-General's Department website.

By this point, intersex activism was much more established and well coordinated in Australia. Several intersex organizations were involved in mainstream activism, most notably Organisation Intersex International Australia (OII Australia) (now Intersex Human Rights Australia [IHRA]) founded in 2010. OII Australia's remit was (and remains) to focus on 'advocacy and work to ensure that the human rights and health of people with intersex variations are recognised and respected' (Intersex Human Rights Australia, 2014). As part of this, the organization regularly makes informed public submissions to government bodies and institutions (Intersex Human Rights Australia, 2021). There were also some notable intersex individuals who had become engaged within political forums, with the first openly intersex person elected to public office in 2012 as a mayor in Australia in Victoria. These developments meant that there was a more coordinated strategy towards raising awareness about intersex issues and engaging with policy makers. This engagement translated into the 2012 round of submissions regarding federal anti-discrimination law including a submission from the Australian Human Rights Commission. Their submission to the Attorney-General's Department referred to a consultation process that they had previously undergone in order to highlight:

> the need to ensure that the protection of the law be as inclusive as possible, including protection on the basis of sex characteristics, gender identity and gender expression in order to achieve the broadest coverage of people of all sex and/or gender identities and to provide improved protection. The Commission also heard of the need to ensure that people who are intersex are expressly included in legislative protections from discrimination. (Australian Human Rights Commission, 2011: para 81)

Following these submissions, in November 2012 the Attorney-General's Department released an 'Exposure Draft' of the Human Rights and Anti-Discrimination Bill 2012 to garner more feedback. In this initial framing of the law 'gender identity' and 'sex' were included but neither sex characteristics nor intersex were separated from these categories (Australian Government, 2012: 34). On 21 November 2012 the Senate referred the exposure draft of the Bill to the Senate Legal and Constitutional Affairs Committee for inquiry and report. Again, submissions were invited from stakeholder groups, some of whom were invited to 'hearings' to speak directly with the Senate.

This round of submissions attracted 595 responses from interested parties. One of the most important, for our purposes, came from OII Australia. In their submission, they noted that 'Intersex is a matter of biology, not gender identity', before going on to note that:

> Intersex is a term which relates to a range of natural biological traits or variations that lie between 'male' and 'female'. An intersex person may have the biological attributes of both sexes, or lack some of the biological attributes considered necessary to be clearly defined as one or the other sex. Intersex is always congenital and can originate from genetic, chromosomal or hormonal variations. In many cases, intersex variations can be determined prenatally, via amniocentesis. (OII Australia, 2012: 1)

They also highlighted that:

> Gender Identity should be defined inclusively. Gender identity should protect all binary and non-binary gender identities, including

> culturally-specific genders, and not only those that are considered mainstream. It should also protect on the basis of gender expression. We do not believe that inclusion of all gender identities would have any new regulatory impact. (OII Australia, 2012: 3)

OII Australia also noted a preference for the term intersex over 'sex characteristics', believing that in light of the history of conflation with trans, intersex specific protections were necessary. Representatives from OII Australia were subsequently invited to speak at the Senate hearings on these issues. On behalf of OII Australia Gina Wilson noted that:

> What concerns us with the draft legislation is that intersex is framed in a way that seems to place us in some way along with gender identity. Intersex is not a matter of gender identity; intersex is something that we are born with. ... Irrespective of whether we identify as, for instance, female and act as a woman and have had 'female' on our birth certificates since the day we were born, we are still subjected to prejudice that is, by and large, a sort of homophobic prejudice. The idea that our anatomy is somehow or other different takes people along the path of viewing us through the lens of 'gay' or 'queer' by nature—that somehow because our anatomy is not perfectly male or perfectly female, or not quite male or not quite female, then somehow the nature of our relationships is uncertain and the way we relate to the rest of the society is uncertain. So we tend to end up being subjected to the same kinds of homophobic abuse and the same kinds of homophobic exclusion as the LGBT group, irrespective of how we identify and irrespective of our sexual orientation. So, what we think is really, really important is that intersex is a protected attribute and is not included as discrimination on the basis of gender identity but included on the basis of discrimination against intersex people. (Legal and Constitutional Affairs Legislation Committee, 2013: 2)

Here we return to the homophobia that links intersex and the broader LGBT community. While OII Australia were keen to highlight that intersex would not be adequately covered by the term 'gender identity' Wilson expresses her experience with reference to the perhaps more socially understandable or intelligible narrative of homophobia. In many ways, this narrative is helpful as it makes the intersex experience clearer. Nonetheless, it also shows the conceptual entanglement of intersex embodiment and LGBT framings and the consequent slippage for the development of law and policy in its responses to homophobic prejudice. Within the LGBT lens there then comes an important subdivision between queer responses that would look to tackle the structural issues and homonormative solutions that look to ensure that the individual fits into heteronormative structures.

The Senate Legal and Constitutional Affairs Committee released its inquiry report on 21 February 2013. With regards to intersex status, the committee recognized that:

> intersex individuals are often the subject of discrimination in public life, and that as such there is a need for protection on the basis of intersex status in Commonwealth anti-discrimination law.
>
> ... The committee agrees ... that intersex status is a matter of biology rather than gender identity, and as such should not be covered within the definition of gender identity in the Draft Bill. Further, the committee considers that the current requirement in the Draft Bill that intersex individuals identify as either male or female is misguided, and is unhelpful for intersex individuals whose biological characteristics do not necessarily accord with a male or female identification.
>
> ... The committee considers, therefore, that intersex status should be listed as a separate protected attribute under the Draft Bill. (Senate Legal and Constitutional Affairs Committee, 2013: paras 7.16–7.19)

The committee went on to recommend that subclause 17(1) of the draft Bill be amended to include 'intersex status' as a protected attribute. However, despite the lengthy consultation process and large volume of feedback, the Human Rights and Anti-Discrimination Bill stalled at the pre-legislative level. A looming election meant that the Bill failed to generate enough political support given the incumbent government's lack of overall majority. In its place the new Sex Discrimination Amendment (Sexual Orientation, Gender Identity and Intersex Status) Bill was introduced in the House of Representatives in March 2013 and passed into legislation in June the same year. For this Bill the House Standing Committee did not call for public submissions as it was aware that the proposed amendments were informed by the wider consultation around the Exposure Draft of the Human Rights and Anti-Discrimination Bill 2012. While much of the previous Bill was jettisoned, in terms of intersex, the new Bill took on board the recommendations of the Senate Legal and Constitutional Affairs Committee. The explanatory memorandum to the Bill noted that:

> A separate ground of discrimination on the basis of intersex status is also introduced. People who are intersex may face many of the same issues that are sought to be addressed through the introduction of the ground of gender identity. However, including the separate ground of intersex status recognises that whether a person is intersex is a biological characteristic and not an identity.

Accordingly, the Act passed in 2013, introducing section 5C into the Sex Discrimination Act 1984, which prohibits discrimination on the basis of a specific intersex status. To make it clear that this is a separate issue from gender identity, section 4 of the Act states that: 'intersex status means the status of having physical, hormonal or genetic features that are: (a) neither wholly female nor wholly male; or (b) a combination of female and male; or (c) neither female nor male.' Reflecting on its passage, it is clear that experiences of intersex people were utilized largely in order to correct the ways in which 'gender identity' had been introduced in the initial 2011 consultation. In many ways, they were successful. Not only did legislation decouple intersex from gender identity, but also layed down relatively clear guidelines for future use in cases like *Norrie v NSW Registrar of Births, Deaths and Marriages*, where the court rejected Norrie's use of the term to encapsulate an indeterminate gender identity. However, while intersex people therefore 'participated' in this legislative process, their participation was in many ways opportunistic. The terms and conditions of their participation had already been constructed through a framework of LGBT embodiment whereby anti-discrimination was seen as an appropriate solution to the problems faced by intersex people. There are two important issues at stake here. Firstly, anti-discrimination law is limited in what it can do, how it can recognize and how it can protect. Secondly, state understanding of intersex through an LGBT lens misrecognizes issues that are issues specific to intersex and has the potential to channel intersex organizations into particular directions. While intersex embodiment was recognized as distinct from the overall LGBT experience by virtue of its congenital basis, the state's framing of the problems that intersex people faced were still understood in relation to (homonormative) LGBT issues. This framing perhaps makes more sense when taking into account that this was the first piece of national legislation to introduce LGBT anti-discrimination provisions. Against that backdrop, aligning intersex strategy with the desires and priorities of the LGBT community makes sense, especially as activists were able to give intersex its own conceptual space.

Moreover, the lack of discussion around non-therapeutic medical interventions on intersex bodies becomes more understandable in a context whereby the Australian Senate's Community Affairs References Committee launched an inquiry into 'Involuntary or coerced sterilisation of intersex people in Australia', also in 2013. The two distinct inquiries of course necessitated differing responses from intersex groups and, indeed, the overlap in terms of time perhaps generated a feeling that the government was capable of resolving the multiple different issues raised by intersex embodiment. In OII Australia's submission to the Australian Senate's Community Affairs References Committee inquiry, they note that:

> Intersex people are medicalised, stigmatised and suffer discrimination due to our distinctive biological characteristics. Intersex variations affect perceptions of our realness as men or women, and society still generally requires people to live and identify as male or female. As a result, intersex bodies do not meet societal expectations and intersex people experience homophobia and prejudice. Cultural, familial and medical attitudes towards our differences from sex norms govern which sex we are assigned, and what surgical and other medical interventions will be made to ensure we conform to those norms. Medical interventions seek to erase intersex differences. (OII Australia, 2013)

Throughout the document they do not engage with issues of anti-discrimination. This highlights that they have kept these issues conceptually distinct in line with the objectives and aims of the inquiries themselves. Clearly, for intersex people, this second inquiry was the most important of the two. Indeed, the findings of the committee, published in October 2013, made a whole series of recommendations that have long been demanded by intersex people.

Contrasting these recommendations with the Sex Discrimination Amendment (Sexual Orientation, Gender Identity and Intersex Status) Act 2013 highlights the stark difference in outcomes dependent on the original framings of the question. The Australian Senate's Community Affairs References Committee Report shows the benefit of engaging with intersex issues without the preconception that the issues intersex people face are equivalent to or derivative of an LGBT lens. Unfortunately, however, a change in federal government in September 2013 to the centre-right Liberal/National Coalition meant that the political will to make changes in this area largely dissipated. Australian intersex people were left in a frustrating position whereby progress and recognition had been made in one area, but in more substantive and important areas continued to be lacking. This has only been highlighted by the decision in *Re Carla (Medical Procedure)*.[24] Australia was frequently cited as an example of how ineffectual such reforms are:

> 'This essentially superficial legislation in Australia is still a way of introducing visibility, it's still a way of getting the concept in front of legislators, people who are patently ignorant on the subject, of general sexuality and gender, and not to mention intersex stuff. I think it's important. But if you want to talk about, "Is this a watershed moment for intersex people?" in my opinion, it is not.' (Respondent 3)

[24] [2016] Fam CA 7 (20 January 2016). See Carpenter (2016).

As a result, the changes made to the Sex Discrimination Amendment (Sexual Orientation, Gender Identity and Intersex Status) Act 2013 can be seen as largely opportunistic rather than part of a broader push for meaningful response or recognition (Garland and Travis, 2018).

In many ways, then, Australia is a working example of some of the earlier concerns about the misdirected focus of states on discrimination rather than rights frameworks built around bodily integrity. The administrative ease of just amending anti-discrimination legislation rather than developing law and policy that challenges current medical practice, combined with the dominant (and misrepresentative) framing of intersex embodiment through an LGBT lens (and global press response), has meant that this type of law reform continues to be the most common state response across the West (Garland and Travis, 2018). As Respondent 3 noted, "So … anti-discrimination stuff, the conflation of gender and sexuality and intersex, aren't the … You've seen it, it garners the most press around the world" (Respondent 3). Our respondents' critique not only centred on the states' failure to address gender-normalizing medical practices, but also on the cyclical effect that such identity-focused legislative reform would have on cultural and institutional misunderstandings: identity-focused reform would perpetuate such misunderstandings and, as a result, leave intersex-specific concerns regarding gender-normalizing surgeries outside the protective legal sphere:

> 'If it's only about registration and nobody's talking about the reality of intersex people, like genital mutilation, then it does more harm … if it's like putting LGBT and it's about registration then … some newspapers [may say that] … intersex can also put an X instead of "male" or "female", then most people think even more that intersex is something like gay or trans. The problem with this first registration thing is that there is no talk about genital mutilation. It's like two different topics.' (Respondent 5)

Since 2013, Australian states and territories have been much more attentive to the specific needs of intersex people within anti-discrimination law and there have been some legal amendments to state-level legislation to better incorporate intersex people. In Tasmania, for example, the Justice and Related Legislation (Marriage and Gender Amendments) Act 2019 removed the word 'intersex' from the Tasmanian Anti-Discrimination Act 1998 and replaced it with the term 'sex characteristics', defining these to mean 'a person's physical, hormonal or genetic features relating to sex, including genitalia and other sexual and reproductive anatomy, chromosomes, genes, hormones, and secondary sex characteristics'.[25]

[25] Although the Act problematically goes on to limit protections to those with intersex variations under section 16(eb).

More significantly, there is some state-level political engagement with issues relating to bodily integrity. At the time of writing, two Australian governments, in response to the 2013 Senate Committee Inquiry into involuntary/coerced sterilization – Australian Capital Territory (Chief Minister, Treasury and Economic Development Directorate, 2021) and the State of Victoria (Department of Health, 2021) – have publicly committed to reform in the area of medical intervention on intersex children. Similarly, in 2020, the Tasmanian Law Reform Institute (a partnership between the government of the state of Tasmania, the University of Tasmania and the Law Society of Tasmania) produced a report on the *Legal Recognition of Sex and Gender*, which recommends a comprehensive body of legal reforms most notably recommending the creation of a crime of performing unnecessary medical intervention to change the sex characteristics of a non-consenting child to be inserted into Tasmania's Criminal Code (Tasmanian Law Reform Institution, 2020). These developments have come from direct engagement with intersex organizations including IHRA, which ensure that relevant issues are addressed at a policy level. This is a very positive step, although the comparative difference between the speed of progression in anti-discrimination law across Australia (nearly 30 years after indeterminate sex was included within NSW's anti-discrimination legislation) is telling of the effects of conceptualizing intersex embodiment through an LGBT frame.

LGBT (homonormative) embodiment and reifying medical frameworks

Throughout this chapter we have demonstrated how anti-discrimination law can be an ineffectual way of tackling intersex issues. Moreover, we have laid out how the focus on anti-discrimination law, despite its lack of success, has largely been the product of framing intersex embodiment through a lens of LGBT. Ultimately, recognition through discrimination law inevitably comes with increased regulation of what those identities/labels mean through the creation of new normativities (Harding, 2010). In the context of intersex embodiment, these normativities largely cohere around the acceptance and reification of understanding intersex through a lens of medical embodiment. A homonormative embodiment framing contributes to the reification of medical frameworks by closing down political discussions, and this final section highlights how the fear of 'difference' can encourage parents to defer to medical understandings and responses. Not only does the medical response to intersex variations leave many individuals too traumatized or fearful to 'come out' as intersex publicly, but large schisms exist within the 'community' itself; indeed, it is not possible to refer to any singular homogenous intersex community at all. In many ways these concerns echo those at the start of intersex activism acknowledged by Sharon Preves in her documentation of ISNA:

> The second, longer lasting split occurred as ISNA continued to associate intersex with gay, lesbian, bisexual, and transgender issues. Given that fear of sexual difference seems to drive medical sex assignment, this conflict should come as no surprise. Some of the support groups have intentionally aligned themselves with GLBT allies. Other groups, especially those run by parents of intersex children, have expressed their reticence to associate intersex with GLBT persons and concerns. In fact, in speaking with parents of intersex children, I have encountered parents' explicit efforts to sever associations between intersex and GLBT issues. Despite this clear divide among interested parties, the Intersex Society of North America has made deliberate appeals to queer activists, press outlets, and medical organizations, framing intersex as an issue of gender and sexuality from its inception in 1993. ISNA's decision to do so has no doubt increased its linkages to GLBT persons and groups, but at the same time alienated itself from the potential support of others who disagree with the organization's framing of intersex in this way. (Preves, 2005: 263)

The potential for institutional misrepresentation that may arise from this LGBT framing has led many intersex embodied people to reject any involvement with LGBT or intersex activism (Garland and Travis, 2020c).[26] As a result, the intersex 'community' has become divided over the way in which understandings and experiences of intersex variations are framed (Garland and Travis, 2020c). Some participants see any legal recognition (even if it misframes intersex embodiment) as positive because it marks the starting point of discussions with the State about meaningful change. Others are more cynical and view legislation as an end point in discussions. Accordingly, problematic legislation works to close down meaningful discussions about change as uninformed policy makers believe that the issues are resolved (Garland and Travis, 2020c).[27] These participants therefore wanted to remain unrecognized by the legal system until they could be recognized on their own terms – with a full acknowledgement of the problems of non-therapeutic medical interventions. As such, the majority

[26] These debates are also internal to LGBT. See for example, Cohen (1997) and Barker (2012).

[27] Again these are similar to debates raised within the LGBT community. See for example, Cohen (1997) and Barker (2012).

of our participants saw framing intersex embodiment as either queer or homonormative potentially misrecognized and marginalized intersex people.

LGBT embodiment, thus can detrimentally affect the mobilization of collective action to push for *effectual* legal reform. Moreover, it also may dangerously strengthen medical power/knowledge in this arena and the continued use of medical interventions to fix intersex children (Carpenter, 2018; Garland and Travis, 2020c). In effect, the individualized nature of anti-discrimination law fails to challenge the structural homophobia inherent to medical frameworks. Furthermore, this linking of intersex, homonormativity and queer embodiment does not challenge the homophobia of the parents of these children who, in the confines of the clinical setting, are unlikely to embrace the potential for gender fluidity and the breakdown of heteronormativity (Holmes, 2009: 6). The structural homophobia in Western society thus diminished the potential for LGBT embodiment to challenge the medical embodiment paradigm. Our respondents understood that identity-focused reforms could reify the division within the intersex 'communities'. Consequently, they wanted legal reform that operated regardless of whether individuals identified as part of an intersex community (Garland and Travis, 2020c). To do so, legislators need to prioritize bodily autonomy and bring about an end to medical interventions designed to 'fix' intersex.

Conclusion

Anti-discrimination law can be an important legislative step towards both legally and politically recognizing intersex as well as addressing broader social inequalities. However, where inappropriately framed, these laws can not only be ineffectual but can be harmful in terms of both perpetuating misunderstandings about intersex embodiment and also reifying medical frameworks. Moreover, by their very design, these laws are ill-equipped to challenge medical norms or the underlying homophobic discriminatory practice that informs medical interventions on intersex bodies. More worryingly, the frequency with which states are introducing anti-discrimination law without any other policy or legislation to protect bodily integrity represents a broader issue of legal and political misdirection that arises when states understand intersex embodiment through a lens of LGBT. This framing is inevitably homonormative.

Close alliances between intersex and LGBT activism have arisen from the shared concerns around homophobia that each group faces. Accordingly, while some have expressed support for such inclusion and increased visibility, others have raised concerns around homonormativity and the ways in which funding has been taken away from intersex groups and the concomitant concealing of intersex voices. More recently, some intersex organizations and activists have fundamental disagreements with being included in LGBT policy and spaces as they feel distanced from LGBT narratives. For these organizations, this type of inclusion has led to a profound confusion about intersex embodiment, with LGBT framings leading to inaccuracies in legal and policy development. This has had institutional and discursive effects that play out in important ways in relation to issues around the ways that intersex concerns can be resolved through law. Seen through a framework of homonormative embodiment, anti-discrimination becomes a valid and useful tool for recognition and for redressing issues of homophobic inequality. At the same time, for some this backdrop may have increased parental desire for their children to undergo non-therapeutic medical interventions, as it means they might avoid their child being associated with LGBT embodiment (Carpenter, 2018). These discursive practices, therefore, have an important framing effect on what intersex is and the necessary policy implications that stem from it. In the Chapter 5 we consider the benefits of tackling the issues of substantive equality that intersex people raise through the legislative context of Malta.

5

Engaging with Intersex Experience: Can Law Disrupt Medical Embodiment?

Introduction

The last two chapters have traced the problems inherent to law and policy framing around intersex embodiment and the consequences of their enactment. Within law, intersex embodiment is most frequently constructed through lenses of LGBT and non-binary embodiment. Perhaps unsurprisingly then, states have turned to anti-discrimination legislation and third markers to redress perceived status disadvantages for intersex people. However, as this book demonstrates, understanding intersex embodiment solely through these lenses is fraught with difficulties. LGBT and non-binary frameworks are ill-equipped to challenge the paradigmatic construction of intersex embodiment as a disorder and cannot redress the systemic disadvantages that arise from the medical management of intersex bodies. Nor can anti-discrimination laws remedy the scope of rights violations identified by international bodies like the UNCRC and the Council of Europe that these non-consensual medical interventions may result in (Garland and Slokenberga, 2018: 1; Office for the Commissioner of Human Rights, 2019; UNCRC, 2019). At best, then, third markers and anti-discrimination legislation are ineffectual and, at worst, harmful as they distract from and potentially silence the core issue at the centre of the intersex movement: bodily integrity (Carpenter, 2018). The result is that the disorder narrative enabled by medical embodiment is in fact perpetuated and strengthened by such state-led measures.

This chapter specifically addresses the question of whether intersex embodiment is disrupted where the law specifically regulates medical interventions. Unlike the last two chapters, this approach attempts to shift the framing of intersex embodiment to one that *draws* upon intersex experience (ontology) rather than *determining* it (epistemology). Since 2015, four states[1] have introduced legislation which directly challenges medical practice and consequently the paradigmatic framing of intersex embodiment as a disorder. In particular, this chapter highlights Malta as the first and longest-standing Western state to prohibit medical interventions on intersex children through legislation in its Gender Identity, Gender Expression and Sex Characteristics Act 2015 (GIGESC Act). The introduction of the GIGESC Act marked a significant moment in intersex legal reform where, for the first time in the West, legislation adopted a children's rights-based approach to intersex issues centred on bodily integrity, autonomy and self-determination. It was met with considerable praise from the activist community for directly exposing and challenging narratives of medical embodiment and referred to as a 'gold-standard' in terms of intersex rights (Garland and Travis, 2018: 606). As the Global Network for Trans Equality stated in response to the introduction of the GIGESC Act:

> The Maltese GIGESC Act not only defends children's rights in Malta, including those of bodily integrity, self-determination and health. It also makes a fundamental contribution to intersex people's human rights by recognizing in law the pervasive role that 'social factors' play in justifying medically unnecessary procedures aimed to 'normalize' intersex bodies. The Maltese Act explicitly exposes the vulnerability of intersex infants, children and adolescents in medical settings, while affirming, at the same time, that this can be successfully addressed as a matter of law. We hope this clear and strong message to be heard and followed not only by other governments around the globe, but also by the World Health Organization. (Cabral, 2015: 196)

This chapter explores the extent to which these reforms in Malta, arguably the most comprehensive of all the current legislative engagements with intersex, have been able to challenge the paradigmatic framing of intersex embodiment as a disorder. To do so, we draw from the two empirical projects set out in Chapter 1 and reflect more broadly on the relationship between legal reform and social change.[2] After setting out Malta's approach, our analysis is two-fold. Firstly, we explore *why* Malta was able to introduce such ground-breaking legislation in a way that has not been possible in other states. As part of this, we highlight the

---

[1] Malta, Portugal, Germany and Greece.

[2] See Chapter 1. Respondents from the SLSA project are identified as 'Respondent XX', while respondents from the British Academy project are identified as 'BA Respondent XX'.

legislation's grounding in queer embodiment, LGBT issues and rights-based frameworks in order to address the productive way in which this has generated success for intersex activists. This has inevitably affected the design and passage of the GIGESC Act, where provisions for intersex people appear appended to the legislation. Secondly, we explore the extent to which the GIGESC Act has successfully disrupted the medical narrative of intersex embodiment. We link this to socio-legal writings on the relationship between law, social movements and social change, which have questioned the efficacy of using law as a strategy to achieve real change. In the Maltese context, we posit that while the prohibition has disrupted the idea of intersex embodiment as 'disordered' on a symbolic level, the GIGESC Act has had little effect on lived experience with an 'implementation gap' existing between law and medical practice. Consequently, the medical narrative of intersex embodiment continues to frame intersex people's lives and experiences. The chapter finally explores the possible reasons for these implementation issues, considering whether legal measures are ever able to disrupt medical framings of embodiment. Ultimately, we note that the subsequent lack of implementation of key services (such as psychosocial care) have meant that intersex embodiment in Malta continues to be understood within a framework of disorder. As a result, we argue that even comprehensive legal challenges informed by intersex experiences struggle to change the conceptualization of intersex embodiment as disordered. In order to do so, there needs to be significant medical buy-in necessitating altered care pathways, changes to clinical classifications and a shift in how medicine understands and frames intersex embodiment. However, we contend that this does not mean that the GIGESC Act represents a failure in terms of the intersex movement. Rather, we argue that social change (and embodiment) should be seen as a dynamic and ongoing concept rather than a movement from one static state to another. Consequently, the Maltese legislation may be seen as a solid starting point for the continued disruption of medical approaches to intersex embodiment and achieving long-term real change.

GIGESC Act: a conceptual shift in intersex embodiment

In 2015, Malta introduced the ground-breaking GIGESC Act, which contained a whole host of rights relating to the recognition and protection of a person's gender identity and sex characteristics. In particular, section 3 affirmed that all citizens of Malta have the right to:

(a) the recognition of their gender identity;
(b) the free development of their person according to their gender identity;

(c) be treated according to their gender identity and, particularly, to be identified in that way in the documents providing their identity therein; and
(d) bodily integrity and physical autonomy.

At its core, then, the GIGESC Act introduced a number of provisions designed to protect bodily integrity, gender autonomy and self-determination. In doing so, the Act powerfully disrupted medicine's framing of intersex embodiment and sex and gender more generally. The majority of the GIGESC Act's 17 sections concern the process of changing recorded gender which, through section 4, is permissible in accordance with the individual's self-determined gender identity; there is no need for medical evidence. Section 7 extends this process to minors, allowing a court order to be made to change the recorded gender of a child as long as it is considered to be in their best interests and that due weight is given to the minor's voice in accordance with their age and maturity. Per section 7(4), the child must be registered within 15 days of birth; however gender does not need to be declared until the child is 18. Significantly, this relieves pressure where an infant is born with ambiguity as to their sex. Most importantly in terms of intersex rights, section 14(1) states: 'It shall be unlawful for medical practitioners or other professionals to conduct any sex assignment treatment and/or surgical intervention on the sex characteristics of a minor which treatment and/or intervention can be deferred until the person to be treated can provide informed consent.' Medical practitioners who break this law can be fined between 5,000 and 20,000 euros and, as a result of Act No XIII of 2018, face up to five years' incarceration (section 14(2) GIGESC Act). However, the legislation does allow for some interventions to be carried out. For example, section14 (1) continues that these interventions 'shall be conducted if the minor gives informed consent through the person exercising parental authority or the tutor of the minor'. Nonetheless, section 14(6) provides that, in this circumstance, the medical practitioner *must* (a) ensure that the 'best interests of the child' as expressed in the Convention on the Rights of the Child be paramount and (b) due weight must be given to the child's voice in light of their age and maturity. Per section 14(3), it is also possible for the person with parental authority and an interdisciplinary team to agree to certain interventions where the minor is unable to give consent. Nevertheless, the Act stresses that 'medical intervention which is driven by social factors without the consent of the minor, will be in violation of this Act'.[3] While we will

[3] Of course, this means that interventions which are not perceived as motivated by social factors are possible. The chapter returns to this point later on.

return to the limitations of these provisions later in the chapter, importantly section 14 represents a significant moment in law reform as it decouples legal regulation from the traditional and dominant medical understandings of intersex embodiment. Through the GIGESC Act, Malta became the first jurisdiction in the world to have legislation designed to protect the bodily integrity of all intersex children.[4] Moreover, it openly challenges the disordered narrative of medical embodiment by recognizing the social motivations behind medical interventions on intersex infants. Indeed, the Act's use of terminology such as 'sex characteristics' rather than 'DSD' highlights its intention to distance itself from medical framings of intersex embodiment. The GIGESC Act (section 2) conceptualizes intersex not as a disorder, but a natural bodily variation: ' "sex characteristics" refers to the chromosomal, gondal and anatomical features of a person, which include primary characteristics such as reproductive organs and genitalia and, or in chromosomal structures and hormones; and secondary characteristics such as muscle mass, hair distribution, breasts and, or structure'. Moreover, the intersex-specific provisions are not designed to simply prohibit medical interventions; it also introduces a number of measures designed to offer holistic support to the individual, further reframing narratives of intersex embodiment. In addition to self-ascribing gender, part of section 14's aim was to establish an interdisciplinary team to oversee the care of intersex individuals. This team was meant to help individuals and parents reach decisions about the care of the individual, including consent to treatment where the minor is unable to consent. This team, through section 14(4), was meant to be appointed by the minister for a period of three years (subject to renewal) and was to be composed of professionals 'whom the Minister consider appropriate' (section 14(5)). In doing so, the Act is designed to set up a network of trained medical professionals specialized in intersex care to provide consistent and appropriate care to individuals across Malta beyond narratives of disorder and fixing (see Garland et al, 2021 for a discussion of the composition of multi-disciplinary teams). Our British Academy respondents emphasized that the GIGESC Act was meant to improve and standardize the medical experience of intersex-embodied people:

> 'What actually the law is meant to do as well and all, sort of create this network of people who are specialized in intersex issues, so that when a very someone goes to an endocrinologist or a gynaecologist or a psychologist or whatever, they would already be familiar

[4] See, however, Garland and Slokenberga (2018) for an examination of Argentina, Chile, and Columbia – as jurisdictions that have attempted to deal with intersex issues outside legislation through either medical protocols or (in the case of Columbia) case law.

> they would be trained on intersex issues, all sorts of, so everyone at least hopefully would get the same level of medical care.' (BA Respondent 1)

Additionally, section 15 ensures that individuals are able to receive appropriate psychosocial support where necessary, stating that: 'All persons seeking psychosocial counselling, support and medical interventions relating to sex or gender should be given expert sensitive and individually tailored support by psychologists and medical practitioners or peer counselling. Such support should extend from the date of diagnosis or self-referral for as long as necessary.' Through sections 14 and 15, then, the GIGESC Act continues to recognize the specialist medical knowledge of healthcare professionals, but does not prioritize it over and above the lived experiences of intersex people (Garland and Travis, 2020a). Indeed, BA Respondent 2 indicated that the interdisciplinary team should consist of not only those with medical expertise but also 'psycho-social professionals, human rights experts, and potentially also intersex persons who could offer peer support together with of course the medical experts, that would make joint decisions and provide information to parents in the early stages'. Accordingly, the GIGESC Act frames healthcare in a way to support the individual's emotional wellbeing. Seemingly committed to wellbeing, the GIGESC Act also amended aspects of Malta's criminal and equality laws. Section 11(2) amended section 83B of the Criminal Code to extend its hate crime legislation where 'an offence is motivated by gender expression and sex characteristics' and section 11(1) makes it an offence to 'insult or revile' any person who has used the provisions within this Act. Section 13(2) further amends Malta's anti-discrimination legislation, confirming that: 'The public service has the duty to ensure that unlawful sexual orientation, gender identity, gender expression and sex characteristics discrimination and harassment are eliminated, while its services must promote equality of opportunity to all, irrespective of sexual orientation, gender identity, gender expression and sex characteristics.' These extensions of anti-discrimination laws are more inclusive than seen in other jurisdictions as they form *part* of a comprehensive package of rights that recognize the multifaceted ways in which individuals experience intersex embodiment. Moreover, the choice of terminology – sex characteristics – ensures that these provisions are accessible by all individuals with intersex variations without the individual having to specifically identify as intersex.[5] This respect towards privacy is present throughout the Act and section 11(1) even makes it an offence for any individual to expose the fact that a person has used a provision.

[5] See Chapters 3 and 4 for more discussion.

Reflecting on the other frameworks explored thus far in this book, it is easy to see why Malta represents a huge conceptual shift in understandings of intersex embodiment. The GIGESC Act breaks away from the typical lenses through which jurisdictions frame intersex and, in doing so, the strategy of law reform used by activists appears successful: Law ostensibly appears to be meeting the primary goal of the intersex movement. The GIGESC Act is a comprehensive piece of legislation that recognizes the need for a wide range of legal measures and reforms to best protect and improve lived experience in terms of core social institutions and, pivotally, wellbeing. While this chapter outlines some of the problematic aspects of this statute's drafting, the intersex-specific provisions introduced by this Act offer a rights-based approach which seemingly implements reform recommendations made by intersex activists and human rights authorities, disrupting medicine's authority over intersex embodiment. As Garland and Slokenberga note, bodies such as the UN and the Council of Europe have not just called upon states to challenge medical practice on the basis that they are non-consensual interventions, but to also recognize that 'interventions violate multiple established rights of children to physical and psychological integrity, as well as rights to identity, privacy, and protection from violence and degrading treatment' (2018, 484). Indeed, the UN has stated that:

> States must, as a matter of urgency, prohibit medically unnecessary surgery and procedures on intersex children. They must uphold the autonomy of intersex adults and children and their rights to health, to physical and mental integrity, to live free from violence and harmful practices and to be free from torture and ill-treatment. Intersex children and their parents should be provided with support and counselling, including from peers. Intersex children and adults should be the only ones who decide whether they wish to modify the appearance of their own bodies – in the case of children, when they are old or mature enough to make an informed decision for themselves. They should have access to support as well as to medical services that respond to their specific health needs and that are based on non-discrimination, informed consent and respect for their fundamental rights … Ending these abuses will also require States to raise awareness of the rights of intersex people, to protect them from discrimination on ground of sex characteristics, including in access to health care, education, employment, sports and in obtaining official documents, as well as special protection when they are deprived of liberty. (Office of the High Commissioner for Human Rights, 2019: 44)

While states that have only modified anti-discrimination law have been accused of having a 'compliance gap between human rights recommendations and law reform' (Garland and Slokenberga, 2018: 1), the GIGESC Act locates intersex within a statutory framework which addresses this broad range of rights violations. Indeed, the final sections of the Act reflect Malta's commitment to upholding human rights standards and medical best practice. Section 16 appoints a working group to oversee the implementation of this Act, comprised of ten members, of which three must be human rights specialists. The remit of this working groups is to 'review the current medical treatment protocols in line with current medical best practices and human rights standards' and to 'issue a report with recommendations for revision of the current medical treatment protocols'. Section 16 therefore was designed to set up a workforce to ensure medical protocols were introduced that translated the GIGESC Act reforms into practice.

Against this backdrop, section 14 of the GIGESC Act has received high praise from the intersex community for enacting real protections which recognize the importance of challenging medical approaches to intersex embodiment. Thus, Malta very quickly became referred to as the gold standard of law reform (Garland and Travis, 2018: 606). For authorities like the UN, Malta is and continues to be a legal benchmark for the rights of intersex persons (Office for the Commissioner of Human Rights, 2019). Our SLSA project interviewed respondents during the passage of the GIGESC Act, with the majority of interviews taking place shortly after the Act had been implemented. All respondents bar one believed that the way to enact positive change for intersex people came through a rights-based approach that both focused on preventing surgeries and offering substantive protections to redress inequalities:

> 'I think it's, again, human rights issues, creating spaces, having laws that are inclusive of intersex folk, but also creating provisions in school, at work, and protections for people who are intersex. And I think as there is more visibility, that will inform more policy. But I think it's important to really … use the UN, human rights decree about the basic things that people need in order to live and to thrive.' (Respondent 15)

For many respondents, Malta offered a model of good practice for other states to follow, having brought in a suite of holistic intersex reforms based on the experiences of intersex people. As one respondent stated, "Malta is a beacon of hope" (Respondent 11).

Therefore, Malta appears best placed in using law to rupture the disorder narrative of intersex embodiment. In contrast to third-gender markers and narratives of LGBT embodiment, legal approaches based around bodily integrity directly challenge the power, knowledge and jurisdiction of medicine by removing intersex subjects from its pathologizing domain. Such shifts relocate intersex embodiment away from the scope of intervention, regulation and surveillance towards equality, emergence and support. This approach takes responsibility for the fact that many of the problems faced by intersex embodied people are caused by institutions and attempts to ameliorate these difficulties. Moreover, this practice encourages state responsibility for the medical profession and seemingly allows for disruptions of and negotiations around medical power and knowledge. The next section now explores *how* Malta moved away from the other lenses of intersex embodiment that we have outlined that continue to dictate legislative responses. Understanding this is key to understanding some of the problems within the Act and its implementation, but also to understanding how activists are best able to instigate state-level change.

Understanding the shift away from medical embodiment

In part, the shift in intersex rights was the product of opportunism in Malta during a wave of reforms relating to trans rights and same-sex marriage. This reform drive began with a significant legal challenge before the Maltese courts regarding the right of a transgender woman to marry her cisgender partner. In 2011, this case, *Joanne Cassar v Malta*,[6] reached the European Court of Human Rights. In an out-of-court settlement Ms Cassar was awarded 10,000 euros and the Maltese government pledged to introduce legislation to allow trans people access to marriage. This promise culminated in the Civil Code (Amendment) Act 2013, which amended the Constitution to state that: 'every person in Malta is entitled to the fundamental rights and freedoms of the individual, that is to say, the right, whatever his … sex, sexual orientation or gender identity.' What followed was a series of legislative reforms, spearheaded by the newly appointed Labour government's commitment to LGBT rights (Muscat, 2013). Following through on its pre-election promises, the Maltese government introduced 'gender identity' as a protected characteristic within Malta's anti-discrimination law;[7] recognized 'gender reassignment' as a legitimate ground for sick leave;[8] and committed to a more thorough Gender Identity Bill in 2015. The government also introduced same-sex civil unions in 2014[9] and same-sex marriage in 2017.[10]

> 'Malta was in Europe quite low when it came to LGBTI rights and within the Maltese government there was just a conscious effort to

---

6 Application no 36982/11.

7 Constitution of Malta (Amendment) Act 2014; Procedural Standards in Examining Applications for Refugee Status (Amendment) Regulations 2014.

8 Equal Treatment in Employment (Amendment) Regulations 2014 (LN 274 of 2014).

9 Civil Union Act 2014.

10 Marriage Act 2017.

> change this. We saw Malta going from a low score on the [ILGA-Europe's annual Rainbow Europe Map and Index] … The current government in Malta seems to see LGBTI actually were not being addressed and so they are looking at it thoroughly.' (Respondent 8)

Initially, intersex rights had not been featured within the social and political upheaval for LGBT rights in Malta. The initial drafting process of the "gender identity, or gender recognition legislation [now GIGESC] … didn't include any references to intersex at all" (Respondent 17). However, the government's commitment to LGBT reform presented an opportunity for intersex to become included within its political agenda. In 2013, the Third International Intersex Forum (a large intersex conference funded by LGBT charity ILGA International and attended by 30 global organizations) was hosted in Malta; the new Director for Civil Liberties and Equalities was invited to attend and did so. Here they heard first-hand accounts of the medical interventions and harms experienced by intersex people. Less than a year on, at the first reading of the GIGESC Bill, intersex issues had been fully included within the objectives of the Bill:

> The objects of this Bill are to provide for the recognition and registration of the gender of a person and to regulate the effects of such a change, and due recognition and protection of the sex characteristics of a person. Gender identity is considered to be an inherent part of a person which may or may not need surgical or hormonal treatment or therapy and the Bill provides for a simplified procedure which respects the privacy of the person requesting that one's official documents be changed to reflect one's gender. Similarly, the sex characteristics of a person vary in nature and all persons must be empowered to make their decisions affecting their own bodily integrity and physical autonomy.

The Bill included articles 15–17, specifically aimed to protect the bodily integrity of intersex minors. Our SLSA respondents attributed Malta's inclusion of intersex specific reforms to this significant moment of policy engagement, where policy makers actively listened and engaged with the needs of intersex people (rather than imagining them or learning about them through broader narratives of queer or homonormative embodiment):

> 'Malta is a very good example of where policy makers have listened to and worked with the community. The Third International Intersex Forum took place there in 2013 and it seems that following that forum, where government officials from Malta attended, they took

> concrete steps and enacted real protections for our community there.' (Respondent 8)

Some of our British Academy respondents similarly stressed the importance of human stories leading to significant institutional shifts:

> 'It's not just about the technical and the … theory but it's also about the personal experiences, the human experiences that parents or children and adults have gone through. … the Minister [for Civil Liberties] at the time was surrounded by two people who have done a lot of work around intersex persons globally and so … had the opportunity to meet a number of intersex activists from around the world when they had … the third international intersex forum that ILGA Europe was conducting in Malta. So the minister had this opportunity, you know, to listen to the stories of so many people and … she felt compelled that she needs to do something about this.' (BA Respondent 4)

However, rather than representing intersex-specific reform, respondents from both the SLSA and British Academy projects considered the intersex provisions to be a drafting afterthought, embedded in law reform predominantly aimed at trans experiences marked through a series of appendages to the title, adapted provisions, and the intersex-specific provisions added to the end of the Act. With opportunism came compromise:

> 'Some … weren't even convinced that [the Bill] should include intersex. Also because … very often trans and intersex are mixed up, they're conflated, many people think that intersex and trans are one and the same thing, or intersex people have the same needs and face the same maybe violations as trans people. So [there were] long discussions about kind of combining or including references to intersex into [the] law. At the same time, again Maltese context here, [they] don't have a long history of progressive governments, and so [their] main concern as LGBTIQ activists was this is a great opportunity.' (Respondent 17)

Drilling deeper into this matter within the British Academy project, however, this is not a universally shared position. One BA respondent thought it was overly simplistic to describe intersex as an 'afterthought' in the political process. Rather intersex was new to the LGBTI activist movement and civil organizations in Malta pushing for change and, consequently, had not been included within the initial tabling of the Gender Identity Bill in 2010. However, "when political will was expressed in terms of passing the

GIGESC Act from the political side, it seemed always intended to include intersex issues" (BA Respondent 2). Attentive to differences, the way in which intersex was framed within the Act remained distinctly separate from trans issues. As Respondent 17 from the SLSA project continued:

> '[They] wanted to have a project from a children's rights perspective rather than [LGBT] - so [they] took a children's right approach. … I'm thinking about other laws that as LGBTIQ activists [they]'ve been involved with. [They]'ve always made the argument about the rights of LGBT people. This was a bit different because [they] approached it from a children's rights perspective, which was a bit different. It was also part of [their] strategy as well.'

Respondent 17 then went on to highlight how there was a recognized need to use children rights to secure the passage of these law reforms:

> 'Strategy-wise … the opposition wasn't about protecting children. People would not object to protecting children. How should I put it? We know what makes the opposition tick. We know that there's anti LGBT or anti gender people. We have them here as well at the Catholic Church. So they would never argue that we should not protect children, because essentially that's what they always used. That's the argument they always use, that we must protect children … In fact, the opposition, or any criticism that [was] received, was mostly around gender identity. [They] did not get any criticism or opposition to kind of stopping the surgeries and medical treatment.'

The intersex-specific additions made to the Bill were largely unchallenged throughout its passage. Of the 26 responses to the Bill's public consultation, nine were from national organizations and institutions, including the Church of Malta, eight from international organizations and institutions, and nine from individuals (with one submission signed by 37 people) (Maltese Government, 2015). Of these submissions, most did not refer to intersex issues or articles 15–17.[11] The main concern both in terms of consultation response and media reception was about gender identity and the registration of gender at birth. At the parliamentary committee, there was also little disagreement on article 15 (now section 14 of the GIGESC Act). Rather,

[11] ADITUS, a Human Rights non-governmental organization, specifically chose to not comment on these articles. The Commissioner for Children and the Maltese Paediatric Association remarked on the fact that the Bill did not distinguish between intersex and trans children, and they questioned the expertise required for the interdisciplinary team.

the debate focused on whether the article should include that the provision was specifically addressed to intersex children and not all newborns. The minister responsible for the law, Dr Helena Dalli, argued that the omission ensured that no unconsented genital surgeries would be allowed, whether the child was born intersex or not; it was more inclusive (Consideration of Bills Committee, 2015: 24–6).[12] The GIGESC Act was finally made law on 1 April 2015, with some notable amendments to the draft. Probably one of the most important amendments related to intersex issues and the ban on genital 'normalizing' surgeries was the introduction of a fine or imprisonment for medical practitioners in breach of article 14 (1).

Given the widespread concern about the cultural silence and invisibility regarding intersex, it is likely that these intersex provisions sailed through the drafting process because they went unnoticed in a Bill designed with trans needs in mind. Dr Nicholas Briffa, a psychologist with special interest in sexual health, noted in their consultation response 'a lot of people inside our country still do not know what the word transgender and intersex means, nor even the difference between the term gender and sex' (Briffa, 2014: 1 translated). Indeed, our British Academy respondents also suggested that the lack of participation by any Maltese intersex people in the drafting process[13] was attributed to this lack of awareness of intersex and social stigma:

> 'Most people don't know what intersex is, and. And it's not just that you know the general public doesn't know what intersex is, I have this feeling that even people who are intersex, don't know that they are intersex, because it is not said, you know, sort of, it's not verbalized, so they know they have a problem most probably likely and, I mean, you know, hormonal issues or CAH or something off the sort you know but they haven't been really mentioned the word intersex hasn't really been mentioned, and the doctors, sort of, they don't realize or else they won't admit, how many people are actually intersex on the island.' (BA Respondent 1)

The introduction of intersex-specific provisions "was more government- than society-led and mainly because there was not a lot of knowledge I would say of civil society on intersex issues" (BA Respondent 2). Moreover, the public consultation and our early findings from the British Academy project suggested limited formal medical engagement with the process.

---

12 This was an important stance, particularly given that the recent law in Germany is limited to intersex, and there are concerns that children simply are not being diagnosed so as to circumvent the legislation.

13 Intersex individuals and organizations engaged in the process were predominantly international.

Crucially, then, the shift in intersex rights in Malta was largely the product of the GIGESC Act's cultural openness towards and grounding in LGBT issues and rights-based frameworks and not limited by the homonormative lens seen in Chapter 4. As we have noted elsewhere, the difference between Malta and other jurisdictions has been 'political openness … marked by the willingness of government officials to listen to intersex testimonies and ensure that these experiences informed the drafting of legislation' (Garland and Travis, 2020a: 322–3). This engagement has enabled policy makers and legislative bodies to understand the problematic nature of the disordered narrative of intersex embodiment. By recognizing inequalities as the product of medical structures rather than being status-based, Malta has been able to commit to introducing legislation with a rights-based focus. The state has been willing to challenge the medical profession's conception of intersex embodiment in a way that has not been seen in other jurisdictions. However, as we discussed in the Chapter 5 there can be dangers when intersex is added to trans-focused reform, even when there is a genuine political commitment to the well-conceptualized intersex provisions contained with that legislation. While this was a marked opportunity without which intersex concerns may not have been addressed at a legislative level, the response and engagement with the passage of the GIGSEC Act suggests that the intersex voice may be lost or assimilated within trans narratives prioritizing a narrative of homonormative LGBT embodiment. This is particularly the case in the *implementation* of this law, whereby almost all the clinical service provision and psychosocial support has been tailored towards trans people. Support for intersex people in medical provision has so far, unfortunately, been marked by a distinct lack of progress, despite the ambition of the legislation.

Law and social change: disrupting the disorder narrative

Much of what we have written thus far in this chapter has been hopeful in terms of law's ability to challenge medical narratives of intersex embodiment and improve lived experience. The frequency with which social movements turn to law to affect change is unsurprising given law's definitive claims over justice, rights and equality. As Lobel states, law 'presents itself both as the exclusive source of authority in a society and as the engine of transformative politics. Law occupies the field of re-form possibilities and reduces a movement's vision to a limited scope of remedies' (Lobel, 2006–07: 955). At a superficial level, Malta's legislative reform has challenged the authority and inevitability of defining intersex embodiment purely in terms of disorder. At a symbolic level then, law *is* directly challenging medical narratives of embodiment not just at the local level but also further afield:

> 'One thing I'm sure is that the law has empowered intersex people abroad, from the reactions we got following the passing of the law. It has been great to see that. I just think we need to focus on the local city origin as well and not forget that most intersex people are still living in secrecy and there's so much stigma around intersex bodies and experiences.' (Respondent 17)

Since Malta's reforms, there has been a ripple effect. Portugal, Greece and Germany have all brought in legislation designed to challenge medical practice, and the Australian States of Victoria and Australian Capital Territory have publicly committed to reform in the area (Tasmanian Law Reform Institution, 2020; Chief Minister, Treasury and Economic Development Directorate, 2021; Department of Health, 2021).

However, there are larger concerns that, despite being a 'fleshed-out' piece of legislation in terms of intersex (particularly in comparison to those frameworks explored in Chapter 3 and 4), the GIGESC Act has not disrupted medical embodiment. This 'failure' is attributable to two key reasons: first, the drafting of the Act is so limited that it does not actually challenge the power of the medical profession but instead continues to privilege them; and, second, there is an implementation gap whereby no medical protocol has been developed to translate legal promises of disruption into practice. Both these issues we address in the following sections. First, however, it is important to reflect on how these issues connect with broader academic concerns about the limitations of law as a vehicle through which to achieve social change. We shall now discuss this prior to looking at the major obstacles behind the slow progress of the GIGESC Act.

Over time, many legal and social movement scholars have become sceptical of law's ability to effect social change (Minow, 1993–94; Barlow et al, 2005; Lobel, 2006–07). Indeed, Lobel argues that 'social movements often overestimate what the law will deliver' (Lobel, 2006–07: 955). For many American scholars, the examples of the civil rights movement and the New Deal labour laws have highlighted the frustrations of working in a legal framework (Crenshaw, 1988: Minow, 1993–94; Lobel, 2006–07). The social progress of these movements has faltered after the initial legal gains. In terms of the civil rights movement, for example, the language of rights, and discrimination has individualized, neutralized and naturalized the presence of racism – ignoring structural issues of racism that require redistribution (Lobel, 2006–07: 948). Indeed, the legal language of rights places issues of redistribution and reparation outside of the realm of the judiciary. As Crenshaw writes: 'Society has embraced the rhetoric of equal opportunity without fulfilling its promise; creating a break with the past has formed the basis for the neoconservative claim that present inequities cannot be the result of discriminatory practices because this society no longer discriminates against Blacks' (Crenshaw, 1988: 1347). Resultantly, the legislation must also be matched by the way that law operates in practice, including failures in implementation, custom and other day-to-day practices (Minow, 1993–94: 174). Such issues have been played out in the context of the anti-discrimination and equality-based reform that this book examined in Chapter 4.

Legal reform has been criticized as it 'narrows the causes, deradicalizes the agenda, legitimizes ongoing injustices, and diverts energies away from more effective and transformative alternatives' (Lobel, 2006–07: 939). In turn, social movements are absorbed into the architecture of law and begin to reinforce dominant social institutions and ideologies (Lobel, 2006–07: 939). Social movements are hampered by the institutional limits of law and, in turn, may be detrimentally affected by engaging with law. In Chapter 4, we traced how engagement with law has actively proved detrimental to the intersex movement, as it has normalized and reified conservative heteronormative values regarding sex and gender. While the GIGESC Act represents a new sort of architecture in the sense that it offers a ground-breaking way of conceptualizing and responding to the concerns of the intersex movement, it is nevertheless developed within the confines of historical legal structures, paradigms and doctrines. These facets of law have historically operated to uphold hierarchies and protect the privileges of the powerful (Barclay et al, 2009: 4). As Barclay et al state: 'Law's structural power is not isolated; instead, legal institutions are enmeshed with other powerful institutions and the discourses they produce' (2009: 7). Accordingly, it may come as no surprise to scholars critical of law's ability to instigate social change that the GIGESC Act contains significant loopholes that enable past medical practices to continue. These loopholes arguably reinforce medical embodiment as the GIGESC Act suggests that problematic practice has, in fact, been challenged and ended by law: the effect is to further legitimize that which is able to continue. Similarly, other scholars have raised doubts about how far law shapes people's day-to-day decision making. As Barlow et al write in the context of cohabitation:

> this … approach has one crucial problem – it implicitly assumes that law can shape social change. … Our findings suggest that this approach is flawed because of its assumption that people are legally rational in this sense. The majority do not choose to [act] because of the legal consequences. This may be because many are unaware of the legal consequences. … But … even when [people] are aware of the legal distinctions, this is hardly ever the basis upon which the decision … is made. … Nor does this all-important knowledge prompt any wide-scale appropriate private ordering, often despite intentions to take the necessary legal steps. (Barlow et al, 2005: 107–8)

Law then may only have a limited effect on the way that people (including practitioners and parents) make decisions, think about their lives and order their worlds.

For some scholars this has encouraged a move away from legal routes to social change in favour of other means of progress and many of our respondents from both the SLSA and British Academy projects did not view law as the chief means to do so. Barclay et al (2009) draw attention to the fact that 'activists are not naively pursuing rights-based legal strategies; they are well aware of the limitations' (2009: 6). In fact, all our SLSA respondents (intersex rights activists) indicated that law was only part of a bigger picture, with education across *all* society depicted as the key mechanism through which to achieve real change. Similarly, all our British Academy respondents identified visibility and raising cultural awareness as the core issue facing intersex communities. Both these themes require responses that change public opinion rather than legal structures: "The media visibility, the continued media visibility and education, which … I think that's where my work is going to fall into, people" (Respondent 3).

However, Lobel argues that the criticisms of legal paths to social change are equally true of all approaches to social change. Moreover, jettisoning law from these approaches might make them more difficult to implement and enforce. Law thus must be seen as only one part of the bigger social movement strategy. Furthermore, this critical conceptualization of legal strategy offers, as Coglianese (2001) highlights, a simplistic understanding of cause and effect between social movement, law and social change. Indeed, Coglianese speaks of the symbiotic relationship between social movements, law and society arguing that they 'interact with one another in a more dynamic, bidirectional fashion than is generally recognised' (2001: 86). Social movements may not affect direct results through law, but their impact may be more subtle and take longer to lead to results. In part, social movements can influence public opinion and non-legal norms of behaviour, which may also bring about social and legal change (Coglianese, 2001: 86). Furthermore, the efforts of law reform can also sway public opinion which in turn affects change, perhaps more so than the legal reform itself (Coglianese, 2001: 86). Accordingly, the perceived limitations we are about to discuss may not reflect a failing, but just reflect the early stages of a radical social (and institutional) shift in intersex embodiment.

The final part of this chapter attempts to understand why the GIGESC Act has not disrupted the medical narrative, looking first at its drafting and second the 'implementation gap'. While legal reforms must be carefully drafted, this alone is not enough to ensure real change. States must be attentive to the *way* in which healthcare responds to legislative change. Rather than seeing the GIGESC Act as a 'failure', we argue that understandings of legal and social change should not be seen in a vacuum. The ability of law to effect societal change is not linear or straightforward. Minow identifies four different schools of thought in this area: that law responds to and is led by social change; that law can prompt small occasional shifts in social values (often unintentionally); that law is capable of shifting cultural perceptions to a large extent; and that law is unable to produce social change (Minow, 1993–94: 171–2). These different perceptions of law's ability to effect social change may depend on the context and examples that are being utilized. Thus, we consider Malta as an example of a legislative approach to social change and its shortcomings before reflecting on this as the *starting point* in an ongoing process of social change.

Limitations of drafting

Quite simply, the major concern with the GIGESC Act is that it has not adequately challenged the established medical narratives of intersex embodiment. The GIGESC Act has not brought about direct change to social, cultural and medical practices that affect intersex people. To have done so, the GIGESC Act would need to cause a fundamental shift in healthcare provision away from medical interventions designed to 'fix' bodies towards an approach which focuses on the emotional wellbeing of the individual. At present, there are several concerns that the legislation itself is limited in its ability to change medical practice, reflecting the aforementioned concern that law actively works against radical change and privileges historical power dynamics. Several loopholes exist which make it possible for medical professionals to circumvent the GIGESC Act. Perhaps most notably, the Act lacks any extra-territorial jurisdiction and thus cannot prevent parents from taking their children abroad to have surgeries in jurisdictions that do not prohibit such practices (Garland et al, 2019; StopIGM, 2019). Malta is small in size, which affects the specialisms available in the health system. In the intersex context, one of our respondents noted that Malta does not have all the specialisms required to treat intersex infants:

> 'We have adult urologists but we don't have paediatric urologists and in fact they refer to, in certain cases, to paediatric urologists abroad like Great Ormond [Street Hospital] etcetera um but and we have general paediatric surgeons here. Um then they have their sort of specialization but not official. You have for example someone who is would tend to carry out surgeries more than others, but officially no paediatric urologists.' (BA Respondent 1)

Consequently, while there are paediatric surgeons in Malta available to carry out certain 'corrective' surgeries like hypospadias, if specialist surgeries are required which are more reconstructive in nature, the lack of specialisms suggest that it will be necessary to refer the patient abroad. This practice would have been unaffected by the Act. Accordingly, where there is a specialism gap, Malta has a history of referring patients to UK hospitals, made possible through the reciprocal health agreement between the government of Malta and the government of the UK first signed in 1975. Thus, even if the GIGESC Act was perfectly designed to stop medical interventions in Malta, there is nothing stopping the established practice of families being referred abroad. Our ongoing British Academy project is examining whether this is in fact a reality. The respondents thus far interviewed indicated a lack of awareness as to whether this occurs, with BA Respondent 2 stating that "I'm not aware, at least, of any cases related to children whose parents have resorted to treatment abroad". BA Respondent 3 did not want to answer the question due to a lack of knowledge. This does not mean it is not happening, however, but rather speaks to the poor record keeping available in regards to intersex persons. Our other respondents were deeply concerned about the lack of knowledge about what is happening to these children. Asked about whether parents were taking their children abroad for treatment, BA Respondent 4 stated:

> 'I'm honestly I'm wondering whether that's happening because if … none of the usual practices, you know, the past practices are being implemented, then I question what is happening. How are these families managing this reality? How are the – because, at this point in time, if any children born after 2015, at this point in time they'll be school age. You know. How have these parents managed, you know, to bring up their children?'

Furthermore, there are concerns relating to decision making in healthcare contexts. Through section 14, it remains possible for minors and/or the adult acting with parental authority to consent to sex-assignment treatments/surgical interventions. There are some procedural safeguards in place. For example, where a minor consents, the medical practitioner *must* consider such treatment to be in the 'best interests of the child' giving due weight to the child's voice in light of their age and maturity (section 14(6)). Nonetheless, these provisions lack sufficient measures to ensure that children meaningfully participate in the decision-making process. Where a minor is unable to consent, parents must reach an agreement with an interdisciplinary team and the Act reiterates that interventions motivated by social factors are prohibited. BA Respondent 2 indicated that an additional process has developed whereby:

> 'The Intersex child that wishes to undergo medical or surgical intervention, is referred to a specific child psychologist and the role

> of the child psychologist is purely to provide assurance to the medical practitioner that there is informed consent on the part of the child and once that report is provided, then and that is endorsed, and the surgery can go ahead.'

However, these measures are not sufficient to protect the bodily integrity of individuals. There is reference to an interdisciplinary team in the context of where a minor cannot give consent and section 16 suggests that treatment protocols should be in line with 'medical best practice' and 'human rights standards'. Yet, there is no indication of what specialisms should be represented on this team, nor that the team should be available to support minors who are able to give consent. The use of an *independent* psychologist to ensure informed consent is positive; however the focus of this psychologist does not appear to be to provide psychosocial support. The absence of such services may mean that both parents and individuals are pressured into giving consent to treatments. This is particularly concerning given that the disorder narrative of intersex embodiment that permeates in clinical settings is a major factor in parental decision making (Streuli et al, 2013; Roen and Hegarty, 2018; Timmermans et al, 2019) and children may still feel pressured to agree to surgery (Garland and Travis, 2018). This was similarly a theme in our SLSA project:

> 'What we and many other intersex people say actually we increase the pressure on the parents because when you don't have a gender in your papers there's a risk that you get outed in kindergarten, school, wherever. Then especially more conservative parents, they would want to have a gender marker, and then comes the doctor and says, "I think it's difficult. I don't know if you can get an M or an F but we make one little surgery and then you can enter it."' (Respondent 6)

> 'When you are seven and you realize that your mother especially and also your father are very stressed, everybody is stressed and it has to do with your genitals, and then you consent out of wish to please or to take this stress away. Everybody knows that most children are doing things because they want to be accepted or liked or because they want to please their parents, and the doctors.' (Respondent 5)

Even the commitment to counselling services and support services within section 15 does not ensure that these subtle yet manifest pressures which can motivate the provision of consent are addressed, as it offers support to individuals 'seeking' counselling and/or psychosocial support rather than mandating its provision to *all* individuals/families. Moreover, the GIGESC Act arguably oversimplifies healthcare needs and interventions performed on intersex individuals. More recently, jurisdictions engaged in reform are introducing, or considering, provisions that contain far more detail about the process of acquiring consent, safeguards, interdisciplinary team specialisms and the need for psychosocial care.[14] For example, the Australian Capital Territory is proposing legislation which distinguishes between simple and complex cases. In simple cases, the Australian Capital Territory is considering reform options which require all families/individuals to be provided with information on the intervention and access to psychological services. And in more complex cases which have a significant human rights implication, the decision should be referred to a specialist panel 'tasked with supporting best practice care for intersex people' (Chief Minister, Treasury and Economic Development Directorate, 2021).

Furthermore, the terms 'best interests' and 'social factors' within the GIGESC Act do not necessarily safeguard minors (Horowicz, 2017; Cannoot, 2020; Fox et al, 2020). Medical interventions on intersex children have long been motivated by the child's 'best interests', particularly to redress the concern that a child with non-normative genitalia would be subject to ridicule and social ostracization (Horowicz, 2017; Fox and Thomson, 2017, Cannoot, 2020). As Kipnis and Diamond write in the context of micropenises: 'The surgeon was immediately concerned about the child's abnormally small penis: technically, a micropenis. Apprehensive about the possibility of the child being shamed in the boys' locker room – psychosocial distress as he matured – the pediatric surgeon was counselling immediate surgical reassignment as a girl' (1998: 398). The GIGESC Act does not define the term 'social factors'. Without such clarification, the Act is unlikely to challenge dominant medical approaches to intersex (Earp et al, 2017). This book has extensively demonstrated how medical interventions on intersex infants have been justified as a clinical rather than social need despite their non-therapeutic nature. These types of definitional requirements become increasingly important in intersex legislation. At present, treatment for conditions such as hypospadias are typically framed as being 'reparative' rather than cosmetic. Three of our British Academy respondents identified that the inclusion of hypospadias under the umbrella of intersex or DSD was hotly contested by the medical profession:

> 'It does seem like that [they have inadvertently] presented something that is very controversial which is the hypospadias issue, especially for the, for the medical community.' (BA Respondent 4)

> 'The only interventions I know of that are still being carried out in Malta are hypospadias repairs, and the issue is that some doctors do not consider hypospadias as an intersex variation, and the way they see

[14] Iceland, chapter II, articles 11–14A.

> it is that they are repairing a problem. They're solving a problem of functionality. So, they are not, because the law states that you cannot change the, the aesthetic and also the appearance of the genitalia. But, so there is a sort of loophole if you're … sorting out the function, you know if it's an issue of function, then that the law, the law allows that. So, in case of hypospadias, you can't really generalize because not every case is the same, but if you have an issue or function, then the law doesn't cover that they would still be allowed. It's not a crime.' (BA Respondent 1)

The possibility that genital ambiguity could be a symptom of serious salt-wasting CAH has led many practitioners to present normalizing genital surgeries as part of the treatment for this emergency (see Chapter 2 and Garland and Travis, 2020b). Genital surgeries thus become presented as medical emergency even though research has demonstrated that it is an entirely separate treatment from the management of salt-wasting (Garland and Travis, 2020b). The vagueness of the term 'social' makes it possible for medical professionals to evade the remit of the GIGESC Act.

While these problems limit the efficacy of the GIGESC Act, they are avoidable where careful drafting is used by legislators. The intersex provisions in the GIGESC Act were rushed through in the context of political opportunism: "Looking back, maybe some things were a bit rushed, but at the same time, given the context that we live in, and not being so sure that we'll have this government that's very supportive, you know, for many years to come, we felt that we should grab the opportunity" (Respondent 17). Therefore, these problems are not necessarily indicative of law being a problematic forum through which to address intersex concerns. Rather it demonstrates the need for social change to be thought of as an ongoing and dynamic process rather than two set static positions. Continuing and ongoing consideration about procedure and consent must be at the forefront of any law reform to avoid such loopholes. Indeed, when asked specifically about loopholes in the legislation, BA Respondent 3 stated that in the absence of a protocol it was not possible to comment on whether there was a loophole as it was not clear what was or was not working within the Act itself. Consequently, "if there is a loophole, then I would say it's the fact that, you know, that that board has not yet produced its report which is not a loophole in the law, but in the implementation of the law" (BA Respondent 3). This quote draws attention to the iterative process of legal reform and social change; GIGESC marks the starting point rather than the end for legal engagement. There is some legal awareness of this contained within the Act, where section 17 provides the minister with powers 'to make regulations to give better effect to any of the provisions of this Act and generally to regulate gender identity in conformity with the provisions of this Act.' The question remains, of course, of how this is approached in the future. To answer this, we must wait to see.

The implementation gap

While many of the aforementioned concerns can be redressed by careful drafting, the major issue with the GIGESC Act is that there has been a total lack of implementation of its core provisions regarding intersex. This lack of implementation perhaps points to bigger problems about law's ability to disrupt medical narratives. Malta's implementation gap has been compounded by the absence of national clinical guidelines on the treatment of intersex children. This is particularly concerning as it demonstrates how even world-leading law can have difficulties permeating medical approaches to intersex embodiment. Part of section 14's purpose was to establish an interdisciplinary team to oversee the care of intersex individuals, to introduce consistent care and ensure medical best practice. However, as yet, no interdisciplinary team has been appointed. Section 16 set out the specific requirements of the working group which was meant to, within one year of the GIGESC Act, review medical protocols and recommend revisions. The first intersex treatment protocol review board was appointed and held its first meetings in 2016 (ILGA Europe, 2017: 160). However, the working group disbanded and it was only in 2020, five years after the Act's passage, that a revised group was reappointed. Without any clinical guidelines in place, there is no homogeneous way in which intersex people are treated, no clear guidance on what happens to intersex people upon birth or referral, and no multidisciplinary team of identified specialists in this area who come together to best address the needs and care pathways of the individual. Thus, medical practice remains the same as pre-Act. Prior to the Act, patient referral to particular specialisms was down to the individual medical practitioner, and this has not changed with the implementation of the GIGESC Act. As BA Respondent 1 stated:

> 'To be perfectly honest I don't think it changed the way medical doctors operate as in not surgically, the way they actually work, because you know they used to refer their own patient to other specialties. And that's what they're still doing since there is no medical protocol. There is no multidisciplinary team now sort of technically officially, there is nothing different from what happened before 2015 … what actually the law is meant to do as well and all sort of create this network of people who are specialized in intersex issues, so that when a very someone goes to an endocrinologist or a gynaecologist or a psychologist or whatever, they would already be familiar they would be trained and intersex issues, all sorts of so everyone at least hopefully would get

the same level of medical care … And the fact that there isn't even the multidisciplinary team in place. Once again, it means that you're sort of the doctor in charge of that particular parish on that particular individual, you know, sort of would choose themselves who to refer the patient to, and also have, and not everyone is actually knowledgeable about intersex issues.'

Referrals were made at the discretion of the individual practitioner, and often these were made on the basis of professional relationships rather than professional expertise. Without national clinical guidelines in place, clinicians are still uncertain what the law allows and what it forbids, hypospadias continuing to be seen as a grey area. At present, in the wake of uncertainty, surgeries are able to continue and it is not clear how practice has been affected. "They don't know what the hell is happening to any children who have been born from 2016 onwards, following the law, whether they've you know they've actually had any surgeries" (BA Respondent 4). Consequently, the GIGESC Act has not yet changed the way in which doctors conceptualize intersex embodiment. Without introducing specialized care and greater input from psychosocial support, it is difficult to see how the GIGESC Act, in practice, can truly challenge the medical understanding of intersex embodiment as disordered.

Similarly, section 15 committed the state to ensuring that individually tailored psychosocial counselling should be available to the individual from the date of diagnosis or self-referral and for as long as necessary. Yet, post-2015, there has been no specific psychological service or psychosocial care set up to offer such support to intersex individuals and their families. In 2018, as part of Malta's LGBTIQ Equality Strategy & Action Plan 2018–22, the SOGIGESC Unit and the Ministry for Health (ODPM) set up the Gender Wellbeing Clinic. This service was designed to offer health services to trans, intersex and gender queer individuals (Maltese Government, 2018: 6). Schedule V of the Social Security Act in early 2019 made treatments for 'Gender Identity and Sex Characteristics' free as part of Malta's NHS. Accordingly, the wellbeing clinic prescribes free hormonal treatments and assessments as well as 'psychosocial support services including psychologist and family therapy sessions' (Gender Wellbeing Clinic, 2021a). However, in the absence of the Intersex Treatment Protocol Review Working Group, it appears that this service is primarily targeted at transgender health. This commitment to intersex healthcare was reiterated in the SOGIGESC Annual Report 2018–19 (Maltese Government, 2018: 16), but in reality, the Gender Wellbeing Clinic specifically targets transgender health, as advertised on its website (Gender Wellbeing Clinic, 2021a). The referral form also appears to solely address transgender people, as does the clinic's generic email address (Gender Wellbeing Clinic 2021b).

Even if the services are available to intersex people, this may not be obvious to them. As a result, there is a lack of psychosocial support available to intersex people and their families even though its provision is embedded within legislation. Initial consultations around infant healthcare, therefore, continue to construct intersex as a disorder rather than using psychosocial care to disrupt this framework and support families with the structural issues around gender that they may be faced with. Again, this highlights the danger of designing structures and institutions for intersex people through a lens of queer or even homonormative embodiment. Consequently, all the elements within the Act specifically designed to change and improve healthcare provision for intersex persons are yet to be more than statutory promises. There are broader questions here about *why* it has not been possible to translate legislative intent into practice. The reasons for the initial working group's disbandment are unknown. It may be that there was a lack of appetite from medical professionals to bring in such changes. As BA Respondent 1 stated, given that some specialisms were not present in Malta "some people may think they may not need a specific protocol as well, because you know sort of why introduce something for something that doesn't happen?"

There may also be jurisdictional difficulties too, alluded to by some of our British Academy respondents:

> 'trying to implement a medical protocol ... is actually trespassing ... in their profession. Taking away from them the authority, ... to make certain decisions. And that can create a bit of a problem. It is a cultural thing you know sort of doctors, most of the time, not all of them but most of the time um they know best, you know, so there's this sort of paternalism. And it's difficult to implement a medical protocol, you know especially if it's implemented by people who are not doctors themselves.' (BA Respondent 1)

Indeed, when directly asked whether the Act would have been better implemented had there been medical buy-in, BA Respondent 2 stated: "... yes, it would have improved, I think. First of all, having a more collaborative approach, would I believe, ensure that both parties feel that they own a part of this. Secondly, obviously it would improve its implementation. The kind of how one implements it." While the Act itself has not yet implemented direct social change, social movement literature suggests the potential of law and social change can arise from the visibility surrounding legal reform attempts (Coglianese, 2001: 86). However, despite the huge legislative potential for intersex reform in Malta, there remains a lack of cultural knowledge about intersex, at least at present. Coupled with the social conservatism in Malta, many people still do not know what intersex is. Intersex remains socially invisible and there are indications that medical professionals continue to use disordered narratives to explain intersex variations:

> 'Intersex hasn't really been mentioned, and the doctors, sort of, they don't realize what it is or they won't admit, how many people are actually intersex on the island.' (BA Respondent 1)

> 'I think what hasn't really changed very much is the visibility of intersex persons within Maltese society. So there has been a bit more contact, especially by the Rainbow Support Services, by the Malta LGBTIQ Rights Movement, and a couple of cases coming forward within the Gender Wellbeing Clinic, but in terms of people who are out as intersex, that hasn't happened yet. … so there's still a huge degree of, I think, stigma in a sense, that seems to be attached.' (BA Respondent 2)

All British Academy respondents thus identified visibility as still the key issue affecting the intersex community in Malta, seven years after the passage of the Act. Education has not been a consequence of the law reform or surrounding discussions. Again, this might be a temporal issue. Requiring a radical change to social understandings of sex and gender may not be possible in seven years; however the lack of even public discussion about intersex and the absence of spaces for dialogue is concerning.

The difficulty in challenging medical authority led to a series of compromises in the GIGESC Act. The original drafting of the GIGESC Act only introduced a small fine up to 5,000 euros attached to a breach of this provision. This was a conscious strategy by activists to ensure the passage of the Bill:

> 'The medical system is a very powerful system. I don't think the strategy should be going against it. So it's a matter of how we position ourselves as policy-makers, as lawyers, as intersex people. So I don't think going against a huge monster like the medical system is the way … you couldn't go against something so big when there are just a handful of you. So groups always tried to work either with the system, or try and move around the system, whether that's the church, or the political class, the … politicians, and other professions as well. ... [Sanctions are] one aspect of the law that we had to find a compromise on. Intersex people call for reparation and compensations for the harm done, and doing that means also finding someone guilty of that harm. That is not included in the Maltese law. So compensation is not included, because that meant criminalizing doctors … it wasn't intended to really scare doctors away.' (Respondent 17)

After international outcry that this made the prohibition inconsequential, the government introduced Act No XIII of 2018, 'to equalise the penalties applicable to intersex genital mutilation to the penalties applicable to female genital mutilation' (Maltese Government, 2018: 7). Doctors now face up to five years' incarceration (section 14(2) of the GIGESC Act). However, there is still widespread concern that these penalties are not actually being enforced (Garland and Travis, 2018; StopIGM, 2019; UNCRC, 2019). Consequently, the UN Committee on the Rights of the Child has called upon Malta to: 'Investigate effectively incidents of surgical and other medical treatment of intersex children without informed consent and provide redress to victims of such treatment, including adequate compensation and rehabilitation' (UNCRC, 2019: 8). The strength of medical power/knowledge has meant that many commentators are concerned that a token fine and the symbolism of criminalizing behaviour is not enough: "only the fear of the judge will make some real change. Because as long as they can just continue with the surgeries and don't have to fear any consequences, they will do a little lip service and just continue with the surgeries" (Respondent 5).

Our project directly asked the British Academy respondents whether medical care had improved for intersex people. For the most part, they felt unable to answer. However, they were hopeful that, even though visibility was an issue, the benefit of these discussions, despite their slow pace, was that it was raising awareness among medical practitioners. As BA Respondent 3 stated: "I would hope that it has had an impact in relation to visibility, at least among medical staff who medical professionals who come into contact with intersex people." Indeed, while much of the critique has focused on a reticent medical profession, arguably the radical nature of the reform is inevitably going to be met by slow-paced implementation. Implementation requires social structures and, to some degree, social change to be underway in tandem with the legal measure. Yet in Malta, without medical buy-in and cultural purchase, this reform was ahead of its (social) time. As BA Respondent 4 observed: "Even the length of time that it has taken. Um And it's not yet finalized for the protocol for intersex persons to be established, I think you know that in itself is a reflection of how unprepared, um, all structures were within Malta for, for, you know, this."

Conclusion

Ultimately, Malta's approach is yet to disrupt the medical framing of intersex embodiment as a disorder and, resultantly, in 2019 the UNCRC reprimanded Malta for the alleged continuation of medical interventions on intersex children (UNCRC, 2019). We argue that this is not necessarily the result of the rights-based framing, but rather from significant gaps in terms of legislation and implementation. Indeed, the UN continues to refer to

Malta as an example of 'good practice' (Office of the High Commissioner for Human Rights, 2019), despite reports of failing to stop medical interventions on children. While we agree that Malta remains the world leader in terms of intersex rights legislation, there are a number of issues that mean that more must be done to help intersex people. To some extent, these issues are related to the drafting of the legislation. In particular, the lack of provision for extra-territorial surgical intervention highlights not only a failure to close loopholes in this area, but also a fundamental misunderstanding of how healthcare provision in Malta was taking place at the time that the legislation was passed. This once again demonstrates the problems with viewing intersex issues through a lens of queer or homonormative embodiment. However, the GIGESC Act does succeed in terms of symbolism and recognition issues remain around the practical effects of such legislative efforts. Again, this may result from the 'opportunistic' ways in which intersex activists are able to engage with policy makers.

Relatedly, we raise huge concerns in Malta around the implementation gap created by this legislation. The GIGESC Act, we would argue, is yet to live up to its promise. So far, the legislation has not implemented an appropriate functioning multidisciplinary team under section 14(4). It has also failed to provide adequate psychosocial care under section 15. Moreover, the legislation's myopic focus on children has meant that psychosocial provision has not been provided for intersex adults. The provision under section 16 to create a working group to oversee the implementation of this Act has also taken five years to achieve. All in all, the afterlife of the legislation highlights the difficulties that rights-based frameworks have disrupting the narrative of medical embodiment. For this type of legal intervention to work there needs to be significant buy-in from medical professionals and, to date, this has not happened in Malta. Seemingly, for the law to better regulate intersex 'normalizing' surgeries, it has to be met with clinical approval or agreement at a medical institutional level. These changes require significant medical buy-in, which would introduce altered care pathways, changes to clinical classifications and a shift in how medicine understands intersex embodiment. However, medicine's long history of self-regulation has left them resistant to legal interference. The rhetoric of harm for intersex bodies is not reflected in medical practice and this presents a significant barrier to legislative prohibition. Overall, the issues with implementation have resulted in a real lack of engagement from stakeholders, leaving Malta's position more symbolic than impactful. In essence this highlights the difficulties of disrupting narratives of 'disorder' even where there is a considerable amount of legal support to do so, and where this has been informed by actual intersex lived experience.

However, it may be helpful to consider the legal situation in Malta outside a simple problem/solution binary. It is clear that the GIGSEC

Act has introduced a number of new issues into the discourse around protecting intersex people. Nonetheless, as Minow argues in the context of deinstitutionalization, this may be a good result, as it has the potential to 'mobilize many people, including patients, to act. It prompts experiments, complete with trial and error, and stimulates a continuing process of reform and reaction. From this vantage point, the failure in result is itself a success in the process of ongoing change' (Minow, 1993–94: 181). In doing so Malta may have created the conditions to remake society through a *process* of social engagement (Minow, 1993–94: 181). As Minow continues:

> The meaning of 'change' may seem obvious. The goal is to alter, revise, renovate, substitute, move. And yet simply shifting from one static position to another, whether the topic is race relations, treatment of persons with disabilities or domestic violence, neglects a deeper notion of change. It is the difference in aiming for results and aiming for a continuing process of change. (Minow, 1993–94: 179)

The social changes enabled by the Maltese legislation, therefore, should not be thought of as an end point, but merely another step in an ongoing project of social change ultimately facilitating bodily integrity for intersex people. As with other legal pathways to social change, what is crucial in the Maltese context is the legislative 'after-care' provided through long-term commitments to implementation and resources (both financial and institutional). Thus, the position in Malta can be both be seen as alarmist and reassuring: alarmist, because in some ways, given how little practice has been challenged in fact, the GIGESC Act appears to have reified the medical control over procedures; and reassuring in that legal reform is one part of a longer strategy and that change must come "slowly, slowly" (BA Respondent 4). In Chapter 6, we consider how far psychosocial care can be used to supplement legal frameworks such as those found in Malta to truly challenge the conceptualization of intersex embodiment as 'disordered'.

6

Intersex as Acceptance and Emergence: Can Psychosocial Frameworks Disrupt Medical Embodiment?

Introduction

While the past three chapters have explored the multifaceted framings of intersex within law and policy, this chapter returns to the realms of healthcare and unpicks the ways in which intersex has been embedded within psychology. We do so to consider the extent to which psychosocial frameworks could disrupt medical embodiment. The institutional location of psychology makes it well placed to instigate an internal rupturing of medical embodiment from *within* the discipline of healthcare itself and thus may offers greater opportunity for change in comparison to the legal frameworks addressed in Chapter 5. Moreover, psychosocial frameworks focus on both the psychological *and* social needs of individuals. Consequently, this framework has significant potential to shape individuals' relationships and dynamic encounters with institutions beyond healthcare, grounded in practices of self-acceptance and destigmatization. While we acknowledge that psychology has a problematic history and raises the possibility of harm, this chapter argues that, if done correctly, this institutional framework has the potential at present to facilitate the reconceptualization of intersex embodiment away from the disorder narrative towards a thicker concept of intersex medical and legal embodiment. The Maltese response had hoped that law, specifically the GIGESC Act, would bring about this reconceptualization of intersex and made space for such psychosocial frameworks. However, as Chapter 5 demonstrated, this internal shift in healthcare provision must happen *in tandem* to legislative responses or else an implementation gap will follow. We consider what is demanded of healthcare provision (chiefly psychosocial care) to improve the medical and legal embodiment of intersex people and how far this has been achieved in practice.

This chapter begins by exploring the long-standing role psychology has played in terms of how intersex is understood and how this has been challenged in recent years. As discussed in Chapter 2, John Money was central in cementing the importance of psychology to intersex management in the 1950s. Accordingly, early psychological constructions of intersex continued the medical legacies set out in Chapter 2 that framed intersex embodiment in terms of a physiological 'disorder' in need of 'fixing'. Money's psychological practices were rooted in determining 'true sex' and its concomitant reliance on heterosexuality as an indicator of 'success'. This influential conceptualization of intersex has dominated psychological approaches towards intersex. The chapter then considers shifts in psychology which have reframed intersex not as a disorder but as 'an [ordinary] aspect of bodily diversity which has psychosocial implications' (Roen, 2019). Whereas Money's use of psychology was to reinforce sex assignment, this revised understanding of intersex focuses on supporting the individual and their emotional well-being (Roen, 2015: 183). Accordingly, in terms of healthcare provision, it demands a more holistic, multidisciplinary approach with professional expertise beyond clinical medics including psychology, social work, bioethics and peer-to-peer support. This reframing has the potential to change the way that psychological provision conceptualizes intersex embodiment and begins to facilitate change from within the discipline of healthcare.

The chapter then explores the extent to which this reframing has translated into practice. Recognition of the importance of psychosocial care resulted in the 2006 consensus statement calling for psychosocial support's 'essential' integration into multidisciplinary teams (MDTs). Yet, in reality, reconceptualization has been piecemeal and patchy. While psychosocial support has become increasingly common, the way that this support has been integrated is far from ideal in terms of when it is delivered, the reasons for its delivery and the extent of support that is offered. The reasons for this variation are dependent, in part, upon how far it is premised upon medical frameworks that understand intersex embodiment as disordered. Better psychosocial support may not be able to successfully disrupt medical narratives from within healthcare; the siloing of expertise and use of jurisdictional boundaries to reassert professional hierarchies limit the disruptive potential of psychology. The state thus has an important role to play in making spaces for psychosocial care possible through law, but also in the provision of services and resources. This chapter explores how, too frequently, 'disordered' and 'fixing' narratives continue to dominate decision making, ultimately sidelining the potential for psychosocial input from MDTs to reframe intersex embodiment. Moreover, these factors can lead to the 'cooption' of psychology where it is used to reaffirm medical embodiment rather than to offer appropriate psychosocial care. Accordingly, there are dangers associated with returning to healthcare to enhance intersex lived experience. In fact, this chapter demonstrates how poorly conceived psychological support can reify clinical medical practice's attempts to 'fix' ambiguity and further pathologize intersex people. Moreover, we recognize that many of the disadvantages faced by intersex people are the product of a society ill-adapted to the reality of intersex bodies. Consequently, there is an acknowledged danger in any implication that the individual and their expectations must adapt or 'be treated' rather than societal norms. Meaningful wellbeing and citizenship requires a bigger social transformation whereby intersex and bodily diversity is celebrated, not merely accepted or tolerated, throughout society. A society which celebrates all bodies would avoid the need for psychosocial support. However, changing societal norms is not an easy task and, as Chapter 5 has highlighted, remains a long-term project, which cannot and should not be rushed.

In the short term then, this chapter argues that a psychosocial framing within healthcare is well placed to enhance lived experience until broader socio-political reform takes place. As such, we conclude by arguing that psychosocial care is an essential element of reframing care for intersex people away from 'fixing' a 'disorder' and towards supporting a person. In order to fulfil this potential, however, psychosocial care requires a bigger shift towards practices that enhance self-acceptance, increase insight, destigmatize intersex bodies and experiences, introduce goal-setting (for individuals, families and MDTs), increase understanding, and to reduce affective, cognitive, behavioural or social barriers to the effectiveness of treatment. Clinical psychologists have the potential to present a range of psychotherapeutic models, such as Acceptance and Commitment Therapy, Systemic Family Therapy, and mindfulness-based cognitive therapy. These are capable of creating targeted support over the life course as well as responding to shorter-term problems as required by a patient-centred approach. These approaches can help to challenge the medical framing of intersex embodiment as 'disordered' and instead help to strengthen a thicker conception of medical and legal embodiment that locates individuals' experiences in their broader social and institutional settings. In turn, this helps to support intersex people in the challenges that they face. However, to maximize the potential of this approach requires institutional buy-in; that is, an active commitment in terms of time, money and resources. These institutions are not limited to medicine but also include law as well as, connectedly, education and the family. However, psychosocial care is, in many instances, yet to reach its full potential and it is therefore unsurprising that Malta's legal reform has also fallen short of its goals to provide tailored psychosocial support to intersex embodied people. While there was 'political will' to pass the GIGESC Act, there has been a distinct lack of post-reform buy-in from policy makers. This has not only delayed the embedding of psychosocial frameworks within healthcare settings, but has also impeded the push for social change. The next section sets out how psychology first contributed to the medical embodiment of intersex and how, promisingly, this has been increasingly challenged over the past 30 years.

Paradigmatic medical embodiment: psychology, surgery and disorder

It is difficult to outline how influential John Money has been in the way that intersex people are understood today. Not only did Money continue the social and medical legacies we traced in Chapter 2; he reinterpreted and reified these narratives through the lens of psychology. In doing so, Money's approach to intersex and, indeed, to gender, has had unprecedented levels of popular appeal. Money's understanding of psychology, however, and its role in the management of intersex people, has significantly affected how intersex is understood and defined and this remains 'the basis for much contemporary thinking about treatment interventions for intersexuality' (Karkazis, 2008: 48). As one respondent put it:

> 'John Money actually was the one that sealed the fate of millions of intersex children in the future and it's still going on. So to go so far as to tell parents not only … and don't tell your family and friends anything but destroy photographs and move house. Just like that. It's unbelievable.' (Respondent 7)

Money began shaping psychology's role in this area when, in 1951, he became the first paediatric psychoendocrinologist at Johns Hopkins bringing his expertise in psychology to the emerging MDT. His PhD, entitled *Hermaphroditism: An Inquiry into the Nature of a Human Paradox* (1952), examined 248 intersex case histories between 1895 and 1951. He also conducted ten interviews with intersex people. Accordingly, Money had particular insight into intersex people, one of the most crucial being that intersex people, for the most part, identified as the sex they were assigned at birth. This was supported by a number of follow-up studies conducted with other colleagues that found that in over 100 intersex people, even those with similar traits who had been assigned different sexes, nearly all were happy with their sex assignment (Money et al, 1955a;Money et al, 1956: 43; Money et al, 1957). Moreover, Money's research revealed that the mental health of intersex people was predominantly positive with 'surprisingly low incidences of psychoses and neuroses despite their atypical anatomical configurations' (Money, 1952; Karkazis, 2008: 50).[1] Accordingly, Money posited that gender itself had psychological components although it was largely predicted through biology and socialization. Importantly, intersex was not seen as a psychological disorder in and of itself, but rather a congenital disorder that could develop into psychological disorders, which, at the time, included gender dysphoria and homosexuality. For Money and his colleagues, then, genital surgeries became 'a kind of pre-emptive psychological treatment' (Morland, 2014: 111). Understanding early non-therapeutic surgical interventions as *psychological* treatment is important for the way that intersex healthcare has been, and continues to be, understood. Under this model, 'successful' surgeries would predict positive psychological outcomes (Roen and Pasterski, 2014: 104). Improvements in surgical technique were consequently understood through a psychosocial lens.

Significantly, Money and his colleagues theorized that all humans were born 'psychosexually neutral or undifferentiated from birth' (Money, 1963: 820) and that 'sexual behaviour and orientation as male or female does not have an innate, instinctive basis' (Money et al, 1955b: 308). Rather 'a person's gender role and awareness is founded in what, from infancy onward, he learns, assimilates and interprets about his sexual status from parents, siblings, playmates and others, and from the way he reads the signs of his own body' (Hampson, 1955: 265; Wilkins, 1957: 209).[2] Accordingly, Money and colleagues pioneered a model of 'assigning sex' and gender management which selected the '*optimal* gender for the individual' (Karkazis, 2008: 55). These beliefs formulated the justification for assigning sex at birth rather than later in childhood. They also provided the justification needed for genital surgery. If children did not recognize their genitals as atypical then they would have less need to question their assigned sex and this would facilitate better gender socialization. Again, medical embodiment through the use of surgery took on a *psychological* veneer. While Money recognized a need for surgery to be delayed as late as possible, this was undermined by an insistence that surgery be performed before the child could demonstrate awareness of their genitalia, typically 18 months (Money and Ehrhardt, 1972).

These surgeries were not only important for the intersex individual, but also for the people around them as responsibility for ensuring a normative gender development fell to parents. It was posited that parents, grandparents, peers and babysitters would all be more accepting of the intersex child's assigned sex if surgery was undertaken. Managing the psychology of the parents and

[1] It is worth noting that Money's method of measuring mental health would not be acceptable or normative in contemporary psychology. While there are many examples of this, particularly problematic would be Money and his team's focus on heterosexuality as a key outcome of measuring 'successful' gender.

[2] As noted in Chapter 2 Money later claimed to have written this piece (Money, 2002).

other carers (potential) adverse reactions to atypical genitalia were seen as key to ensuring the child accepted their own gender. Surgeries ensured the acceptance of the child's assigned sex by others – thus, reinforcing the child's assigned sex. Intersex surgeries were no longer about the functional, sexual and medical adult issues that they had been understood as prior to Money, but rather a new psychological management tool for children to facilitate psychological wellbeing and 'the development of normative gender identity' (Roen, 2015: 185). Early psychological approaches continued to be grounded in notions of medical embodiment which foregrounded the idea of 'fixing' children into a binary, with heterosexuality being viewed as a key measure of success.

Although non-therapeutic surgical interventions had been recast as a psychological tool, Money advocated continued psychological support be on offer for the intersex child and their families (see, for example, Money et al, 1955a: 291–6). Money et al wrote that 'the more manifest the signs of hermaphroditism, the more necessary are psychologic guidance and follow-up' (Money et al, 1955a: 292). However, the details of this psychological 'support' are equal parts unknown, idiosyncratic and abusive (Colapinto, 2000). Money's interventions were running completely unopposed and without ethical oversight due to his prominence in the field and position at Johns Hopkins. The 'support' that was given to intersex people and their families was designed to affirm the sex that had been assigned by the MDT at Johns Hopkins. As Morland highlights:

> Money cast the role of the consulting psychologist in intersex cases as not to defend genital diversity, but to oversee its prompt surgical elimination: in doing so, Money took up the established … imperatives of plastic surgery – to operate early in life, to foreclose self-consciousness of atypical appearance, to prevent teasing, and to reduce parental anxiety. (Morland, 2015: 84)

Writing on the infamous John/Joan case (discussed below), Money detailed the sorts of support that parents would receive:

> In particular, [the parents] were given confidence that their child can be expected to differentiate a female gender identity, in agreement with her sex of rearing. They were broadly informed about the future medical program for their child and how to integrate it with her sex education as she [grew] older. They were guided in how to give the child information about herself to the extent that the need arises in the future; and they were helped with what to explain to friends and relatives, including their other child. Eventually, they would inform their daughter that she would become a mother by adoption, one day,

> when she married and wanted to have a family. (Money and Ehrhardt, 1972: 119)

Money and Ehrhardt's book was highly significant and influential in the context of the sexual revolution, the second-wave feminist movement and the development of women's and LGBT rights. The book propelled Money into a level of celebrity that was unheard of for medical professionals of the time. It was also hugely influential in terms of developing how psychology (as a discipline) understood gender. Early psychological approaches thus continued earlier medical legacies that conceptualized intersex embodiment in terms of medicine and disorder. Psychology was seen as an extra component necessary to 'fix' children into a binary gender and to prevent later psychological disorders and not a place for discussing the issues and barriers that intersex people might face (partly as a result of the so-called 'normalizing' surgeries) (Liao, Tacconelli et al, 2010; Engberg et al, 2016; Schweizer et al, 2017).

Reframing clinical practice towards psychosocial framings: the need for 'less cutting and more talking'

For the next 40 years, Money's approach to intersex and indeed sex/gender dominated 'virtually all academic writing on sex and gender' (Kessler, 1990; Morland, 2015: 86) producing over 40 books and 400 scientific papers (Karkazis, 2008: 62) (there was, of course, some dissent – particularly from Milton Diamond – which we shall go on to discuss). The impact of this was not only to shape theory in this area, but also practice – with a number of paediatric specialists and medical practitioners incorporating his work into their own protocols (Kessler, 1990; Karkazis, 2008: 62). Money and his colleagues' research was considered to be the definitive writing in this area (Reis, 2009: 104). However, in the 1990s a number of academics and activists (including ISNA) began to openly critique Money's work (Kessler, 1990, 1998; Diamond and Sigmundson, 1997). Not only were Money's theories based on very few case studies (Kessler, 1990), but his most infamous study, the John/Joan case, was exposed as false. After a botched circumcision, Money had convinced David Reimer's (known in the literature as John) parents to raise him as a girl (referred to as Joan) and accordingly performed feminizing surgery on him before he was 18 months old. Money had published extensively on the 'success' of this treatment in many medical journals, claiming David to be a well-adjusted girl. However, several sources began to expose that the John/Joan case had not transpired in the way that Money had claimed. A 1980 BBC documentary (*Open Secret: The First Question*) questioned the long-term prognosis of David's transition (Williams, 1980). This was followed up by Milton Diamond and David Reimer's local psychiatrist Keith Sigmundson in 1997 exposing Money's claims to be false and that David had suffered psychological distress throughout this entire process, eventually transitioning to a boy at age 14 (Diamond and Sigmundson, 1997). At a similar time, David Reimer gave an interview to John Colapinto for *Rolling Stone* magazine, giving an insight into the actual person who had undergone this process (Colapinto, 1997). These texts exposed the harms of Money's work, appealing to a public perception that gender identity was not simply determined by sex assignment surgery and sex of rearing. Importantly, the exposure of the case highlighted the dangers of using psychology to *manage* rather than support. As David Reimer reflected:

> My childhood. It comes to me. I don't go and think about it … Memories of how I used to look. Memories of being belittled by my classmates. Memories of just trying to survive. If I had grown up as a boy without penis? Oh, I would still have had my problems, but they wouldn't have been compounded the way they are now. If I was raised as a boy, I would have been more accepted by other people. I would have been way better off if they had just left me alone, because when I switched back over, then I had *two* problems on my hands, not just one, because of [their] trying to brainwash me into accepting myself as a girl. So you got the *psychological* thing going in your head. When I'm intimate with my wife it sometimes *haunts* me. (Reimer quoted in Colapinto, 2000 261–2)

The exposure of the David Reimer case shone a light onto the ways in which intersex people had been *psychologically* as well as physically harmed by the optimal gender rearing model. Such harms were highlighted by our SLSA respondents:

> 'Most intersex, at least I know, are very, very traumatized and suffer from physical and psychological harm of these genital surgeries during childhood.' (Respondent 6)

> 'I've met a lot of currently adults who actually were subject to normalization surgery as an infant … When you see the psychological trauma those individuals have to go through when the wrong genitals were picked. I mean, if they think that's the right genitals even.' (Respondent 12)

While Money's claims were being exposed, the 1990s also saw a push from within psychology and early intersex activism to reconceptualize intersex embodiment. Notably, socio-psychologist and feminist Suzanne Kessler (1990, 1998) critiqued Money's medical model for its heteronormative basis and argued that intersex should be depathologized. In ground-breaking research, Kessler interviewed clinical practitioners about the diagnosis and treatment of intersex people, revealing that decisions about genital surgeries and the disordered framing of intersex embodiment were rooted in practitioners' *cultural* beliefs that genitals fell into the category of either male or female (Kessler, 1990). Practitioners considered genitals which are not wholly masculine or feminine to be 'deformed' or 'disfiguring' and therefore in need of corrective surgery (Kessler, 1998). Challenging Money's assumptions, Kessler argued that genitalia was not 'naturally dimorphic'; intersex was part of normal variation in human genitalia (1990, 1998: 7; Preves, 2001). Moreover, the psychological distress experienced by individuals and families was not caused by 'abnormal' genitalia but the social and medical *response* that such genitalia elicited – in particular, the strict adherence to gender binarism that led to the disordered narrative. Kessler was also concerned that: 'In the literature of intersexuality, issues such as announcing a baby's gender at the time of delivery, postdelivery discussions with the parents, and consultation with patients in adolescence are considered only peripherally to the central medical issues – etiology, diagnosis and surgical procedures' (Kessler, 1990: 2). Accordingly, her book *Lessons from the Intersexed* was described as 'one of the most influential texts on the ethics of sexual assignment surgery for [intersex] infants' (Baker, 2017: 448) and called for intersex management to involve 'less cutting and more talking' (Kessler, 1998, 125). While Kessler recognized that parental distress was problematic, unlike Money she believed that surgery was not the answer. Rather, input from mental health professionals and the careful use of sensitive language by the medical team when interacting with parents were key to ensuring the individual's (and family's) wellbeing.

Kessler's call for clinical reform has been echoed by other commentators in this area (Preves, 2001, 2003, 2005; Reiss, 2009, 2019; Feder, 2014; Davis, 2015; Roen, 2015, 2019; Carpenter, 2018; see also Chapter 2) and there is a growing mass of research continuing to evidence how stigma and shame are rooted in social and medical responses to intersex rather than from the intersex variation itself (see Chapter 2). Accordingly, an increasing number of healthcare professionals and advocates since the 1990s have called for a 'new paradigm' in clinical practice with improved interdisciplinary care, greater collaboration between parents, patients and practitioners where psychological input was the central aspect of clinical management (Wilson and Reiner, 1998; Carmichael and Alderson, 2004; Liao and Boyle, 2004). Together, the push from what Preves terms the medical reform movement and intersex activism led to greater change in clinical practice (2003) and the effects of this can be seen in the recognition of psychology in the International Consensus Statement 2006. Notably, the consensus statement saw two important interventions in terms of psychological approaches to intersex healthcare. Firstly, psychological support was deemed essential in the healthcare provision of intersex children (Lee et al, 2006: e492). When the consensus was updated ten years later, it was emphasized that 'education and psychological support was needed … to [allow individuals to] make sense of the condition, relate to their community and establish relationships' (Lee et al, 2016: 170). Secondly, the psychologist was to be part of a MDT capable of working together to determine the best outcomes for the child (Lee et al, 2006: e490). Such inclusion was significant as it brought with it the potential to destabilize medical embodiment by shifting focus from immediate surgeries towards a new focus on self-acceptance, growth and the way in which individuals develop through their interactions with the social environment around them. This new model offered the potential to reframe intersex embodiment as emergence. However, as we shall go on to outline in later in the chapter, the consensus statement is beset by significant problems that delimit the transformative potential of these new approaches.

Before we consider how psychosocial support has been incorporated into practice we set out *why* psychology has an important role in terms of intersex embodiment. In particular, we focus on new approaches to psychology that seem to foreground the embodiment of intersex people and view them outside the disorder/fixing paradigmatic medical embodiment framework. These embodied approaches to psychology are attentive to the harm done by these interventions; the way that these harms are framed; and, at the same time, focus on enhancing the long-term wellbeing of individuals. We are, in many ways, hesitant to fall so readily into the acceptance of psychology given its problematic, regulatory and carceral legacies. However, in shifting the lens from fixing to support or wellbeing we do see the potential of psychology to help facilitate justice for intersex people and to shift conceptions of intersex embodiment away from the medical framework of disorder. We would therefore support a move from the current endocrinologist/urologist-based model to a psychosocial model with 'psychological health care [being] the foundation upon which other kinds of health care may be built as needed' (Roen, 2019: 517). Such an approach can prioritize self-acceptance, enhance insight, destigmatize, focus on goal-setting (for individuals, families and MDTs), improve understanding, and reduce affective, cognitive, behavioural or social barriers to the effectiveness of treatment. All these aspects challenge the framework of intersex embodiment as a disorder that can be 'fixed'.

The consensus statement: clinical recognition of the importance of psychosocial care

While the last section set out *why* psychosocial care contains so much potential in terms of intersex embodiment, this next section traces how far this framework has been able to disrupt medical embodiment in practice. As aforementioned, the push for medical reform did result in a change in clinical practice, primarily through the International Consensus Statement 2006. Notably, the consensus statement recognized the importance of psychosocial care and the integration of MDTs. However, as we shall go on to outline in the next section, the consensus statement is beset by problems which have ultimately limited the radical transformative potential that psychosocial frameworks may contain. The consensus statement is dominated by an endocrinologist-led interventionist approach grounded in a medical understanding of embodiment rather than one that attempts to support self-acceptance. The meeting that led to the consensus statement was attended by 11[3] psychologists – although these had a range of specialisms, some of which were unrelated to clinical support such as brain-imaging and neuroscience. Moreover, some of the psychologists' beliefs were biologically essentialist. For instance, Heino Meyer-Bahlburg has outlined their theory that same-sex attraction is caused by brain chemistry (Kotulak, 2003). Kenneth Zucker, in turn, has been criticized for his controversial 'conversion therapy' approach to trans healthcare (Marusic, 2015). The consensus statement therefore seemed to pay lip service to psychology rather than being informed by the principles of psychology. It also failed to include eminent psychological bodies such as the American Psychiatric Association or the British Psychological Society.

As Liao and Roen note, the document was 'a professional response to a troubled and troubling area of medicine and a strategic development to facilitate basic science research on the horizon' (2014: 1). The consensus statement was therefore an important milestone as it called for psychosocial care to be a core feature within comprehensive, integrated and standardized multidisciplinary care (Ernst et al, 2018). However, as this chapter goes on to address, this integration has not materialized (Rolston et al, 2017, Crerand et al, 2019, Liao and Roen, 2019, Lampalzer et al, 2021). The reason for this is twofold. Firstly, the way in which psychology was incorporated within the statement was not a complete radical departure from the medical model developed by Money; and secondly, the clinical management of intersex has rested on dual and conflicting understandings of what intersex is. Ultimately this has introduced an implementation gap and relegated psychosocial care to a secondary role in intersex care pathways. This implementation gap resonates with that seen in Chapter 5 and draws attention to the state's need to help facilitate change to practice. We now address the shortcomings of the consensus statement.

[3] These were: Sheri Berenbaum, Polly Carmichael, Peggy Cohen-Kettenis, Jay Giedd, Richard Green, Melissa Hines, Heino Meyer-Bahlburg, Hertha Richter-Appelt, David Sandberg, Ute Thyen and Kenneth Zucker (see Lee et al, 2006: e497).

The consensus statement: a not-so-new paradigm in psychosocial care

As aforementioned, the consensus statement formalized the role of psychology as an essential part of the care management of intersex. Indeed, its section on psychosocial care begins by stating: 'Psychosocial care provided by mental health staff with expertise in DSD should be an integral part of management in order to promote positive adaptation' (Lee et al, 2006: e492). However, despite the consensus statement's apparent commitment to the role of psychological intervention, in reality the provision of psychosocial support has been lacking (Rolston et al, 2017, Crerand et al, 2019, Liao and Roen, 2019, Lampalzer et al, 2021). Children are unlikely to be referred to MDTs purely on the basis of psychosocial support. Liao et al carried out a review of 50 girls and young women seen at a specialist DSD clinic over a six-month period. They found that although 70 per cent of girls and young women were referred on the basis of urological or gynecological reasons, 46 per cent required ongoing psychological input (Liao, Tacconelli et al, 2010). Only 14 per cent of people had been referred for psychosocial reasons. The increased need for psychosocial support for intersex people was replicated in the UK's 2017 LGBT survey which noted that 'Twenty-five per cent of intersex respondents had accessed mental health services in the 12 months preceding the survey. A further 13%, however, had tried to access mental health services but had been unsuccessful' (Government Equalities Office, 2018b: 243). Intersex participants in that survey were more likely to state that accessing mental health services had been difficult (37 per cent compared to 28 per cent of non-intersex service users) (Government Equalities Office, 2018b: 243) and to rate the mental health services they had accessed as mainly or completely negative (27 per cent in comparison to 21 per cent of non-intersex service users) (Government Equalities Office, 2018b: 246). These findings need to be situated in a context where studies have found that young intersex people and their parents find that conversations with healthcare professionals can lead to emotional struggle and feelings of being overwhelmed (Boyse et al, 2014; Sanders & Carter, 2015). Other studies have found that intersex adolescents report turning down offers of psychological support because were not comfortable talking about their variations (Engberg et al, 2016; Ernst et al, 2018; Ernst et al, 2020).

Parents of intersex children have reported similarly, with one study finding only 7 per cent of parents feeling that counselling was available when they needed it (Lampalzer et al, 2021: 236). Of the counselling that had been received, 80 per cent reported a negative experience (Lampalzer et al, 2021: 236). Parents felt like they needed access to psychosocial support at a variety of different moments over the child's life course, including when they first learnt of the child's intersex variation, dealing with everyday situations, before the onset of puberty, and during puberty (Lampalzer et al, 2021: 236).

Of those that had received psychosocial support, parents felt like there was a lack of discussion around sexuality, being open about variations, and limitations and risks of medical interventions (Lampalzer et al, 2021: 236). Other risk factors for distress include 'severity of illness' (Sharkey et al, 2018) although anxiety was seen to reduce over time. Additionally, lower income, increased medical care and travel expenses, and having no other children have all been found to increase parental distress (Perez et al, 2019). Overall, therefore, we can speculate that the mental health needs of intersex people and their parents have not been met and, crucially, may have been exacerbated by previous psychological approaches grounded in a framework of medical embodiment that prioritized surgical interventions. Indeed, and as discussed in previous chapters, there is emerging evidence that repeated normalizing surgeries increase the rates of dissatisfaction and shame felt by intersex children (Liao, Tacconelli et al, 2010; Engberg et al, 2016; Schweizer et al, 2017). In these studies, it is the surgeries themselves that are seen as the cause of psychological discomfort rather than the intersex variation (Liao, Tacconelli et al, 2010; Engberg et al, 2016; Schweizer et al, 2017).

Resultantly, a question arises as to how far the consensus statement addressed the mental health needs of intersex people and their families. In England, recent research has highlighted that psychosocial care for children is, for the most part, being integrated into MDTs (Garland et al, 2021) with 86 per cent of MDTs having access to a psychologist or psychiatrist – although, prior to this study, one of the leading providers of intersex healthcare in the UK was extensively criticized for failures to provide psychological support to patients (Kirkland, 2017). Internationally, this figure is speculated to be far lower, with a review of 329 parents finding that 50 per cent felt that they did not have access to adequate psychosocial support (Bennecke et al, 2015). The question then is *why* psychosocial care has been so absent from care pathways, particularly given the strong push for medical reformists and the ever-growing evidence base that talking, not cutting, is the key to positive outcomes. The differences between the poor mental health of adults and the perceived availability of support for children perhaps highlight difficulties in the way that psychological support is structured, when it is introduced as well as the aims of this psychosocial care (Chadwick et al, 2014; Garland et al, 2021). The next sections explore two key stumbling blocks.

The framing of psychology in the consensus statement

One of the reasons for poor integration of psychosocial care originates from the consensus statement itself. Its proposal to introduce MDTs that include psychological expertise was not in fact a radical departure from the medical model; as we have seen in this chapter and Chapter 2, in reality Johns Hopkins had been working as a MDT since 1955. The consensus statement was not so much a radical departure, therefore, but a standardization of practice based on the Johns Hopkins paradigmatic model of medical embodiment rather than Kessler's approach. Here we see a disguised 'cooption' of psychological practices into the medical embodiment model.

If we return to the consensus statement's section on psychosocial care it states: 'Psychosocial care provided by mental health staff with expertise in DSD should be an integral part of management in order to promote positive adaptation' (Lee et al, 2006: e492). While the understanding that psychosocial care is an essential aspect of supporting intersex people and their families is welcome, the statement raises several questions that point to the retained dominance of the medical embodiment framing. Firstly, what does the phrase 'promote positive adaptation' mean? Adaptation implies change rather than, for example, acceptance or even support. This focus on change is supported by the following sentence in the consensus statement: 'This expertise can facilitate team decisions about gender assignment/reassignment, timing of surgery and sex hormone replacement' (Lee et al, 2006: e492). Even though the consensus statement highlights elsewhere that the research supporting early 'normalizing' intersex surgery is, at best, equivocal, it seems to assume here that these surgeries will be happening regardless. Indeed, studies have shown that healthcare practitioners' views continue to be shaped by the belief that surgery prevents parental distress (Liao et al, 2019) despite studies contesting this (Michala et al, 2014, Wolfe-Christensen et al, 2017). As a result, we get a sense that the psychologist's role is to promote positive adaption *after* surgical interventions have taken place. The consensus statement's imagined role for the psychologist, therefore, fails to offer alternatives to intersex children that fall outside the surgical intervention foregrounded by the medical embodiment paradigm. Indeed, despite their potential for 'facilitating' they are not introduced into the support of intersex children and their families at the beginning of their interactions with MDTs. Instead, as we will discuss more in the following section, psychologists are used to manage the emotional aftermath of surgeries (and their failures). Again, this point is reinforced by the next sentence in the consensus statement which notes that: 'Psychosocial screening tools that identify families at risk for maladaptive coping with a child's medical condition are available' (Lee et al, 2006: e492). Promoting positive adaptation to the child's 'new' gender role and the support of 'maladaptive' families form the duties of the imagined psychologist in this field.

The role for psychology imagined by the consensus statement, therefore, was neither radical nor progressive. At the same time, the statement's ostensible commitment to psychosocial care as essential makes it able to hide its commitment to medical embodiment in plain sight. While the document goes on to stress the need for including the child in decision making once they are able to participate in decision making (Lee et al, 2006: e492) it does not really challenge the orthodoxy established by John Money that surgeries are a tool of psychology. Indeed, the document goes on to play down any concerns about assigning the wrong gender:

> Reassignment discussions should recognise that childhood gender dissatisfaction often remits and is not synonymous with cross-sex behaviour, and that gender reassignment should be patient initiated. Atypical gender role behaviour is more common in children with DSD than in the general population, but should not be taken as an indicator for gender reassignment. (Lee et al, 2006: e492)

The consensus statement fails to reflect that these behaviours offer evidence for deferring surgery as long as possible.

In the final sentence of the section on psychosocial care the text does briefly raise the issue of the effect of surgeries on mental health: 'Medical interventions and negative sexual experiences may have fostered symptoms of post-traumatic stress disorder and referral to a qualified mental health professional may be indicated' (Lee et al, 2006: e492). This is the only point at which medical interventions are postulated as having potential negative mental health outcomes and it is interesting that this does not warrant more attention in the document as it has the potential to radically reorientate healthcare in this area. Nonetheless, we can see that the consensus statement, despite its designation of psychosocial care as essential, failed to differentiate its practices from those formulated by John Money in the 1950s. For the consensus statement, surgical intervention still forms the basis for intersex treatment, and this can be seen as a missed opportunity to ground intersex healthcare primarily in psychosocial care and support particularly given that 'the primary challenges faced by parents of children newly diagnosed with a DSD are informational and psychosocial, not medical or surgical' (Ernst et al, 2018:1). In some ways this is unsurprising given that the consensus statement was primarily drafted by endocrinologists. Even so, the document continues to have profound effects in practice on the way that psychologists continue to be integrated into MDTs. Ultimately, as Liao and Roen note:

> MDT approaches with psychological involvement were endorsed by the Consensus Statement which, however, did not differentiate between multidisciplinary in the historical sense, of medicine and psychology … that justified 'normalising' medical treatment, and multidisciplinary in the contemporary sense, of integrated care to de-stigmatise bodily differences and promote self-acceptance. It is this latter, integrated approach that could provide opportunities for innovative and transformative psychological contribution. (Liao and Roen, 2021: 203)

As we will discuss in the next section, therefore, psychosocial care in this area seems to be caught between these two conflicting senses of what multidisciplinary *means*, which itself is based on differing conceptions of what intersex *is*. The consensus statement therefore does not challenge Money's disorder-based medical model of embodiment.

Aims of psychosocial care

As outlined in the previous section, if psychosocial care is grounded in the disorder narrative of medical embodiment it is then used as an afterthought to deal with the emotional impact of surgeries, which undermines the potentially positive aspects and internal disruption that psychology could bring to this area of healthcare in offering alternative clinical pathways (Liao and Roen, 2021). The primacy of surgical intervention as the dominant healthcare approach to intersex children is confirmed through studies that focus on medical professionals working within MDTs. Studies, such as those run by Liao and Roen (2021), have highlighted that the structure of MDTs often deprioritizes the voices of psychologists and confirms their introduction into the team only once surgeries have already been undertaken. Liao and Roen conducted interviews with 32 MDT members and found psychologists are routinely marginalized as their expertise is seen as peripheral. This can see them working in parallel and separate to the main MDT (Liao and Roen, 2021: 208): "the centrality of a medical process … was taken for granted rather than negotiated. The classification of intersex traits as pathological dictates clinical priorities and hierarchical arrangements, leaving very little space for psychosocial staff to formulate different ideas and solutions' (Liao and Roen, 2021: 213). The consensus statement and subsequent national guidelines advocate that paediatric endocrinologists should be in charge of MDTs, ensuring that their *medicalized* construction of intersex embodiment are prioritized. The consensus statement's lack of ambition or vision for psychosocial care has consequently frustrated the actual *integration* of psychology into MDTs. As Chadwick et al note, although 'multi-disciplinary care pathways for … DSDs often allude to the importance of psychological interventions, [they] … are usually set up without due considerations of them' (Chadwick et al, 2014: 131).

The consensus statement's conceptual grounding in a medical embodiment framework has thus ensured the prevention of alternative care pathways being offered by psychologists either as part of or outside the MDT. The dominance of surgical intervention was highlighted by Garland et al (2021), who found evidence that at least in some MDTs surgeons were far more likely to be present for initial clinical meetings than psychologists. This framing would have a substantial effect on the way that clinical pathways are understood by parents (Streuli et al, 2013; Hegarty and Roen, 2018; Timmermans et al, 2019).

This research is replicated by international studies focussing on healthcare professionals present at *initial* meetings with parents. Kyriakou et al (2016), for example, in their research found that only 53 per cent of initial evaluations had a child psychologist present. Essentially, the medical model facilitates the siloing of medical expertise and the establishment of jurisdictional boundaries to reassert professional hierarchies which place urology and endocrinology at the top and psychology near the bottom. This further limits the disruptive potential of psychology both in healthcare but also in its potential to reshape and formulate other social institutions. The downplaying of psychosocial support within MDTs has important consequences for the ways in which parental concerns are understood and addressed. Timmermans et al's direct observations of interactions between healthcare providers and caregivers in DSD clinics found that clinicians' continue to frame gender through a lens of medical embodiment, thus skewing the process of gender assignment. Informed by caregivers' already pre-conceived expectations regarding the child's future gender, clinicians are able to 'marshal information strategically to make certain decisions seem more appropriate than others' (Timmermans et al, 2019: 1534). Clinicians and parents thus coproduce gender using a 'medical rationale that absolves clinician and parents from making the "wrong" choice' (Timmermans et al, 2019: 1534). Other research has raised important concerns over the potential for healthcare professionals to 'lead' parents into making certain decisions through the way they frame information (Hegarty and Roen, 2018: 978). This was also reflected in our findings:

> 'There are just still so many … who are at the mercy of doctors who are misinforming them when their intersex children are born.' (Respondent 14)

> I think parents are presented with this issue and then they are almost kind of duped into these [thinking these] surgeries are beneficial for the children and then parents are left alone to kind of figure this out, to sort out by themselves.' (Respondent 15)

> 'Doctors largely dissuade intersex people from contacting intersex support and advocacy groups rather than encourage participation.' (Respondent 2)

This framing may, in practice, shut down dialogue between parents and medical professionals by presenting information as a single unified collective (Davis, 2015). As Davis writes: 'While this model can disperse medical decision-making power, it also can reassert the authority of medical professionals over intersex traits by vesting it in a group, not simply an individual' (Davis, 2015: 85). Moreover, the lack of MDT representation from psychiatrists, social workers and broader fields such as ethics, bioethics, law, sociology, or anthropology, may be due to their greater potential to 'reject essentialist beliefs about sex, gender and sexuality' (Davis, 2015: 86).

The need for, and limits of, psychosocial support

Overall then, we can trace multiple problems with the historical development of psychology, its integration within MDTs and its uncritical acceptance of the medical embodiment framing of intersex as a disorder. There have been, and continue to be, several harms that are associated with psychology's role within healthcare. These include, but are by no means limited to, conversion therapy, regulatory and carceral responses to mental distress, and interpersonal difficulties in the therapeutic relationship. Much of the practical work and academic literature in clinical psychology has been grounded in a framework that is committed to classifications of variation in human behaviour as 'disorders' (for example, through psychiatric diagnostic tools such as the DSM 5 or ICD 10 classifications of mental disorders). These moves within psychology are consistent with the expansion of medical governance, which has led to all of us being 'asymptomatically, presymptomatically ill – and perhaps all suitable cases for treatment' (Rose, 2009: 71). A shift towards preventative medicine has seen the medical profession extending its authority into spheres to which it would not traditionally have access; issues such as obesity are now understood in terms of a 'health crisis' (Rose, 2009: 71), highlighting the (perhaps) unlimited potential of medicine to colonize other areas and knowledge bases. Pickersgill has traced similar shifts in relation to psychiatry. Discussing changes in the American Psychiatric Association's *Diagnostic and Statistical Manual of Mental Disorders* (*DSM*), Pickersgill notes an increasing medicalization of everyday or routine experiences (Pickersgill, 2014: 522). This does not mean that we should jettison psychology – but does mean we must be attentive to the ways in which psychological practice operate, the logics it conforms to and the power relations it destabilizes or reifies. As Pickersgill notes in relation to the *DSM*:

> we might usefully consider whether scholars and other commentators … could broaden out their arguments over whether diagnostic entities … are 'right' or 'wrong' – or even 'good' or 'bad' – and reflect more fully on the kinds of rights and responsibilities that different diagnoses and diagnostic tools enable and constrain. By this I mean, for instance, where and how diagnoses are used both to facilitate and exclude individuals from accessing particular services and benefits, and indeed how they are employed in the actual design of services. (Pickersgill, 2014: 524)

Engaging with this call, we focus on psychology that foregrounds the experiences of intersex people and views them outside the disorder/fixing paradigmatic medical embodiment framework. These experiential approaches to psychology are attentive to the harm done by these interventions and the way that these harms are framed and at the same time are focused on enhancing the long-term wellbeing of individuals. We are, in many ways, hesitant to fall so readily into the acceptance of psychology given its problematic, regulatory and carceral legacies. Similarly, our respondents were tentatively supportive of the need for psychosocial support, but also raised caution about the historical legacies of the psychological frameworks that are available to them:

> 'We need much more psychological input, people need to be offered counselling, parents, intersex people themselves, etc., and I say yes, but where do these psychologists get their information from, and if their criteria on what constitutes success is for someone to be normatively gendered and have a normative gender expression, behaviour, etc., that's not what we are advocating for.' (Respondent 4)

Despite the risks, there is still need for appropriately framed psychosocial support that challenges the paradigmatic medical model of intersex embodiment. This is not because individuals are 'disordered' but rather the need arises because of the extent to which the sex/gender binary is entrenched within cultural and institutional contexts. The strong normative expectations and beliefs that are attached to the binary are challenged by the birth of an intersex child, and the way in which families, practitioners and broader society respond to this challenge can produce long-term negative psychosocial effects on the individual. A study in 2017 of 110 intersex adults found: 'Impaired psychological well-being is an unfortunate outcome in many people with DSD, and we conclude that specialized interdisciplinary care with a focus in particular on psychological care is needed to improve well-being' (Bennecke et al, 2017: 642). Such implications arise from the shame and stigma experienced by intersex people and can affect a broad range of factors, including self-acceptance, family dynamics, the experience of otherness and overall social and psychological wellbeing (Roen, 2019; Lampalzer et al, 2021). Clinical psychology in this area must pivot, therefore, towards enhancing self-acceptance, increasing patient insight, destigmatizing intersex variations, introducing the setting of goals (for individuals, families and MDTs), increasing understanding, and to reducing affective, cognitive, behavioural or social barriers to the efficiency of treatment. Clinical psychologists are capable of introducing important psychotherapeutic models such as Acceptance and Commitment Therapy, Systemic Family Therapy, and mindfulness-based cognitive therapy (third wave CBT). These types of therapy are able to ensure targeted support over the life course as well as responding to shorter-term problems as required by a patient-centred approach. These approaches can help to challenge the idea of intersex embodiment as 'disordered' and instead help to focus on supporting them in the challenges that they face. Psychologists are also able to alter the use of pathologizing medical terminology in discussions with children with variations of sex development shifting narratives of 'disorder'. Where medical terminology is routinely used to frame discussions around children's bodies it can reinforce a self-understanding of disorder. Such an approach can hugely influence the 'need' for medical 'solutions'. As outlined above, this need for psychosocial support is often heightened where individuals have had unnecessary and non-consensual medical interventions:

> 'The grand majority of kids born with an intersex trait or variation is sex anatomy are damn healthy. Most of them really are. And there are kids who are born with a battery of difficult stuff, of disorders, and intersex stuff just happens to be just part of it, but most people born with intersex traits actually are healthy, they're fine. It's the medical intervention that really fucks with them.' (Respondent 3)

However, the question that this poses is that, if the issue lies in societal responses, why should responses focus on the individual rather than on changing structural and institutional responses? We agree that the long-term goal should be to change binary ideologies and normative expectations regarding bodily diversity at the cultural and institutional levels (Cooper and Renz, 2016). Inevitably, psychosocial support as a strategy is limited in terms of what it can achieve even where perfectly implemented. It focuses on the individuals' self-acceptance and growth rather than on societal change. As MacDougall (2001) comments in the context of same-sex rights, meaningful and positive participation in social life requires not just compassion or condonation (that is acceptance of diversity), but also celebration as 'stopping short denotes inferiority; it indicates that there is thought to be something problematic with the group and its members' (257). Accordingly, psychosocial frameworks must reflect that the problems that intersex people face are structural and external to the individual. Consequently, real change requires a shift in cultural attitudes towards bodily diversity where celebration rather than acceptance, tolerance or even compassion is the response to intersex bodies.

Yet, social change is not an easy task. Indeed, Fineman stresses that cultural disparities are harder to change than biological disparities, as 'to state that something is socially constructed … is to concede that it is powerful and resistant to change' (Fineman, 1992: 14, fn 25). It is therefore important not to overlook the distress individuals experience as a result of this systemic discrimination. Many of our respondents ultimately believed that, while broader societal shifts were key to positive outcomes, the immediate concern was ending surgical interventions on children and this required direct intervention with parents to depathologize the child:

> 'Because it's not just the children but it's just like how do we afford children in their most tender years, in their most vulnerable periods, but how do we strengthen the resilience of parents to sort of protect their children? What supports do we have for parents? So that one, that they are not subjecting their children to invasive surgeries but also what are the psychosocial supports for parents? … I think parents are presented with this issue and then they are almost kind of duped into these [thinking these] surgeries are beneficial for the children and then parents are left alone to kind of figure this out, to sort out by themselves. So the thing is that I feel like this should not solely be on the back for children but I think it's about also really educating and informing parents and giving support to parents to raise intersex children because they are ones who are going to be ultimately advocating for their kids.' (Respondent 15)

The turn to holistic healthcare practice is not to further pathologize and diagnose mental health problems, but rather to provide psychosocial support benefits from being framed around wellbeing and positive psychological adjustment (Sandberg et al, 2017: 280). As Hegarty and Roen (2018) state in the context of care pathways for hypospadias, the hope is that:

> Shifting parents' attention to the love for their child, and creating hopeful expectations for their child, could demedicalize the experience of having a child with hypospadias more than information about the risks of early surgery alone can do. Accordingly, the best interests of children with hypospadias may well be served when psychological pathways are properly conceptualized as focused on psychological qualities, including affect, well-being, and unconditional positive regard, that are beyond medical understandings of personhood. (Hegarty and Roen, 2018: 978)

The need to support parents as soon as possible on the birth of a child with atypical genitals has been highlighted in the research (Mednick et al, 2009; Creighton et al, 2018) and our British Academy respondents similarly alluded to this: "Those are difficult moments for parents to navigate and … they could do with some support, some social and emotional support apart from just the medical facts." (BA Respondent 3). High-level parental stress can lead to unhelpful coping and there is evidence of a link between maternal health and wellbeing and the psychological adaptation of the child (Immelt, 2006, Creighton et al, 2018). Recent research has demonstrated a strong case for psychological input showing that 'talking' is helpful for both parents of intersex children and intersex people themselves (Liao and Simmonds, 2013; Boyse et al, 2014; Lundberg et al, 2016; McCauley, 2017; Ernst et al, 2018; Lampalzer et al, 2021) and that parental stress can be alleviated where parents are adequately informed and have an opportunity to speak to other parents in a similar situation (Baratz et al, 2014; Creighton et al, 2018: 4). In a recent study Lampalzer et al (2021) found that 93 per cent of parents of intersex children felt that 'talking with other parents' helped them and 60 per cent reported 'understanding and emotional support' as being helpful (Lampalzer et al, 2021: 233). 60 per cent of parents also found that 'talking with persons with intersex/dsd conditions' was helpful (Lampalzer et al, 2021: 233). Moreover, while much of this section has focussed on supporting parents, intersex people also reported that talking with other intersex people was helpful (81 per cent) (Lampalzer et al, 2021: 233). 'Understanding and emotional support' was more likely to be found helpful for intersex adults (67 per cent) than parents of intersex children (Lampalzer et al, 2021: 233). Discussion of intersex variations allows for the 'normalization' of the different issues that intersex people face (Boyse et al, 2014; McCauley, 2017). One example of psychosocial support that decentred pathologizing and medicalized narratives was conducted by Chadwick et al (2014). In this study, the researchers ran a one-day workshop for women with Turners Syndrome. This particular group of women often report negative self-evaluation. There is very little research, however, into how women with Turners Syndrome can be psychosocially supported or how to improve their mental health. The workshop encouraged the group to challenge 'the taken-for-granted notion that having TS made the women unworthy' (Chadwick et al, 2014: 132). Three months later, during a follow-up meeting with the researchers, participants expressed a newfound ability 'to draw more positive meanings from their experience of living with TS' (2014: 132), 'felt less different from other women' and 'had started to place a more positive value on being "different"' (2014: 132). As Creighton et al state: "The research in a variety of paediatric contexts makes a strong case for sustained psychological input for parents in paediatric gynaecological care" (Creighton et al, 2018: 4).

Consequently, aside from emergency lifesaving treatment (in the case of salt-wasting CAH for example, which as we outlined in Chapter 2 is largely the basis for the disorder framework) we would argue that psychosocial support ought to be the primary motivator of MDTs. It is concerning, therefore that Liao, Green et al have found that although 'it is obvious that parents affected by DSD first and foremost require sustained psychological support … this does not seem to be the central focus in paediatric management'

(Liao, Green et al, 2010: 193–9). Moreover, the absence of psychologists from initial discussions with families becomes even more concerning when taking into account that 'they are likely to be the only team members with advance training in communication in emotive environments' (Liao and Roen, 2021: 203). This is problematic, as the birth of a child with an intersex variance can often be a time of immense distress for parents. Along with the usual complications, emotions, and exhaustions of parenthood, they are also faced with a need to understand information relating to complex medical and genetic variations, stigma, ambiguity regarding gonadal tumour risk, a lack of certainty about future gender identity, and uncertainty regarding fertility potential (Ernst et al, 2018: 1). Psychosocial care, therefore, forms a key component of supporting intersex people over the life course. It is vital for both intersex individuals and the familial institutions in which they find themselves.

Questions remain as to who should deliver this type of support (psychiatrists, counsellors, or peer support networks) (Lampalzer et al, 2021: 233) and how far they should be independent of any MDTs (Lampalzer et al, 2021: 237). But the need for this type of support is clear, particularly as 27 per cent of parents may have no opportunity to discuss the issues that they face as they do not feel comfortable disclosing information to family members or friends (Sandberg et al, 2017). In the context of intersex then the need to minimize surgical interventions and to maximize psychological support becomes apparent.

There are several barriers to establishing these sorts of psychosocial improvements, many of which rest upon the fact that medical embodiment narratives of 'disorder' are better understood and, subsequently, better funded. These include accessing resources, a lack of knowledge about the issues, and difficulties accessing localized treatment (Ernst et al, 2019: 2). Studies have found that even where psychosocial support is available a lack of funding to access those services or to travel to them means that intersex people are unable to utilize them (Lampalzer et al, 2021: 238). In other places, however, funding is needed to ensure the provision of services. As Ernst et al explain: 'Current care models frequently do not offer adequate financial support for complex multidisciplinary care, and traditional fee-for-service payment systems may not support the provision of behavioural health within a subspecialty clinic' (Ernst et al, 2018: 3).

Moreover, healthcare models are increasingly built around 'financial models that disincentivize the extra time required to coordinate integrated care' (Ernst et al, 2019: 2). The small number of specialist services available also creates difficulties around accessing localized support. Lampalzer et al found that 57 per cent of intersex adults and 53 per cent of parents of intersex children reported travelling more than 200 kilometres to access peers support, counselling offers and structures (2021: 230). Consequently, their respondents identified a high need for localized services with parents in particular placing emphasis on this (81 per cent) (236). Finally, there are difficulties around the amount of psychosocial care-workers who are trained to provide this type of support (Lampalzer et al, 2021: 238; see also Ernst et al, 2019). As Lee et al note: 'the paucity of psychologists with training and experience with individuals born with ambiguous genitalia makes [psychological assessment and counselling of parents and family members] an ongoing challenge' (Lee et al, 2020: 3). This may account for the difficulties in Malta in providing tailored support for intersex individuals.

However, as we have mentioned throughout this chapter, we do not view psychology or psychosocial care as the final step or ideal solution for ameliorating disadvantages currently faced by intersex embodied individuals nor for facilitating wellbeing. Rather, like the legal reforms seen in Chapter 5, psychology is one part of a strategy through which to meaningfully destabilize medical embodiment and begin to undo its direct and associated harms. There remains, however, a need to shift the identity of intersex from something that is devalued and in need of 'fixing' to a lived experience that is celebrated, recognized and valued in ways that are meaningful to intersex people (Overboe, 1999: 23). Part of this strategy going forwards must hinge around a state obligation to meet the psychological needs of intersex children and their families. This requires significant state buy-in in terms of time, money and resources. Malta's law reforms have great potential; the GIGESC Act actively makes space for the provision of psychosocial frameworks to be extended and recognized. Law, thus, continues to play an important place to carve space for these changes. However, states must be dynamic and active after legislative reform has gone through; Chapter 5 highlighted the perils of stagnant law reform that does not retain political momentum. As BA Respondent 4 emphasized, part of the failure to yet implement the medical protocol and psychosocial frameworks was state (and political) apathy: "I think there are far too few people who are pushing for intersex issues to be you know, on the agenda, and for this to be, um, put in place."

Legal embodiment and psychosocial support

Grounding our understanding of intersex in the lived experience of our participants allows us to push back on psychological narratives that might advocate for (or are premised upon) a medical embodiment model lens of disorder. Focussing on the contextuality of embodiment directs us to foreground the material body as the means through which we interact with and experience institutions and discourse. Interventions on the body are therefore often biographical, shaping our interactions with institutions, life experiences and subsequent choices (Fox and Thomson, 2017, Garland et al, 2021). Embodiment helps us to understand the essential role of the body in the developing lives and identities of children and alerts us to the potential shaping effect of non-therapeutic interventions on the way that intersex people experience the world. As Roen writes: 'The scarring, the aesthetic difference, the changes to sensation are lived continuously. They are necessarily imbricated in the process of an emerging self' (Roen, 2009: 21). While the approaches of clinicians to their patients clearly differ (Hegarty and Roen, 2018: 978) where the body is treated as an abstract 'malleable object', the role of the body in constituting the emerging subject and selfhood is ignored (Roen, 2009: 21). Legal and psychological approaches to intersex embodiment, therefore, must be established on the basis of this understanding of the harms created by surgical interventions. As Roen writes: 'surgery does reach beyond the superficial and even beyond the material, enabling a different reality for the emerging self. For those who undergo surgery, the embodied self is necessarily remoulded: surgery is never simply a "cosmetic" endeavour' (Roen, 2009: 15). For these reasons, legal and psychological responses to intersex people must aim at deferring intersex surgeries and instead promote a range of tools aimed at self and familial acceptance and, ultimately, celebration. This has the potential to profoundly disrupt the paradigmatic medical embodiment lens of intersex – moving away from narratives of fixing and disorder towards supporting the emerging subjectivity and protecting the future interests of the intersex child (Fox and Thomson, 2017). In addition, it necessitates a break from John Money's conceptual legacy of the role of psychology in intersex care. In some way, we see this attempt in Malta with its legal shift towards psychosocial approaches, although the delivery of this has been patchy.

This shift within psychology (or perhaps the promise of psychology yet to come) echoes recent legal work on bodily integrity. Following Priaulx's recognition that bodily integrity is a fundamental 'psychological need' (Priaulx, 2008: 179) Fox and Thomson have begun to push for recognition of the concept of embodied integrity within law (Fox and Thomson, 2017; Fox et al, 2020; Garland et al, 2021). This seeks to recognize not only the traditional 'protective' functions of bodily integrity doctrine – the injunction to refrain from unwanted interference with the body – but also the shaping, biographical and psychological effects of surgeries.

In some senses Fox and Thomson's work in this area serves as a critique of traditional conceptions of bodily integrity that they see as 'grounded in a mind/body dichotomy that prioritizes the physical body, conceptualized as bounded territory or property to be policed and defended against the encroachment of others' (Fox and Thomson, 2017: 503). They note that this leads to carceral responses from the legal system in addition to problems with 'indeterminacy and cultural contingency, as well as the gendered and racialized ways [bodily integrity] operates in practice' (2017: 502). In particular, Fox and Thomson illustrate the gendered and racialized components of how bodily integrity is operationalized through the example of female genital cutting.

Counter to this model of bodily integrity, Fox and Thomson offer an approach based on embodied integrity. This approach 'enriches conventional accounts by integrating physical and psychological dimensions of integrity in recognition of the child's emerging legal subjectivity' (Fox and Thomson, 2017: 503). Additionally, embodied integrity, 'requires human bodies to be understood as inherently relational, experiential, and subject to change by interactions with society' (515). This expansion of bodily integrity can be traced in a nascent line of European Court of Human Rights judgments. For example, in the *Glass v UK* case, David Glass's article 8 rights were recognized as encompassing both his physical and personal integrity.[4] Donnelly and Kilkelly highlight that this judgment focusses on both David's physical and psychological integrity (2011: 49). This judgment was followed by the decision of *Storck v Germany* where the European Court of Human Rights found that states must secure citizens' rights to 'physical and moral integrity'[5].

A developing focus on the psychological aspects of bodily integrity within legal reasoning works in tandem with Fox and Thomson's call to protect the emerging subjectivity of the child and to protect the future interests of the child. In terms of protecting the emerging subjectivity of the child, an embodied approach would recognize the child as being subject to both development and change. Psychological support can help to work through such changes in light of current social stigma – whereas surgeries may curtail them in psychologically damaging ways. As Fox and Thomson write: 'The value of embodied integrity lies precisely in how it underpins the child's emergent subjectivity, meaning that her needs are never synonymous with those of others, or merely an extension of them' (Fox and Thomson, 2017: 523). In relation to protecting the future interests of the child, Fox et al draw upon Feinberg to highlight a need for 'autonomy rights that are held in trust for the adult that the child will become' and that 'parents and others should refrain from actions that limit or deny options that the child should have when she reaches adulthood' (Feinberg, 1994; Fox et al, 2020: 299). Fox et al bring this into connection with the work of Cornell to argue that embodied integrity should be understood as an open-ended process that maximizes the subjects' capacity for choice (Cornell, 1995; Fox et al, 2020: 299) even where such decision making is supported (Harding and Taşcıoğlu, 2018).

As a consequence, we can see the ways in which law and psychology can co-constitute the supportive environment needed for intersex people

4 [2004] 1 FLR 1019.

5 61603/00 [2005] ECHR 406.

to flourish. Law is able to provide the scaffolding, momentum and force necessary for psychology to revitalize medical conceptions of intersex embodiment. Psychology, in tandem, is able to provide law with a thicker conception of bodily integrity – one that maximizes individual autonomy, choice and flourishing. For these reasons we see the entanglement of psychology and law as vital to challenging and, ultimately, reorientating the paradigmatic medical conception of intersex embodiment.

Conclusion

In conclusion, we can see that the conceptual legacies of John Money have been grounded within and reified medical embodiment approaches to intersex that focus on disorder and fixing. With them, come the concomitant criticisms of psychology as a framework with huge baggage around conversion therapy, carceral approaches to mental distress and problematic power dynamics between patients and clinicians. Despite these, within psychology are the seeds of a new approach to intersex embodiment that is capable of reorienting healthcare towards self-acceptance and support. Disentangling these seeds is not easy, but the conceptual rewards of reorientating medical embodiment from within are potentially vast.

Consequently, of the frameworks explored so far, the psychosocial framework which focuses on supporting the individual and emotional wellbeing is most suited to challenging the lens of intersex as a medically embodied 'disorder' through its focus on self and societal acceptance. However, despite considerable efforts from the medical reform movement, current approaches to intersex healthcare continue to be based on biomedical approaches that privilege narratives of 'disorder' through 'normalizing' surgeries rather than prioritizing psychosocial care demonstrating the huge difficulties around shifting the paradigm of medical embodiment (Liao and Roen, 2021). This has led to a situation where intersex people are far more likely to have experienced medical intervention than psychosocial support (Lampalzer et al, 2021: 238). Psychologists involved in multidisciplinary work continually find themselves marginalized or otherwise being unable to challenge narratives grounded in medical embodiment (Liao and Roen, 2021). The provision of psychosocial care is crucial in order to 'encourage self-acceptance, process trauma, accept the experienced otherness and improve sexual satisfaction, as well as overall psychosocial well-being' (Lampalzer et al, 2021: 228). Yet, despite the aforementioned benefits of psychosocial care, for the most part, psychological interventions that promote self-acceptance of difference (rather than 'fixing') have not been engaged with by the medical profession. Nonetheless, 'cognitive behavioral and problem-solving psychosocial interventions have demonstrable efficacy in improving the psychosocial functioning of patients and families in other pediatric conditions' (Ernst et al, 2018: 3).

Disrupting narratives of disorder requires a focus on self and societal acceptance. As a result, normalizing the experience of counselling as an integrated part of intersex healthcare becomes paramount. Healthcare providers need to work to ensure that offers of psychosocial support are not understood as being only for those with mental health issues or in need of 'therapy' (Bennecke et al, 2015). Rather than focussing on a particular mental health need, psychosocial support benefits from being framed around wellbeing and positive psychological adjustment (Sandberg et al, 2017: 280). As Roen notes, in order to ensure that healthcare is built upon a psychosocial framework we need to ensure that we make 'regular conversations with a psychosocial professional a standard part of the process for all families involved in diagnostic and treatment processes'(Roen, 2019: 522). Similarly, peer support needs to be better integrated into healthcare pathways (Ernst et al, 2019; Lampalzer et al, 2021: 233).

At the same time, while we advocate the merits of psychosocial approach, engagement with healthcare must be cautious as poorly conceived psychological support could reify clinical medical practice's attempts to 'fix' ambiguity and further pathologize intersex people. In order to meaningfully reorient healthcare towards a grounding in psychosocial care (Roen, 2019; Liao and Roen, 2021), therefore, improvements need to be made to include 'easily accessible psychosocial support' (Lampalzer et al, 2021: 237), specialization and training in intersex issues and some provision of independence from medical doctors (Ernst et al, 2019; Lampalzer et al, 2021: 237), non-pathologizing peer-led counselling and support for parents (Lampalzer et al, 2021: 237), and education and concomitant qualifications of practitioners (Ernst et al, 2019; Lampalzer et al, 2021: 238). If these changes were to be introduced then we might begin to see substantial improvements to the psychosocial health of intersex people through empowering them and enhancing their autonomy. Consequently, we can see that, done correctly, psychosocial approaches can move beyond frameworks of disorder, LGBT and non-binary in favour of offering support, self-acceptance and familial bonding to intersex people. This 'supportive' framework seriously challenges the framing of intersex embodiment as a 'disorder'. If healthcare could be reorientated in this direction it would significantly change the experiences of intersex people for the better. In order to do this, however, healthcare would need to reflect on its own involvement in the creation and reification of disorder narratives and look to go beyond them. Without these shifts it is difficult to see how law reform, like the GIGESC Act, could ever improve the relationship between healthcare and intersex individuals. At the same time, the dominant narratives within healthcare may require institutions such as law to help carve space for meaningful inclusion of psychosocial frameworks and state commitment to ensure that it happens in practice. All this is necessary against a backdrop of social change which moves from acceptance and tolerance to celebration.

7

Conclusion: Intersex Embodiment

This book set out to examine what intersex embodiment means in the 21st century in predominantly Western societies. In doing so, it has demonstrated that there are multiple disjointed and fragmented accounts of intersex embodiment which are produced through a range of different regulatory frameworks. Each of these frameworks arguably set out to improve the lived experience of intersex embodied individuals. In reality, they often misconceptualize 'intersex' and consequently serve to disempower intersex embodied individuals.

The professionalization of medicine in the 19th century saw a change in the way that intersex embodiment was constructed. Conceptualizing intersex embodiment as a 'disorder' has prevented legal and political questions about intersex equality to be taken forward. Instead, governing logics of 'fixing' intersex people have dominated the ways that intersex embodiment is understood. This process of 'fixing', in turn, is committed to logics of binary sex and heteronormativity (Dreger, 1998; Malatino, 2019). Since the early 20th century, medical professionals have attempted to 'normalize' intersex children through surgical and hormonal interventions to ensure they adhere to the sex binary. While the motivations of these interventions are not to harm, but to 'better' the lives of their 'patients' by enabling heteronormative social participation, the need for interventions are based on social anxieties rather than scientific evidence; no longitudinal studies exist which prove that lived experience has actually improved as a result of such interventions. In fact, these interventions are usually non-therapeutic, and can lead to severe life-long physical and psychological problems. Surgical interventions tend to occur within the first 18 months of the child's birth, and this, combined with the culture of secrecy that accompanies intersex variations, has led to an erasure of intersex embodiment in political and legal discourse. There have been few constructions of intersex embodiment outside the medical profession, and the shame and stigma attached to a 'disorders of sex development' label prevents families and individuals from speaking out.

Indeed, many families go to great lengths to hide such a 'diagnosis' (Hegarty and Chase, 2000; Davis, 2015).

The construction of intersex embodiment as a disorder is not natural, inevitable or apolitical. The notion of intersex embodiment as a disorder is loaded with meaning that influences how intersex people understand their own bodies and choices (Karkazis and Feder, 2008: 2016). Similarly, framing intersex embodiment as a disorder impacts how parents understand their children and the medical options that are available to them (Reis, 2007: 536, Timmermans et al, 2019). Given law's role in determining who can legitimately participate in society, the failure to offer an alternative construction of intersex embodiment in any meaningful way has perpetuated, if not exacerbated, the problems that intersex people face. Legal silence tacitly legitimizes the medical account of intersex embodiment as 'fixable' disorders, outside the terrain of appropriate legal supervision. Thus, law aligns itself with the biomedical discourse of intersex embodiment, depicting such bodies as deviant or in need of correction (Travis, 2015: 182). In doing so, law reaffirms a binary understanding of sex (Dreger, 1998) and prevents intersex individuals from engaging with the law. Law's silence is therefore not neutral; rather it perpetuates the existence of a striking power imbalance between intersex people, their families and the medical profession (Garland and Travis, 2018). Treatment and diagnoses, therefore, must be understood through a general cultural, social and state acceptance of sex as binary. Medical knowledge that reifies existent cultural norms is privileged over the lived experiences of individuals who challenge the idea that sex is binary. Intersex individuals who question the sex binary continue to be framed as a very small, unrepresentative minority (Ahmed et al, 2016), a representation that fails to consider the ways in which epistemologies influence ontology.

Intersex embodiment has also often been constructed as a synonym for non-binary. Germany's Gesetz zur Änderung personenstandsrechtlicher Vorschriften (Personenstandsrechts-Änderungsgesetz— PStRÄndG) 2013 introduced an alternative construction of intersex embodiment into German law. Nonetheless, this framing of intersex embodiment has led to little uptake and much criticism from intersex people. While some intersex people identify as non-binary, the majority of our respondents were happy to define as male or female. More importantly, however, was the fact that policy and legislation that understands intersex embodiment as non-binary unintentionally strengthens medical power over intersex people (Carpenter, 2018). Parents of intersex children were keen to have their children placed *within* the gender binary and this led to an earlier uptake of surgeries (Travis, 2015; Amnesty International, 2017). Legislation in Germany has starkly outlined the issues in this area, when non-binary becomes the predominant lens through which intersex embodiment is understood. Such legislative and policy approaches risk failing to give broader recognition to those that need them while *misrecognizing* many intersex people.

Intersex embodiment has also been produced through LGBT framings which have grown from the close political and community alliances between intersex and LGBT activism. Some of our participants expressed support for the inclusion and increased visibility that working within a queer framing of embodiment could provide. Others, however, raised concerns about how amalgamation (or coopting) into the production of a homonormative embodiment had meant that funding was siphoned away from intersex issues and that intersex voices were not listened to (by either LGBT activists or policy makers). In turn, some intersex organizations and activists – particularly those led by parents of intersex children – raised fundamental disagreements with being included in LGBT policy and spaces as they felt that it misrepresented the issues that intersex children face. At the same time, association with the LGBT community may have increased parental desire for their children to undergo non-therapeutic medical interventions, again failing to challenge the paradigmatic construction of intersex embodiment as a disorder (Carpenter, 2018).

Despite these concerns, homonormative framing has had a powerful effect on how intersex embodiment is understood in law and policy. Seen through a homonormative lens, adding intersex people to contemporary anti-discrimination law becomes an important aspect of recognition and equality. Anti-discrimination law has, in some jurisdictions, allowed for an alternate legal and political recognition of intersex embodiment. However, these legal approaches can, in reality, reify existing medical frameworks based on 'disorder'. Indeed, the individualized design of anti-discrimination laws means that they are poorly suited to challenging dominant medical norms. Nonetheless, the 'ease' with which anti-discrimination law can be amended (in comparison to challenging medical frameworks) has meant that this type of legal intervention is among the most popular methods of intersex 'inclusion'. Yet, without reference to bodily integrity our participants saw this type of law as failing to offer an empowering sense of intersex embodiment.

Even so, in jurisdictions that have prioritized the prohibition of non-therapeutic surgical interventions, there were problems with the way that intersex embodiment was framed. Malta's creation of the GIGESC Act in 2015 received plaudits when the Act was introduced, but is yet to deliver on its potential to disrupt the framing of intersex embodiment as a disorder. This was highlighted by the UNCRC's reprimand of Malta for the alleged continuation of medical interventions on intersex children (UNCRC, 2019). While the legislation itself is progressive there are several problems that limit its efficacy. In particular, the lack of provision for extra-territorial surgical intervention highlights not only a failure to close loopholes in this area, but also a fundamental misunderstanding of how healthcare provision in Malta was taking place at the time that the legislation was passed.

Relatedly, our research reveals significant concerns in Malta around the way that this legislation has been implemented. The impact of the GIGESC Act has been hampered by its inability to deliver upon its potential. So far, the legislation has not introduced an appropriate functioning MDT as promised by section 14(4). Adequate psychosocial care as pledged by section 15 is also yet to be delivered for either adults or children. The working group provided for under section 16 has been beset by delay and difficulties. In sum, Malta's legislative potential highlights the difficulties that are raised where legal and medical frameworks interact. Reform is needed at an institutional level within medicine for this type of legal intervention to work and this is yet to occur in Malta. Overall, the issues with implementation have resulted in a real lack of engagement from stakeholders leaving Malta's position more symbolic than impactful. This showcases the complexities of challenging narratives of intersex embodiment grounded in 'disorder' even where law is geared towards empowering intersex people. Medicine, it seems, must transform its own narrative of intersex in tandem with legal reform in order to instil real change. It also draws attention to the complex relationship between law and social change. In doing so, we also recognize that social change is a dynamic and ongoing process rather than a shift between two static concepts. Malta has introduced a positive first step in offering an alternative conception of intersex embodiment – one grounded in the lived experience of intersex people. What happens next, however, relies on greater state and political buy-in to ensure that the proposed changes take place.

The psychosocial framework offers an alternative approach to intersex embodiment that focuses on supporting individual and emotional wellbeing through a narrative of self and societal acceptance. It also offers a space to disrupt medical narratives from within the discipline of healthcare itself. Despite overtures to the contrary, the role of psychosocial care still seems to be minimized on MDTs (Garland et al, 2021, Lampalzer et al, 2021, Liao and Roen, 2021). Healthcare providers need to work to ensure that offers of psychosocial support are not understood as being only for those with mental health issues or in need of 'therapy' (Bennecke et al, 2015). Psychosocial support benefits from being framed around wellbeing and positive psychological adjustment rather than been only targeted at immediate crisis level interventions (Sandberg et al, 2017: 280). At the same time, while the psychosocial approach has many important benefits, poorly conceived psychological support could reify paradigmatic medical approaches to intersex embodiment that attempt to 'fix' ambiguity and further pathologize intersex people. Instead, if grounded in the empowerment of intersex people and the enhancement of their autonomy, psychosocial approaches can move beyond frameworks of disorder, homonormative and non-binary in favour of offering support, self-acceptance and familial bonding. Medical accounts of intersex embodiment could be reorientated in this direction. However, in order to do so, healthcare institutions would need to reflect on their own involvement in the creation, perpetuation and desire for narratives of intersex embodiment grounded in disorder within their governing logics. States need to meaningfully commit to funding and supporting the development of infrastructure that can enable the delivery of well-crafted psychosocial care. In this arena, law and the state continue to play an important function ensuring the formal inclusion of psychosocial care in healthcare settings.

These substantive chapters highlight the usefulness of an approach attentive to legal embodiment. As we have seen in the preceding chapters, definitions of what intersex *means* is dependent upon the institutional context in which it is raised and upon the discursive and cultural framework in which it is embedded. As a result, intersex embodiment is inherently pluralistic. To some extent the book has begun to address Karkazis's call to 'understand and interrogate what these meanings imply for lived experience' (Karkazis, 2008: 14) and provided further elaboration on Holmes' understanding of intersex embodiment as "not one but many sites of contested being, temporally sutured to biomedical, political, and social imperatives in play in each moment" (Holmes, 2009: 2). Similarly, the book resonates with Karkazis' reminder that "What intersexuality is and how it should be treated (if at all) are questions always subject to the constraints of time and place; that is understandings of these conditions and their treatment are culturally and historically contingent and thus subject to change." (Karkazis, 2008: 290). This important point gives further credence to the view that we should be attentive to the lived experiences of intersex people (Monro et al, 2021).

Returning to our initial outline of embodiment, we can see that intersex variations have a profoundly material dimension. They are congenital – present from birth (even if they are not detected until much later). Chromosomes, hormones, receptors and genitals all have a corporeal presence. They exist, they are identifiable and are capable of cataloguing and documentation. Where variations in these bodily materialities are present, it may be indicative of an intersex variation. It is not decisive, however, as the inclusion of some variations remains deeply disputed (Griffiths, 2018a) particularly around hypospadias, CAH, Turners Syndrome and Klinefelters Syndrome. These variances also have genetic and molecular existence that complicates binary models of sex, which Rosario has argued leads us to a 'polymorphic and multifactorial' model of 'quantum sex' (Rosario, 2009: 269). Alongside bodies, however, harm also has a material dimension. The surgeries that some of these children are subject to have far-reaching material consequences (Roen, 2009). Nonetheless these harms are often minimized on the basis that children lack the capacity to vocalize these harms (Fox et al, 2020). Harm, however, is also culturally produced (Giliani, 2020: 3) with some of the harms around clinical intervention being understood as benefits. For some intersex people, their families and their doctors, harms are understood through this medical lens. In doing so, social understandings of how intersex embodiment should be clinically managed are culturally produced. This type of approach fails to fully address 'the future desires of the intersex person, or the future political perspective and social opportunities of the intersex person, and issues to do with the complex involvement of the body in the process of becoming' (Roen, 2009:19). The multiple directions in which the intersex person can emerge become much more limited (Griffiths, 2021). As Timmermans et al conclude from their observations within MDTs:

> The future presented in the clinic thus reinforces medical interventions as the solution to problems of embodied intersex differences for self and society. Even if the success of the medical interventions remains unclear, the core issue is that parents and clinicians feel they have a measure of control over the process and outcomes. … Biological sex is presented as relatively plastic: external and internal sex traits can be removed, brought down, enlarged, shortened, or sculpted; while hormonal processes of development during puberty can be supplemented or suppressed. Clinicians present surgery and hormone therapies not simply as sex normalising but as sex-gender realignment techniques. (Timmermans et al, 2019: 1528–9)

The approaches observed by Timmermans et al leave little room for the child to emerge on their own terms rather than responding to the future imagined for them by their parents and medical professionals (Roen, 2009). While the material dimension of intersex variations are clear, what these somatic components *mean*, however, is even more contested. Meaning, especially for sex and gender, is always culturally and institutionally produced (Butler, 1993; Fausto-Sterling, 2000, Holmes, 2008a). Interpretation of these variations – as disorders, as non-binary, as queer or homonormative – is determined by the cultures in which they are embedded. As Holmes notes:

> Intersexuality is a historical and cultural construction rather than a simple biological phenomenon. The categorization of intersex is related to ideological commitments to a presumed binary 'nature' of male and female, coupled with a paradoxical assumption that gender is so fluid that we are entitled to make of infants and children whatever we will. (Holmes, 2008a: 154)

This effect of interpreting intersex variations through culture seems to be one dimensional. Intersex variations, for their part, have done little to rupture our cultural understandings of sex and gender as binary or natural

(Fausto-Sterling, 2000). As Fausto-Sterling writes: 'our beliefs about gender affect what kinds of knowledge scientists produce about sex' (Fausto-Sterling, 2000: 3).

Importantly, while sometimes discourse and these institutions are in harmony, at other times they will construct intersex embodiment in ways that conflict. Embodiment thus highlights the pluralistic ways in which intersex bodies are situated within their legal, social, medical and political contexts. This is important not only because it recognizes the dynamism within the term intersex but also because it allows for the tracing of the framing effects that are then played out in law and policy. We live in a time where we are lucky to have an increasing amount of visible intersex people willing to share their priorities, needs and desires (Holmes, 2008a; Carpenter, 2018, 2021; Davis, 2015; Rubin, 2017; Malatino, 2019). Their role is pivotal in increasing visibility, and two of our British Academy respondents reflected on how the absence of such role models in Malta made it difficult to instigate social change:

> 'We're educating people out there about intersex conditions and but there isn't anyone visibly intersex appearing on, on media and talking about their experience, unlike all of the other identities within the LGBT community. So, I think that makes it quite difficult for, for other intersex persons to reach out to, to be part of the Community and to have Community support.' (BA Respondent 4)

Through our interview process, this book has sought to centre those experiences and ensure they are at the forefront of policy development in this area. We remain attentive to the limitations of these projects as highlighted in Chapter 1: they cannot be said to represent a whole community. Nonetheless, the empirical work has demonstrated that although many of the framings of embodiment that we outline are structural – intersex people understand their lived experience *through* these frameworks. As a result, it is vital to recognize that intersex people remain deeply divided over terminology, medical interventions, human rights and inclusion within LGBT spaces. Crucially, this gives us reason to reflect on the fact that intersex people are imbricated within these systems of embodiment and are themselves invested in particular types of meaning – ontology is constructed through epistemologies.

For some, identifying their variance as a disorder that lays outside the scope of the LGBT community is essential to the way that they understand the world and how they navigate and experience society. In some contexts and cultures, and for some intersex embodiment is simply medical and not an issue of identity or law. These internalizations of medical approaches to embodiment highlight its power to construct the subject. As Karkazis notes: 'Far from existing outside culture, biomedicine is a cultural entity that not only has unparalleled discursive and practical powers to define and determine what is to be normatively human but also to withstand alternative constructions and challenges to its version of normativity' (Karkazis, 2008: 5). In many ways, medicine's power is self-generating. Many intersex people are not faced with (explicit) alternate conceptions of intersex embodiment (particularly in the area of law). This can lead to a situation whereby 'sex diversity is seen exclusively through a medical lens, which leads to most research being done from a medical perspective and many families believing that the only people they can talk to about their affected children are medical professionals' (Roen, 2019: 512; see also Sandberg et al, 2017). This has led many intersex people to embrace the term DSD as it has the potential to minimize the experience of being intersex. A DSD is something that you *have* rather than an identity that you *are*. As Davis has noted, acceptance of the term DSD provides certain benefits including 'supportive relationships with medical providers and family members' (Davis, 2015: 146). While we have problematized the way that medical embodiment draws upon binary understandings of sex and gender and heteronormative hierarchies, this does not make them any less valid for intersex people who experience them. While it is important to be attentive to the individual experiences of this system it also highlights a need to ensure that focus is paid to the structural inequalities that are generated in its wake. Just because some individuals do not mind these inequalities or, indeed, seek to perpetuate them does not bring them within the ambit of intersex justice.

For others, their self-understandings are markedly different. Intersex embodiment is constructed through a lens of identity, and this carries significant political dimensions. As Davis notes: 'Intersex people who reject DSD language tend to reject the idea that sex, gender, and sexuality are biologically proscribed bodily phenomena and instead embrace intersex itself as a powerful identity' (Davis, 2015: 146). For these people, intersex embodiment challenges institutional structures that are based around binary conceptions of sex and gender. Fundamentally, this means challenging the medical profession and holding them accountable for the ways in which they have treated intersex people. Many of these individuals' distance themselves from medical self-understandings as being overly pathologizing and placing too much power in the hands of medical professionals. For most of these intersex people, their more politicized self-understanding draws them towards LGBT spaces through a shared sense of political and institutional struggle. Katrina Roen uses the term queer in order to 'imagine the spaces where difference may be embraced and celebrated, rather than needing to be erased' (Roen, 2009: 35). In doing so, she challenges medical professionals to further consider their role in 'facilitating queer embodied relationships, as part of a process of enabling queer embodied subjects to feel loveable and participate in adult relationships' (Roen, 2009: 35). Again, an emphasis is placed on support, self-determination and the acceptance of difference as opposed to the shame and stigma that have become associated with medical embodiment constructions of disorder. While such an approach is more focused on the structural issues faced by intersex people it still highlights the pluralistic and interdisciplinary means needed to enable intersex justice. Law is not the only, nor even the primary, tool through which intersex needs can be met. Buy-in from healthcare professionals is necessary to shift paradigmatic conceptions of intersex embodiment and address the long-term goals of intersex people. Our research on Malta highlighted what can happen where the aims of law and healthcare are misaligned.

This is not to say that the legal frameworks that we have presented in this book are completely unhelpful in terms of their conceptualization of intersex embodiment. Some intersex embodied people *are* non-binary; some identify as LGBT, and some do not. These varied experiences require specific measures to support and protect the individual's rights and wellbeing. However, the major failing of most of the legal constructions of intersex embodiment set out in this book (in addition to failing to challenge medical power/knowledge) is that they each present a fragmented account of intersex embodiment, depicting it to be wholly one thing or another: intersex *is* non-binary or intersex *is* LGBT. This typical legislative approach fails to understand the rich multifaceted ways in which intersex individuals understand their own embodiment. While Malta went some way towards a more enriched understanding of intersex, the fragmentation between law and medicine has significantly hindered the progress that the GIGESC Act was designed to bring. Law must not only have medical buy-in to be effective, but it must be carefully crafted so as to avoid this reductive account of intersex embodiment. To ensure this, it must *meaningfully* engage with the intersex community by speaking with and listening to a wide range of individuals and not over-rely on secondary sources of information to produce and devise law and policy. We too classify this book as a secondary source and are conscious that it should never take the place of these conversations between legislators, policy makers and intersex communities. While we draw on interviews with intersex people which have helped us examine the impact of law in depth, neither author speaks for the intersex communities. Consequently, those who are in a position of power and instilling change must create platforms where they can elicit dialogue.

Regardless of whether intersex *individuals* understand themselves through medical or other frameworks they are broadly aligned on the idea that non-therapeutic medical interventions should be prohibited. Surgeries have a lasting effect on the body. Surgeries produce subjects – telling individuals who they are, what they are capable of and what their bodies are for. As Roen notes: 'These effects of medicalization inevitably are part of the process of embodied becoming: the surgically altered child does not come into being as an embodied subject without such medical interventions on the body having an impact' (Roen, 2009: 32). These surgeries can shape individual narratives – indeed, reflecting on John Money's work, this was the rationale for performing these surgeries. For some, John Money's vision came true – the surgeries help confirm their place *within* the sex binary. For others, however, surgeries produce a different narrative either confirming their place as disordered (Asch, 2006) or placing them (at least in terms of self-narrative) outside the sex binary (Holmes, 2002, 2008; Roen, 2009: 21). The ambiguity of the shaping effects these surgeries have on individual psyches and the lack of longitudinal data justifying their continuance is enough to rationalize their prohibition until an individual can consent to such interventions. In their place we need to ensure that intersex embodiment is constructed through a lens of care which empowers intersex people – supporting them to live the lives and identities that they want to live. Where surgery closes down options – delaying surgical interventions allows multiple possibilities for intersex people to determine their own futures (Griffiths, 2021). Intersex justice, therefore, is characterized by its place 'as a technology of subject formation, object of knowledge, analytic category, and mode of dis/identification – trouble[ing] the notion that only with a common language or onto-epistemology can one belong in world of differences' (Rubin, 2017: 147). Intersex justice is inherently pluralistic in its self-understanding and its acceptance that similar interventions and harms can be experienced very differently.

Intersex embodiment, consequently, must be seen as inherently pluralistic in its production through materiality, institutions and cultural knowledge that are contingent to particular times, places, contexts and regulatory frameworks. These different intersecting dimensions produce diverse understandings of intersex embodiment at different times and places. Understanding these different approaches, and how they – in turn – are understood by intersex people has been a core aim of this book, and we call upon all researchers, legislators and policy makers to meaningfully engage with intersex embodied people. To finish, we hope that we have articulated a conception of intersex embodiment that goes beyond traditional categories of disorder and identity in order to outline a more situated, contextful and considered account of intersex people.

Once more, we are indebted to those intersex individuals who have given up their time to contribute to this project.

References

Ahmed, S.F., Achermann, J.C., Arlt, W., Balen, A.H., Conway, G., Edwards, Z.L. et al (2016) 'UK guidance on the initial evaluation of an infant or an adolescent with a suspected disorder of sex development (revised 2015)', *Clinical Endocrinology* 84: 771–88.

Althoff, N. (2018) 'Gender diversity in law: the German perspective' in J.M. Scherpe, A. Dutta, and T. Helms (eds) *The Legal Status of Intersex Persons*, Cambridge: Intersentia, pp 393–412.

Amnesty International (2017) *First Do No Harm; Ensuring the Rights of Children with Variations of Sex Characteristics in Denmark and Germany*, London: Amnesty International.

Anonymous (2016) 'Austrian intersex person denied 'third gender' passport', *The Local*, [online] 11 October, www.thelocal.at/20161011/austrian-intersex-person-denied-third-gender-passport [Accessed 17 June 2021].

Asch, A. (2006) 'Appearance-altering surgery, children's sense of self, and parental love' in E. Parens (ed) *Surgically Shaping Children: Technology, Ethics and the Pursuit of Normality*, New York: Johns Hopkins University Press, pp 227–52.

Ashley, F. (2018) 'Don't be so hateful: the insufficiency of anti-discrimination and hate crime laws in improving trans well-being', *University of Toronto Law Journal* 68: 1–36.

Associated Press in Denver (2015) 'Colorado resident sues US government to put third gender option on passports', *The Guardian*, [online] 26 October, www.theguardian.com/world/2015/oct/26/passports-third-gender-option-lawsuit-colorado-resident [Accessed 17 June 2021].

Australian Civil Liberties Union (2001) 'Chapter 18 – gay, lesbian, bisexual, transgender and intersex rights', *Australian Civil Liberties Union*, [online] www.angelfire.com/folk/aclu/gaylesbianrights.htm [Accessed 17 November 2021].

Australian Government (2011) 'Consolidation of Commonwealth anti-discrimination laws discussion paper', *Australian Government*, [online] www.ag.gov.au/Consultations/Documents/ConsolidationofCommonwealthanti-discriminationlaws/Consolidation%20of%20Commonwealth%20Anti-Discrimination%20Laws.pdf [Accessed 17 November 2021].

Australian Government (2012) 'Exposure draft of the Human Rights and Anti-Discrimination Bill 2012', *Australian Human Rights Commission*, [online] December https://humanrights.gov.au/sites/default/files/20121206_hrad_bill.pdf [Accessed 17 November 2021].

Australian Human Rights Commission (2011) 'Consolidation of Commonwealth discrimination law: Australian Human Rights Commission submission to the Attorney-General's Department', *Australian Human rights Commission*, [online] 6 December https://humanrights.gov.au/our-work/legal/consolidation-commonwealth-discrimination-law#Heading266 [Accessed 17 November 2021].

Australian Senate Community Affairs Committee Secretariat (2013) *The Involuntary or Coerced Sterilisation of Intersex People in Australia*, Canberra: Parliament House, Senate Printing Unit.

Baker, L.L. (2017) 'Gender by *Dasein*? A Heideggerian critique of Suzanne Kessler and the medical management of infants born with disorders of sexual development', *Theoretical Medicine and Bioethics* 38: 447–63.

Baker, S. and Edwards, R. (2012) 'How many qualitative interviews is enough? Expert voices and early career reflections on sampling and cases in qualitative research', *National Centre for Research Methods Review Paper*, Southampton: National Centre for Research Methods.

Baratz, A., Sharp, M.K. and Sandberg, D.E. (2014) 'Disorders of sex development peer support' in O. Hiort and S.F. Ahmed (eds) *Understanding Differences and Disorders of Sex Development (DSD)*, Basel: Karger, pp 99–112.

Barclay, S., Bernstein, M. and Marshall, A. (2009) 'The challenge of law: sexual orientation, gender identity and social movements' in S. Barclay, M. Bernstein and A. Marshall (eds) *Queer Mobilizations: LGBT Activists Confront the Law*, London: New York University Press, pp 1–19.

Barker, N. (2012) *Not the Marrying Kind: A Feminist Critique of Same-Sex Marriage*, Basingstoke: Palgrave.

Barlow, A., Duncan, S., James, G. and Park, A. (2005) *Cohabitation, Marriage and the Law: Social change and Legal Reform in the 21st Century*, Oxford: Hart Publishing.

Benetti-Pinto, C., Bedone, A., Magna, L.A. and Marques-Neto, J. (2002) 'Factors associated with the reduction of bone density in patients with gonadal dysgenesis', *Fertility and Sterility* 77: 571–5.

Bennecke, E., Thyen, U., Grüters, A., Lux, A. and Köhler, B. (2017) 'Health-related quality of life and psychological well-being in adults with differences/disorders of sex development', *Clinical Endocrinology* 86: 634–43.

Bennecke, E., Werner-Rosen, K., Thyen, U. et al. (2015) 'Subjective need for psychological support (PsySupp) in parents of children and adolescents with disorders of sex development (dsd)', *European Journal of Pediatrics* 174: 1287–97.

Benson, S.R. (2005) 'Hacking the gender binary myth: recognizing fundamental rights for the intersexed', *Cardozo Journal of Law and Gender* 12(1): 31–64.

Bettcher, T.M. (2015) 'Intersexuality, transgender, and transsexuality', in L. Disch and M. Hawkesworth (eds) *The Oxford Handbook of Feminist Theory*, pp 407–27.

Bird, J. (2005) 'Outside the law: intersex, medicine and the discourse rights', *Cardozo Journal of Law and Gender* 12(1): 65–80.

Blackless, M., Charuvastra, A., Derryck, A., Fausto-Sterling, A., Lauzanne, K. and Lee, E. (2000) 'How sexually dimorphic are we? A review article', *American Journal of Human Biology* 12: 151–66.

Bowcott, O. (2019) 'UK refusal to issue gender-neutral passports unlawful, appeal court told', *The Guardian*, [online] 3 December www.theguardian.com/world/2019/dec/03/home-office-taken-to-court-of-appeal-over-refusal-of-gender-neutral-passports [Accessed 17 June 2021].

Boyse K.L., Gardner, M., Marvicsin, D.J. and Sandberg, D.E. (2014) '"It was an overwhelming thing": parents' needs after infant diagnosis with congenital adrenal hyperplasia', *Journal of Pediatric Nursing* 29: 436–41.

Bracton, H. (1968) *Henry de Bracton, On The Laws and Customs of England 1240–1260 vols 1–4* (trans. S.E. Thorne), Cambridge, MA: Harvard University Press.

Braun, V. and Clarke, V. (2006) 'Using thematic analysis in psychology', *Qualitative Research in Psychology* 3: 77–101.

Briffa, N. (2014) 'White Paper – Identita' tal-ġeneru – Suġġerimenti' *Maltese Government Public Consultations*, [online] 6 December https://meae.gov.mt/en/Public_Consultations/MSDC/Documents/2014%20-%20GIGESC/Nicholas%20Briffa.pdf [Accessed 18 November 2021].

Broster, L.R. (1953) 'Adrenal pseudohermaphroditism', *British Medical Journal* 12: 1288.

Butler, J. (1993) *Gender Trouble: Feminism and the Subversion of Identity*, London: Routledge.

Cabral, M. (2015) 'Statement from GATE – Global Action for Trans* Equality', *Reproductive Health Matters* 23: 196.

Cabrielli, D. (2020) *Employment Law in Context*, Oxford: Oxford University Press.

Callens, N., Van Kuyk, M., van Kuppenveld, J., Drop, S., Cohen-Kettenis, P. and Dessens, A. (2016) 'Recalled and current gender role behavior, gender identity and sexual orientation in adults with disorders/differences of sex development', *Hormones and Behavior* 86: 8–20.

Cannoot, P. (2020) 'Do parents really know best? Informed consent to sex assigning and "normalising" treatment of minors with variations of sex characteristics', *Culture, Health & Sexuality* 23: 564–78.

Carmichael, P. and Alderson, J. (2004) 'Psychological care in disorders of sexual differentiation and determination' in A. Balen, S. Creighton, M. Davies, J. MacDougall and R. Stanhope (eds) *Paediatric and Adolescent Gynaecology*, Cambridge: Cambridge University Press, pp 158–78.

Carpenter, M. (2012) 'An annulment of marriage due to being intersex in the Family Court: in the marriage of C and D (falsely called C)' *Intersex Human Rights Australia*, [online] 12 February https://oii.org.au/16808/annulment-marriage-due-intersex-marriage-falsely-called/ [Accessed 1 July 2021].

Carpenter, M. (2014) 'High Court: NSW Registrar of Births, Deaths and Marriages v. Norrie' *Intersex Human Rights Australia*, [online] 1 February, https://oii.org.au/24421/high-court-nsw-registrar-v-norrie/ [Accessed 11 November 2021].

Carpenter, M. (2016) 'The Family Court case Re: Carla (Medical procedure) [2016] Fam CA 7' *Intersex Human Rights Australia*, [online] 8 December, https://oii.org.au/31036/re-carla-family-court/ [Accessed 11 November 2021].

Carpenter, M. (2018) 'The "normalization" of intersex bodies and "othering" of intersex identities in Australia', *Journal of Bioethical Inquiry* 15(4): 487–95.

Carpenter, M. (2021) 'Intersex human rights, sexual orientation, gender identity, sex characteristics and the Yogyakarta Principles plus 10', *Culture, Health & Sexuality* 23: 516–32.

Chadwick, P.M., Smyth, A. and Liao, L-M. (2014) 'Improving self-esteem in women diagnosed with Turner Syndrome: results of a pilot intervention', *Journal of Pediatric and Adolescent Gynecology* 27: 129–32.

Charlebois, J.B. (2014) 'Intersex women: the extreme political subject of feminism', *Recherches Feminists* 27(1): 237–55.

Chase, C. (2017) 'Hermaphrodites with attitude: mapping the emergence of intersex political activism' in B.K. Scott, S.E. Cayleff, A. Donadey and I. Lara (eds) *Women in Culture: An Intersectional Anthology for Gender and Women's Studies* (2nd edn), West Sussex: Blackwell Publishing, pp 300–14.

Chief Minister, Treasury and Economic Development Directorate (2021) 'Protecting the rights of intersex people in medical settings' *Australian Capital Territory Government*, [online] www.cmtedd.act.gov.au/policystrategic/the-office-of-lgbtiq-affairs/protecting-the-rights-of-intersex-people-in-medical-settings [Accessed 15 November 2021].

Chowdhury, T. (2020) *Time, Temporality and Legal Judgement*, Oxon: Routledge.

Clayton, P.E., Miller, W.L., Oberfield, S.E., Ritzén, E.M., Sippell, W.G. and Speiser, P.W., ESPE/ LWPES CAH Working Group (2002) 'Consensus statement on 21-hydroxylase deficiency from the European Society for Paediatric Endocrinology and the Lawson Wilkins Pediatric Endocrine Society', *Hormone Research* 58: 188–95.

Clune-Taylor, C. (2019) 'Securing cisgendered futures: intersex management under the "disorders of sex development" treatment model', *Hypatia* 34: 690–712.

Coglianese, C. (2001) 'Social movements, law, and society: the institutionalization of the environmental movement', *University of Pennsylvania Law Review* 150(1): 85–118.

Cohen, C. (1997) 'Punks, bulldaggers, and welfare queens: the radical potential of queer politics', *GLQ* 3: 437–65.

Cohen-Kettenis, P. (2005) 'Gender change in 46, XY persons with 5α-Reductase-2 Deficiency and 17β-Hydroxysteroid Dehydrogenase-3 Deficiency', *Archives of Sexual Behavior* 34(4): 399–410.

Coke, E.D.W. (1628) *The First Part of the Institutes of the Laws of England*, London: Society of Stationers.

Colapinto, J. (1997) 'The true story of John/Joan', *Rolling Stone*, 11 December, 775: 54, 56–8, 60–2, 64, 66, 68, 70–2, 92, 94–7.

Colapinto. J. (2000) *As Nature Made Him: The Boy Who Was Raised as a Girl*, London: Quartet.

Collins, H. (2003) 'Discrimination, equality and social inclusion', *Modern Law Review* 66: 16–43.

Commissioner for Human Rights (2021) 'Human rights of lesbian, gay, bisexual, transgender and intersex people (LGBTI)' *Council of Europe*, [online] www.coe.int/en/web/commissioner/thematic-work/lgbti [Accessed 15 November 2021].

Consideration of Bills Committee (24 March 2015) 'Bill No. 70 – Gender Identity, Gender Expression and Sex Characteristics Bill' *House of Representatives Standing Committees for the Consideration of Draft Laws, Malta*, [online] 20150324_046d_kun.docx (live.com) [Accessed 30 November 2021].

Cooper, D. and Renz, F. (2016) 'If the state decertified gender, what might happen to its meaning and value?', *Law and Society* 43: 483.

Cornell, D. (1995) *The Imaginary Domain: Abortion, Pornography and Sexual Harassment*, London: Routledge.

Council of Europe (2015) *Human Rights and Intersex People: Issue Paper*, Strasbourg: Council of Europe.

Cowan, S. (2009) 'Looking back (to)wards the body: medicalization and the GRA', *Social & Legal Studies* 18(2): 247–52.

Creighton, S., Alderson, J., Brown, S. and Minto, C.L. (2002) 'Medical photography: ethics, consent and the intersex patient', *BJU International* 89: 67–72.

Creighton, S., Balen, A., Breen, L. and Liao, L-M. (2018) 'An introduction to pediatric and adolescent gynaecology practice' in S. Creighton, A. Balen, L. Breen and L-M. Liao (eds) *Paediatric and Adolescent Gynaecology: A Problem-Based Approach*, Cambridge: Cambridge University Press, pp 1–7.

Creighton, S., Chernausek, S.D., Romao, R., Ransley, P. and Salle, J.P. (2012) 'Timing and nature of reconstructive surgery for disorders of sex development – introduction', *Journal of Pediatric Urology* 8: 602–10.

Creighton, S., Michala, L., Mushtaq, I. and Yaron, M. (2014) 'Childhood surgery for ambiguous genitalia: glimpses of practice changes or more of the same?', *Psychology and Sexuality* 5: 34–43.

Creighton, S., Minto, C.L. and Steele, S.J. (2001) 'Objective cosmetic and anatomical outcomes at adolescence of feminising surgery for ambiguous genitalia done in childhood', *The Lancet* 358: 124–5.

Crenshaw, K. (1988) 'Race, reform and retrenchment: transformation and legitimation in anti-discrimination law', *Harvard Law Review* 101: 1331–87.

Crerand, C.E., Kapa, H.M., Litteral, J.L., Nahata, L., Combs, B., Indyk, J.A. et al (2019) 'Parent perceptions of psychosocial care for children with differences of sex development', *Journal of Pediatric Urology* 15: 522, e1–.e8.

Crouch, M. and McKenzie, H. (2006) *The Logic of Small Samples in Interview-Based Qualitative Research*, London: SAGE Publications.

Crouch, N.S., Liao, L-M., Woodhouse, C.R.J., Conway, G.S. and Creighton, S. (2008) 'Sexual function and genital sensitivity following feminizing genitoplasty for congenital adrenal hyperplasia', *Journal of Urology* 179: 634–8.

Darlington Statement (2017) 'The Darlington Statement' *Intersex Human Rights Australia*, [online] 10 March https://ihra.org.au/darlington-statement/ [Accessed 10 November 2021].

Daston, L. and Park, K. (1985) 'Hermaphrodites in Renaissance France', *Critical Matrix* 1: 1.

Davidson, H. (2014) 'Third gender must be recognised by NSW after Norrie wins legal battle' *The Guardian*, [online] 2 April www.theguardian.com/world/2014/apr/02/third-gender-must-be-recognised-by-nsw-after-norrie-wins-legal-battle [Accessed 17 June 2021].

Davis, G. (2015) *Contesting Intersex: The Dubious Diagnosis*, New York: New York University Press.

Department of Health (2021) 'I am equal: future directions for ACT's intersex community' *Victoria State Government*, [online] www.health.vic.gov.au/publications/i-am-equal [Accessed 15 November 2021].

Deutscher Ethikrat (2012a) 'German Ethics Council: intersex people should be recognized, supported and protected from discrimination' [online] 23 February www.ethikrat.org/en/press-releases/2012/german-ethics-council-intersex-people-should-be-recognized-supported-and-protected-from-discrimination/ [Accessed 17 June 2021].

Deutscher Ethikrat (2012b) *Intersexualität Stellungnahme*, Berlin: Herausgegeben vom Deutschen Ethik.

Dewhurst, C.J. and Gordon, R.R. (1969) *The Intersexual Disorders*, London: Baillière, Tindall and Cassell.

Diamond, M. and Sigmundson, K. (1997) 'Sex reassignment at birth: long-term review and clinical implications', *Archives of Pediatrics and Adolescent Medicine* 151: 298–304.

Dietz, C. (2018) 'Governing legal embodiment: on the limits of self-declaration', *Feminist Legal Studies* 26(2): 185–204.

Dietz, C. and Pearce, R. (2020) 'Depathologising gender: vulnerability in trans health law' in C. Dietz, M., Travis and M. Thomson (eds) *A Jurisprudence of the Body*, Cham: Palgrave Socio-Legal Studies, pp 179–203.

Dietz, C., Travis, M. and Thomson, M. (2020) 'Nobody, anybody, somebody, everybody: a jurisprudence of the body' in C. Dietz, M. Travis, and M. Thomson (eds) *A Jurisprudence of the Body*, Cham: Palgrave Socio-Legal Studies, pp 1–13.

Doell, R.G. and Longino, H.E. (1988) 'Sex hormones and human behaviour: a critique of the linear model', *Journal of Homosexuality* 15: 55–78.

Donnelly, M. and Kilkelly, U. (2011) 'Child-friendly healthcare: delivering on the right to be heard', *Medical Law Review* 19: 27–54.

Dreger, A. (1998) *Hermaphrodites and the Medical Invention of Sex*, Cambridge, MA: Harvard University Press.

Dreger, A. and Herndon, A. (2009) 'Progress and politics in the intersex rights movement: feminist theory in action', *GLQ: A Journal of Lesbian and Gay Studies* 15: 199–224.

Duggan, L. (2002) 'The new homonormativity: The sexual politics of neoliberalism' in R. Castronovo and D. Nelson (eds) *Materializing Democracy: Toward a Revitalized Cultural Politics*, Durham, NC: Duke University Press, pp 175–94.

Duggan, L. (2003) *The Twilight of Equality? Neoliberalism, Cultural Politics, and the Attack on Democracy*, Boston, MA: Beacon.

Dunne, P. and Mulder, J. (2018) 'Beyond the binary: towards a third sex category in Germany?', *German Law Journal* 19(3): 627–48.

Earp, B., Hendry, J. and Thomson, M. (2017) 'Reason and paradox in medical and family law: shaping children's bodies', *Medical Law Review* 25: 604–27.

Easten, R. (2003) 'Research Brief No 2003/02 Protecting transgender rights under Queensland's Discrimination Law Amendment Act 2002' *Queensland Parliamentary Library*, [online] 27 July, www.parliament.qld.gov.au/documents/explore/researchpublications/researchbriefs/2003/200302.pdf [Accessed 11 November 2021].

Ellens, R., Bakula, D.M., Mullins, A.J., Scott Reves, K., Austin, P., Baskin, L. et al (2017) 'Psychological adjustment in parents of children born with atypical genitalia one year after their child undergoes genitoplasty', *Journal of Urology* 198(4): 914–20.

Engberg, H., Möller, A., Hagenfeldt, K., Nordenskjöld, A. and Frisén, L. (2016) 'The experience of women living with Congenital Adrenal Hyperplasia: impact of the condition and care given', *Clinical Endocrinology* 85: 21–8.

Ernst, M.M., Chen, D., Kennedy, K., Jewell, T., Sajwani, A., Foley, C. et al (2019) 'Disorders of sex development (DSD) web-based information: quality survey of DSD team websites', *International Journal of Pediatric Endocrinology* 1: 1–11.

Ernst, M.M., Kogan, B.A. and Lee, P.A. (2020) 'Gender identity: a psychosocial primer for providing care to patients with a disorder/difference of sex development and their families [individualized care for patients with intersex (Disorders/differences of sex development): Part 2]', *Journal of Pediatric Urology* 16: 606–11.

Ernst, M.M., Liao, L-M., Baratz, A.B. and Sandberg, D.E. (2018) 'Disorders of sex development/intersex: gaps in psychosocial care for children', *Paediatrics* 142: 1–4.

European Parliament (2017) *Promoting the Human Rights of and Eliminating Discrimination against Intersex People* (Resolution 2191).

Fausto-Sterling, A. (2000) *Sexing the Body: Gender Politics and the Construction of Sexuality*, New York: Basic Books.

Feder, E. (2014) *Making Sense of Intersex: Changing Ethical Perspectives in Biomedicine*, Indianapolis: Indiana University Press.

Feder, E.K. (2021) 'Feminist theory and intersex activism: thinking between and beyond', *Philosophy Compass*, e12764 [online] https://doi.org/10.1111/phc3.12764.

Feinberg, J. (1994) *Freedom and Fulfilment: Philosophical Essays*, Princeton, NJ: Princeton University Press.

Fineman, M. (1992) 'Feminist theory in law: the difference it makes', *Columbia Journal of Gender and Law* 2: 1–23.

Fineman, M. (2008) 'The vulnerable subject: anchoring equality in the human condition', *Yale Journal of Law and Feminism* 20: 1–23.

Fineman, M. (2010) 'The vulnerable subject and the responsive state', *Emory Law Journal* 60: 251–75.

Fineman, M. (2012) '"Elderly" as vulnerable: rethinking the nature of individual and societal responsibility', *The Elder Law Journal* 20: 101–41.

Fineman, M. (2014) 'Vulnerability, resilience, and LGBT youth', *Temple Political & Civil Rights Law Review* 23: 307–29.

Fineman, M. (2017) 'Vulnerability and inevitable inequality', *Oslo Law Review* 4: 133–49.

Fineman, M. (2020) 'Reasoning from the body: universal vulnerability and social justice' in C. Dietz, M. Travis and M. Thomson (eds) *A Jurisprudence of the Body*, Cham: Palgrave Socio-Legal Studies, pp 17–34.

Foucault, M. (1980) *Herculine Barbin*, New York: Pantheon Books.

Fox, M. and Murphy, T. (2013) 'The body, bodies, embodiment: feminist legal engagement with health' in V. Monro and M. Davies (eds) *The Ashgate Research Companion to Feminist Legal Theory*, London: Ashgate, pp 249–67.

Fox, M. and Thomson, M. (2005) 'Short changed? The law and ethics of male circumcision', *The International Journal of Children's Rights* 13: 161–82.

Fox, M. and Thomson, M. (2010) 'HIV/AIDS and circumcision: lost in translation', *Journal of Medical Ethics* 36: 798–801.

Fox, M. and Thomson, M. (2012) 'The new politics of male circumcision: HIV/AIDS, health law and social justice', *Legal Studies* 32: 255–81.

Fox, M. and Thomson, M. (2017) 'Bodily integrity, embodiment, and the regulation of parental choice', *Journal of Law and Society* 44: 501–31.

Fox, M., Thomson, M. and Warburton, J. (2020) 'Embodied integrity, shaping surgeries and the profoundly disabled child' in C. Dietz, M. Travis and M. Thomson (eds) *A Jurisprudence of the Body*, Cham: Palgrave Socio-Legal Studies, pp 281–314.

Fraser, N. (2003) 'Social justice in the age of identity politics' in N. Fraser and A. Honneth (eds) *Redistribution or Recognition? A Political-Philosophical Exchange*, London: Verso, pp 7–109.

Fredman, S. (2016) 'Substantive equality revisited', *International Journal of Constitutional Law* 14: 712–38.

Furtado, P., Moraes, F., Lago, R. and Barros, L. (2012) 'Gender dysphoria associated with disorders of sex development', *Nature Reviews Urology* 9(11): 620–7.

Garland, F. (2014) 'Section 15 Property (Relationships) Act 1976: compensation, substantive equality and empirical realities', *New Zealand Law Review* 3: 355–81.

Garland, F. and Travis, M. (2018) 'Legislating intersex equality: building the resilience of intersex people through law', *Legal Studies* 38(4): 587–606.

Garland, F. and Travis, M. (2020a) 'Making the state responsible: intersex embodiment, medical jurisdiction, and state responsibility', *Journal of Law and Society* 47: 298–324.

Garland, F. and Travis, M. (2020b) 'Temporal bodies: emergencies, emergence, and intersex embodiment' in C. Dietz, M. Travis and M. Thomson (eds) *A Jurisprudence of the Body*, Cham: Palgrave Socio-Legal Studies. Palgrave Macmillan, pp 119–47.

Garland, F. and Travis, M. (2020c) 'Queering the queer/non-queer binary: problematizing the "I" in LGBTI+' in S. Raj and P. Dunne (eds) *A The Queer Outside in Law*, Cham: Palgrave Macmillan, pp 143–64.

Garland, F., Lalor, K. and Travis, M. (2022) 'Exploring the scalar limitations of the United Nations: intersex activism and international legal recourse', *Human Right Law Review*, doi: ngac020.

Garland, F., Samuelsen, N. and Travis, M. (2019) 'Law and intersex in Norway: challenges and opportunities', [online] https://pdfs.semanticscholar.org/e3d0/1b8a91c05d9c29f628cc8ccc13b820f4fbf9.pdf [Accessed 14 November 2021].

Garland, F., Thomson, M., Travis, M. and Warburton, J. (2021) 'Management of "disorders of sex development"/intersex variations in children: results from a freedom of information exercise', *Medical Law International* 21: 116–46.

Garland, J. and Slokenberga, S. (2018) 'Protecting the rights of children with intersex conditions from non-consensual gender-conforming medical interventions: the view from Europe', *Medical Law Review* 27: 482–508.

Gender Wellbeing Clinic (2021a) 'Transgender health & psycho-social care service' *Gender Wellbeing Clinic*, [online] https://genderwellbeingclinic.business.site/ [Accessed 18 November 2021].

Gender Wellbeing Clinic (2021b) 'Referral form to the Gender Wellbeing Clinic' *Gender Wellbeing Clinic*, [online] https://deputyprimeminister.gov.mt/en/forms/Documents/Gender_Wellbeing_Clinic_Referral_Form.pdf [Accessed 17 June 2021].

Gilani, S. (2020) 'On the discursive-material enactment of criminal violence: how death and injury come to matter to the criminal law' *Law Culture and the Humanities* https://doi.org/10.1177/1743872120966814.

Gilani, S. (2021) 'Bionic bodies, posthuman violence and the disembodied criminal subject', *Law and Critique* 32: 171–93.

Goodrich, P. (2000) 'Rhetoric and somatics: training the body to do the work of law', *Law Text Culture* 2: 241–70.

Government Equalities Office (2018a) 'LGBT action plan: improving the lives of lesbian, gay, bisexual and transgender people' *Government Equalities Office*, [online] July https://assets.publishing.service.gov.uk/government/uploads/system/uploads/attachment_data/file/721367/GEO-LGBT-Action-Plan.pdf [Accessed 15 November 2021].

Government Equalities Office (2018b) 'National LGBT survey: research report' *Government Equalities Office*, [online] https://assets.publishing.service.gov.uk/government/uploads/system/uploads/attachment_data/file/721704/LGBT-survey-research-report.pdf [Accessed 23 November 2021].

Government Equalities Office (2019) 'Call for Evidence on Variations of Sex Characteristics' *Government Equalities Office*, [online] https://assets.publishing.service.gov.uk/government/uploads/system/uploads/attachment_data/file/771459/VSC_call_for_evidence_Web_Accessible.pdf [Accessed 05 July 2022].

Government of the Netherlands (2018) 'Equal rights for lesbian, gay, bisexual and transgender and intersex (LGBTI)' *Government of the Netherlands*, [online] www.government.nl/topics/human-rights/human-rights-worldwide/equal-rights-for-lesbian-gay-bisexual-and-transgender-and-intersex-lgbti [Accessed 15 November 2021].

Grabham, E. (2012) 'Bodily integrity and the surgical management of intersex', *Body and Society* 18: 1–26.

Graham, A. (2019) 'A theory of discrimination law, written by Tarunabh Khaitan', *Journal of Moral Philosophy* 5: 666–70.

Grear, A. (2006) 'Human rights–human bodies? Some reflections on corporate human rights distortion, the legal subject, embodiment and human rights theory', *Law and Critique* 17: 171–99.

Grear, A. (2007) 'Challenging corporate "humanity": legal disembodiment, embodiment and human rights', *Human Rights Law Review* 7: 511–43.

Greenberg, J. (2012) *Intersexuality and the Law*, New York: New York University Press.

Greenhow, A. and Weinert, K. (2019) 'Diversity, equity and inclusion (or exclusion) in sport: a review of the Caster Semenya case', *Griffith Journal of Law and Human Dignity* 7: 248–74.

Greenwood, E. (1957) 'Attributes of a profession', *Social Work* 2: 45–55.

Grenfell, L. (2003) 'Embracing law's categories: anti-discrimination laws and transgenderism', *Yale Journal of Law and Feminism* 15: 51–98.

Griffiths, D.A. (2018a) 'Shifting syndromes: sex chromosome variations and intersex classifications', *Social Studies of Science* 48: 125–48.

Griffiths, D.A. (2018b) 'Diagnosing sex: intersex surgery and "sex change" in Britain 1930–1955', *Sexualities* 21: 476–95.

Griffiths, D.A. (2021) 'Queering the moment of hypospadias "repair"', *GLQ* 27: 499–523.

Grosz, E. (1994) *Volatile Bodies: Toward a Corporeal Feminism*, Bloomington: Indiana University Press.

Guba, E. (1990) 'The alternative paradigm dialogue' in E. Guba (ed) *The Paradigm Dialogue*, London: Sage, pp 17–29.

Hampson, J. (1955) 'Hermaphroditic genital appearance, rearing and eroticism in hyperadrenocorticism', *Bulletin of the Johns Hopkins Hospital* 96: 265–73.

Harding, R. (2010) *Regarding Sexuality: Legal Consciousness in Lesbian and Gay Lives*, Oxon: Routledge.

Harding, R. and Taşcıoğlu, C (2018) 'Supported decision-making from theory to practice: implementing the right to enjoy legal capacity', *Societies*, 8(2): 25.

Hegarty, P. and Chase, C. (2000) 'Intersex activism, feminism and psychology: opening a dialogue on theory, research and clinical practice', *Feminism & Psychology* 10(1): 17–132.

Hegarty, P. and Roen, K. (2018) 'Shaping parents, shaping penises: how medical teams frame parents' decisions in response to hypospadias', *British Journal of Health Psychology* 23: 967–81.

Helms, T. (2018) 'Germany (the 2013 German Law)' in J.M. Scherpe, A. Dutta and T. Helms (eds) *The Legal Status of Intersex Persons*, Cambridge: Intersentia, pp 369–82.

Herdt, G. (1993) 'Introduction: third sexes and third genders' in G. Herdt (ed) *Third Sex, Third Gender: Beyond Sexual Dimorphism in Culture and History*, New York: Zone Books, pp 21–81.

Higgins, T., Williams, D. and Nash, D.F.E. (1951) *The Urology of Childhood*, London: Butterworth and Co.

Hirschfeld, M. (1906) 'Drei Falle von irrtfimlicher Geschlechtsbestimmung', *Medizinische Reform, Wochenschrift for Soziale Medizin* XIV: 614.

Holmes, M. (2002) 'Rethinking the meaning and management of intersexuality', *Sexualities* 5: 159–80.

Holmes, M. (2004) 'Locating third sexes', *Transformations* 8: 1–14.

Holmes, M. (2008a) *Intersex: A Perilous Difference*, Selinsgrove: Susquehanna University Press.

Holmes, M. (2008b) 'Mind the gaps: intersex and (re-productive) spaces in disability studies and bioethics', *Journal of Bioethical Inquiry* 5(2–3): 169–81.

Holmes, M. (2009) 'Introduction: straddling past, present and future' in M. Holmes (ed) *Critical Intersex*, Surrey: Ashgate, pp 1–12.

Holstein, J.A. and Gubrium, J.F. (1995) *The Active Interview*, London: Sage.

Hooley, J. (2006) 'Normalising transgender and policing transgression: anti-discrimination law reform ten years on', *Australian Feminist Law Journal* 25: 79–98.

Horowicz, E. (2017) 'Intersex children: who are we really treating?', *Medical Law International* 17: 183–218.

Hughes, I., Nihoul-Fékété, C., Thomas, B., and Cohen-Kettenis, P.T. (2007) 'Consequences of the ESPE/LWPES Guidelines for Diagnosis and Treatment of Disorders of Sex Development', *Best Practice & Research Clinical Endocrinology & Metabolism* 21: 351–65.

Hughes, I.A. (2010) 'The quiet revolution: disorders of sex development. Best practice & research', *Clinical Endocrinology & Metabolism* 24: 159–62.

ILGA Europe (2017) 'Malta' *ILGA Europe Annual Review*, [online] www.ilga-europe.org/sites/default/files/2017/malta.pdf [Accessed 15 November 2021].

Immelt, S. (2006) 'Psychological adjustment in young children with chronic medical conditions', *Journal of Paediatric Nursing* 31: 362–77.

Intersex Greece (2021) 'Press release about the Bring-IN research project' *Intersex Greece*, [online] 2 November https://intersexgreece.org.gr/en/2021 November 02/press-release-about-bring-in-research-project/ [Accessed 10 November 2021].

Intersex Human Rights Australia (2014) 'Welcome!' *Intersex Human Rights Australia* [online] 4 April https://ihra.org.au/19853/welcome/ [Accessed 15 November 2021].

Intersex Human Rights Australia (2021) 'Public submissions' *Intersex Human Rights Australia*, [online] https://ihra.org.au/category/articles/submissions/ [Accessed 15 November 2021].

Jarvis, J. (2018) 'First Dutch gender-neutral passport issued to intersex citizen' *The Evening Standard*, [online] 19 October www.standard.co.uk/news/world/first-dutch-genderneutral-passport-issued-to-intersex-citizen-a3966891.html [Accessed 17 June 2021].

Johnson, P. (2010) '"An essentially private manifestation of human personality": constructions of homosexuality in the European Court of Human Rights', *Human Rights Law Review* 10: 67–97.

Jones, C. (2022) '"This is what I am and who I am": exploring authorship and ethics in intersex research and reflective diaries' in M. Walker (ed) *Interdisciplinary and Global Perspectives on Intersex*, Cham: Palgrave Macmillan, pp 89–105.

Jones, T., Hart, B., Carpenter, M., Ansara, G., Leonard, W. and Lucke, J. (2016) *Intersex: Stories and Statistics from Australia*, Cambridge: Open Book Publishers.

Karkazis, K. (2008) *Fixing Sex: Intersex, Medical Authority, and Lived Experience*, Durham, NC: Duke University Press.

Karkazis, K. and Feder E. (2008) 'Naming the problem: disorders and their meanings', *The Lancet* 372: 2016–17.

Kessler, S. (1990) 'The medical construction of gender: case management of intersexed infants', *Signs: Journal of Women in Culture and Society* 16(1): 3–26.

Kessler, S. (1998) *Lessons from the Intersexed*, London: Rutgers University Press.

Keywood K. (2000) 'My body and other stories: anorexia nervosa and the legal politics of embodiment', *Social & Legal Studies* 9: 495–513.

Keywood, K. (2010) 'Vulnerable adults, mental capacity and social care refusal', *Medical Law Review* 18: 103–10.

Khaitan, T. (2015) *A Theory of Discrimination*, Oxford: Oxford University Press.

Kipnis, K. and Diamond, M. (1998) 'Pediatric ethics and the surgical assignment of sex', *The Journal of Clinical Ethics* 9: 398–410.

Kirkland, F. (2017) 'Great Ormond Street Hospital failing intersex children' *BBC News*, [Online] 12 October www.bbc.co.uk/news/uk-41593914 [Accessed 8 July 2021].

Kloppel, U. (2016) *Zur Aktualitat kosmetischer operationen 'uneindeutiger' genitalien im kindesalter*, Berlin: zentrum fur transdisziplinare geschlecterstudien der Humbolt-Universitat zu Berlin.

Knouse, J. (2005) 'Intersexuality and the social construction of anatomical sex', *Cardozo Journal of Law and Gender* 12(1): 135–54.

Kolbe, A. (2009) 'Intersex, a blank space in German law?' in M. Holmes (ed) *Critical Intersex*, Oxon: Routledge, pp 147–70.

Kotulak, R. (2003) 'Homosexuality may be issue of brain chemistry', *Chicago Tribune*, 17 November.

Koyama, E. and Weasel, L. (2002) 'From social construction to social justice: transforming how we teach about intersexuality', *Women's Studies Quarterly* 30(3/4): 169–78.

Kyriakou, A., Dessens, A., Bryce, J. et al (2016) 'Current models of care for disorders of sex development – results from an international survey of specialist centres', *Orphanet Journal of Rare Diseases* 11: 155–65.

Lachmund, J. (1998) 'Between scrutiny and treatment: physical diagnosis and the restructuring of 19th century medical practice', *Sociology of Health & Illness* 20: 779–801.

Lampalzer, U., Briken, P. and Schweizer, K. (2021) 'Psychosocial care and support in the field of intersex/diverse sex development (dsd): counselling experiences, localisation and needed improvements', *International Journal of Impotence Research* 33: 228–42.

Landau, T. (1903) 'Uber Hernaphroditen. Nebst einigen Bemerkungen fiber die Erkenntnis und die rechtliche Stellung dieser Individuen', *Berliner Klininische Wochenschrift* 15: 339–42.

Latham, J.R. (2017) '(Re)making sex: a praxiography of the gender clinic', *Feminist Theory*, 18(2): 177–204.

Legal and Constitutional Affairs Legislation Committee (2013) 'Human Rights and Anti-Discrimination Bill 2012' *Parliamentary Information*, [online] 24 January https://parlinfo.aph.gov.au/parlInfo/download/committees/commsen/cad30f53-4fdd-4b84-97b0-664c4a1ac185/toc_pdf/Legal%20and%20Constitutional%20Affairs%20Legislation%20Committee_2013_01_24_1618_Official.pdf;fileType=application%2Fpdf#search=%22committees/commsen/cad30f53-4fdd-4b84-97b0-664c4a1ac185/0000%22 [Accessed 15 November 2021].

Lee, P., Nordenstrom, A., Houk, C.P., Ahmed, S.F., Auchus, R., Baratz, A. et al (2016) 'Global disorders of sex development update since 2006: perceptions, approach and care', *Hormone Research in Paediatrics* 85: 158–80.

Lee, P.A., Fuqua, J.S., Houk, C.P., Kogan, B.A., Mazur, T. and Caldamone, A. (2020) 'Individualized care for patients with intersex (disorders/differences of sex development): part I', *Journal of Pediatric Urology* 16: 230–7.

Lee, P.A., Houk, C.P., Ahmed, S.F. et al, in Collaboration with the Participants in the International Consensus Conference on Intersex Organized by the Lawson Wilkins Pediatric Endocrine Society and the European Society for Paediatric Endocrinology (2006) 'Consensus statement on management of intersex disorders', *Paediatrics* 118: e488–e500.

Leiboff, M. (2015) 'Towards a jurisprudence of the embodied mind – Sarah Lund, *Forbrydelsen* and the mindful body', *Nordic Journal of Law and Social Research* 2: 77–92.

Liao, L-M. and Boyle, M. (2004) 'Surgical feminism: the right approach', *The Psychologist* 17: 459–62.

Liao, L-M. and Roen, K. (2014) 'Intersex/DSD post-Chicago: new developments and challenges for psychologists', *Psychology and Sexuality* 5: 1–4.

Liao, L-M. and Roen, K. (2019) 'The role of psychologists in multi-disciplinary teams for intersex/diverse sex development: interviews with British and Swedish clinical specialists', *Psychology and Sexuality* 12: 202–16.

Liao, L-M. and Roen, K. (2021) 'The role of psychologists in multi-disciplinary teams for intersex/diverse sex development: interviews with British and Swedish clinical specialists', *Psychology & Sexuality* 12: 202–16.

Liao, L-M. and Simmonds, M. (2013) 'Communicating with clients affected by diverse sex development' in J. Wiggins and A. Middleton (eds) *Getting the Message Across: Communication with Diverse Populations in Clinical Genetics*, Oxford: Oxford University Press, pp 42–60.

Liao, L-M., Green, H. Creighton, S., Crouch, N. and Conway, G. (2010) 'Service users' experiences of obtaining and giving information about disorders of sex development', *British Journal of Obstetrics & Gynaecology* 117: 193–9.

Liao, L-M., Hegarty, P., Creighton, S., Lundberg, T. and Roen, K. (2019) 'Clitoral surgery on minors: an interview study with clinical experts of differences of sex development', *BMJ Open* 9: 1–7.

Liao, L-M., Tacconelli, E., Wood, D., Conway, G. and Creighton, S.M. (2010) 'Adolescent girls with disorders of sex development: a needs analysis of transitional care', *Journal of Pediatric Urology* 6: 609–13.

Lobel, O. (2006–07) 'The paradox of extralegal activism: critical legal consciousness and transformative politics', *Harvard Law Review* 120: 937–89.

Loir, J.N. (1854) *Des sexes en matière d'état-civil: comment prévenir les erreurs résultant de leurs anomalies*, Paris: Cotillon. Ovide.

Lundberg, T., Hegarty P. and Roen, K. (2018) 'Making sense of "intersex" and "DSD": how laypeople understand and use terminology', *Psychology & Sexuality* 9: 161–73.

Lundberg, T., Roen, K., Hirschberg, A.L. and Frisén, L. (2016) '"It's part of me, not all of me": young women's experiences of receiving a diagnosis related to diverse sex development', *Journal of Pediatric and Adolescent Gynecology* 29: 338–43.

MacDougall, B. (2001) 'The celebration of same-sex marriage', *Ottawa Law Review* 32: 235–67.

Mak, G. (2005) 'Doubtful sex in civil law: nineteenth and early twentieth century proposals for ruling hermaphroditism', *Cardozo Journal of Law & Gender* 12: 197–212.

Mak, G. (2012) *Doubting Sex: Inscriptions, Bodies and Selves in Nineteenth-Century Hermaphrodite Case Histories*, Manchester: Manchester University Press.

Malatino, H. (2019) *Queer Embodiment: Monstrosity, Medical Violence, and Intersex Experience*, Lincoln: University of Nebraska Press.

Malta Declaration (2013) 'Public statement by the Third International Intersex Forum' *Intersex Human Rights Australia*, [online] https://ihra.org.au/24241/public-statement-by-the-third-international-intersex-forum/ [Accessed 9 November 2021].

Maltese Government (2015) 'Gender Identity, Gender Expression and Sex Characteristics Act' *Maltese Government*, [online] https://meae.gov.mt/en/Public_Consultations/MSDC/Pages/Consultations/GIGESC.aspx [Accessed 9 November 2021].

Maltese Government (2018) 'LGBTIQ Equality, Strategy and Action Plan 2018–2022' *Maltese Government*, [online] https://humanrights.gov.mt/en/Documents/Annual%20Report%20Web%20Final.pdf# [Accessed 9 November 2021].

Marusic, K. (2015) 'Hooray! A big, bad conversion therapy clinic for trans youth in Canada is shutting down' *MTV News*, [online] 17 December www.mtv.com/news/2690170/canada-camh-child-youth-and-family-gender-identity-clinic-shutting-down/ [Accessed 23 November 2021].

Matta, C. (2005) 'Ambiguous bodies and deviant sexualities: hermaphrodites, homosexuality, and surgery in the United States, 1850–1904', *Perspectives in Biology and Medicine* 48: 74–83.

McCauley, E. (2017) 'Challenges in educating patients and parents about differences in sex development', *American Journal of Medical Genetics* 175: 293–9.

Mednick, L., Gargollo, P., Oliva, M., Grant, R. and Borer, J. (2009) 'Stress and coping of parents of young children with bladder exstrophy', *Journal of Urology* 181: 1312–17.

Mendez, J.E. (2013) *Report of the Special Rapporteur on Torture and Other Cruel, Inhuman or Degrading Treatment or Punishment*, Office for the High Commissioner on Human Rights, A/HRC/22/53.

Mendez, J.E. (2016) *UN Human Rights Council, Report of the Special Rapporteur on Torture and Other Cruel, Inhuman or Degrading Treatment or Punishment*, Office for the High Commissioner on Human Rights, A/HRC/31/57.

Meoded Danon, L. (2018) 'Time matters for intersex bodies: between socio-medical time and somatic time', *Social Science & Medicine* 208: 89–97.

Michala, L., Liao, L-M., Wood, D., Conway, G.S. and Creighton, S.M. (2014) 'Practice changes in childhood surgery for ambiguous genitalia?', *Journal of Pediatric Urology* 10: 934–9.

Mieszczak, J., Houk, C.P. and Lee, P.A. (2009) 'Assignment of the sex of rearing in the neonate with a disorder of sex development', *Current Opinion in Pediatrics* 21: 541–7.

Minow, M. (1993–94) 'Law and social change', *UKMC Law Review* 62: 171–83.

Minto, C., Liao, L-M., Woodhouse, C.R.J., Ransley, P.G. and Creighton, S. (2003) 'The effects of clitoral surgery on sexual outcome in individuals who have intersex conditions with ambiguous genitalia: a cross-sectional study', *The Lancet* 361: 1252–7.

Money, J. (1952) *Hermaphroditism: An Inquiry into the Nature of Human Paradox* (PhD Dissertation, Harvard University).

Money, J. (1955) 'Hermaphroditism, gender and precocity in hyperadrenocorticism', *Bulletin of Johns Hopkins Hospital* 96: 253–64.

Money, J. (1963) 'Cytogenic and psychosexual incongruities with a note on space-form blindness', *American Journal of Psychiatry* 119: 820–7.

Money, J. (2002) *A First Person History of Pediatric Psychoendicrinology*, New York: Kluwer Academic.

Money, J. and Ehrhardt, A. (1972) *Man and Woman, Boy and Girl: The Differentiation and Dimorphism of Gender Identity from Conception to Maturity*, Baltimore, MD: Johns Hopkins University Press.

Money, J., Hampson, J. and Hampson J. (1955) 'Hermaphroditism: recommendations concerning assignment of sex, change of sex and psychologic management', *Bulletin of Johns Hopkins Hospital* 97: 284–300.

Money, J., Hampson, J. and Hampson J. (1955a) 'An examination of some basic sexual concepts: the evidence of human hermaphroditism', *Bulletin of Johns Hopkins Hospital* 97: 301–19.

Money, J., Hampson, J. and Hampson J. (1956) 'Sexual incongruities and psychopathology: the evidence of human hermaphroditism', *Bulletin of Johns Hopkins Hospital* 98: 43–57.

Money, J., Hampson, J. and Hampson J. (1957) 'Imprinting and the establishment of gender role', *American Medical Association Archives of Neurology and Psychiatry* 77: 333–6.

Monro, S., Carpenter, M., Crocetti, D., Davis, G., Garland, F., Griffiths et al (2021) 'Intersex: cultural and social perspectives', *Culture, Health & Sexuality* 23:4: 431–40.

Monro, S., Crocetti, D., Yeadon-Lee, T., Garland, F. and Travis, M. (2017) *Intersex, Variations of Sex Characteristics, and DSD: The Need for Change*, Huddersfield: University of Huddersfield.

Mora, S., Weber, G., Guarneri, M.P., Nizzoli, G., Pasolini, D. and Chiumello, G. (1992) 'Effect of estrogen replacement therapy on bone mineral content in girls with Turner Syndrome', *Obstetric Gynaecology* 79: 747–51.

Morland, I. (2014) 'Intersex', *Transgender Studies Quarterly* 1: 111–15.

Morland, I. (2015) 'Gender, genitals and the meaning of being human' in L. Downing, I. Morland and N. Sullivan (eds) *Fuckology*, Chicago, IL: University of Chicago Press, pp 69–99.

Morrison, S. (2013) 'Special report: intersex women speak out to protect the next generation' *The Independent*, [online] 30 November www.independent.co.uk/news/uk/home-news/special-report-intersex-women-speak-out-protect-next-generation-8974892.html [Accessed 17 June 2021].

Moss, P. and Dyck, I. (1999) 'Body, corporeal space, and legitimating chronic illness: Women diagnosed with M.E.', *Antipode* 31: 372–97.

Mulcahy, S. (2021) 'Dances with laws: from metaphor to methodology', *Law and Humanities* 15: 106–33.

Murphy, T. (1997) 'Feminism on flesh', *Law Critique* 8: 37–59.

Muscat, J. (2013) 'Malta for all key proposals from the 2013 electoral manifesto' *Maltese Government*, [online] www.um.edu.mt/__data/assets/pdf_file/0006/207348/PLElectionManifesto2013Key.pdf [Accessed 18 November 2021].

Naderifar, M., Goli, H. and Ghaljaei, F. (2017). 'Snowball sampling: a purposeful method of sampling in qualitative research', *Strides in Development of Medical Education*' 14: 1–4.

Naffine, N. (2003) 'Who are law's persons? From Cheshire cats to responsible subjects', *The Modern Law Review* 66: 346–67.

Naffine, N. (2009) *Law's Meaning of Life: Philosophy, Religion, Darwin and the Legal Person*, Oxford: Hart Publishing.

Newbery-Jones, C. (2018) 'Judging the judges: the image of the judge in the popular illustrated press' in J. Gregory, D.J.R. Grey and A. Bautz *Judgment in the Victorian Age*, London: Routledge, pp 161–81.

Ng, E. (2013) 'A "post-gay" era? Media gaystreaming, homonormativity, and the politics of LGBT integration', *Communication, Culture & Critique* 6: 258–83.

Nokoff, N., Palmer, B., Mullins, A.J., Aston, C.E., Austin, P., Baskin, L. et al (2017) 'Prospective assessment of cosmesis before and after genital surgery', *Journal of Pediatric Urology* 31: 28e1–e6.

Oakley, A. (1972) *Sex, Gender and Society*, London: Maurice Temple Smith Ltd.

Office of the High Commissioner for Human Rights (2019) 'Background note on human rights violations against intersex people' *Office of the High Commissioner for Human Rights*, [online] October www.ohchr.org/EN/Issues/Discrimination/Pages/BackgroundViolationsIntersexPeople.aspx [Accessed 15 November 2021].

OII Australia (2012) 'Submission on the proposed federal Human Rights and Anti-Discrimination Bill' *Parliament of Australia*, [online] www.aph.gov.au/Parliamentary_Business/Committees/Senate/Legal_and_Constitutional_Affairs/Completed%20inquiries/2010-13/antidiscrimination2012/submissions [Accessed 15 November 2021].

OII Australia (2013) 'Submission on the involuntary or coerced sterilisation of people with disabilities in Australia' *Intersex Human Rights Australia*, [online] 25 February https://ihra.org.au/21727/involuntary-sterilisation/ [Accessed 15 November 2021].
Orr, C.E. and Watson, A.D. (2021) ' "Usually the mother:" Dilation and the medical management of intersex children' in R. Bannerjee, and K. Mukhida (eds) *From Band-Aids to Scalpels: Motherhood Experiences in/of Medicine*, Bradford: Demeter Press, pp 65–83.
Overboe, J. (1999). 'Difference in itself: validating disabled people's lived experience', *Body & Society*, 5: 17–29.
Parsons, V. (2021) 'Progress Pride flag gets 2021 redesign to better represent intersex people' *Pink News*, [online] 7 June www.pinknews.co.uk/2021/06/07/progress-pride-flag-intersex-flag/ [Accessed 17 June 2021].
Patel, S. (2021) 'Gaps in the protection of athletes gender rights in sport – a regulatory riddle', *The International Sports Law Journal* 21: 257–75.
Perez, M.N., Delozier, A.M., Aston, C.E., Austin, P., Baskin, L., Ming Chan, Y. et al (2019) 'Predictors of psychosocial distress in parents of young children with disorders of sex development', *The Journal of Urology* 202: 1046–51.
Piaggio, L.A. (2014) 'Congenital adrenal hyperplasia: review from a surgeon's perspective in the beginning of the twenty-first century', *Frontiers in Pediatrics* 1(50): 1–7.
Pickersgill, M.D. (2014) 'Debating DSM-5: diagnosis and the sociology of critique', *Journal of Medical Ethics* 40: 521–5.
Preves, S. (2001) 'Sexing the intersexed: an analysis of sociocultural responses to intersexuality', *Signs: Journal of Women in Culture and Society* 27: 523–56.
Preves, S. (2003) *Intersex and Identity: The Contested Self*, London: Rutgers University Press.
Preves, S. (2005) 'Out of the O.R. and into the streets: exploring the impact of the intersex media activism', *Cardozo Journal of Law and Gender* 12(1): 247–88.
Priaulx, N. (2008) 'Rethinking progenitive conflict: why reproductive autonomy matters', *Medical Law Review* 16: 169–200.
REF 2021 (2019) Guidance on Submissions, [online] ref-2019_01-guidance-on-submissions.docx (live.com) [Accessed 30 November 2021].
Reilly, E. (2005) 'Radical tweak – relocating the power to assign sex – from enforcer of differentiation to facilitator of inclusiveness: revising the Response to Intersexuality', *Cardozo Journal of Law and Gender* 12(1): 297–336.
Reis, E. (2007) 'Divergence or disorder?: the politics of naming intersex', *Perspectives in Biology and Medicine* 50: 535–43.
Reis, E. (2009) *Bodies in Doubt: An American History of Intersex*, Baltimore, MD: Johns Hopkins University Press.

Reis, E. (2019) 'Did bioethics matter? A history of autonomy, consent, and intersex genital surgery', *Medical Law Review* 27: 658–74.

Renz, F. (2020a) 'Genders that don't matter: non-binary people and the Gender Recognition Act 2004' in S. Raj and P. Dunne (eds) *The Queer Outside in Law*, Switzerland: Palgrave Macmillan, pp 143–64.

Renz, F. (2020b) 'The challenge of same sex provision: how many girls does a girls' school need?', *feminists@ law* 10: 1–29.

Roen, K. (2009) 'Clinical intervention and embodied subjectivity: atypically sexed children and their parents' in M. Holmes (ed) *Critical Intersex*, Surrey: Ashgate, pp 15–40.

Roen, K. (2015) 'Intersex/DSD' in C. Richards, and M.J. Barker (eds) *The Palgrave Handbook of the Psychology of Sexuality and Gender*, London: Palgrave Macmillan, pp 183–97.

Roen, K. (2019) 'Intersex or diverse sex development: critical review of psychosocial health care research and indications for practice', *Journal of Sex Research* 56: 511–28.

Roen, K. and Pasterski, V. (2014) 'Psychological research and intersex/DSD: recent developments and future directions', *Psychology and Sexuality* 5: 102–16.

Rogers, L. and Walsh, J. (1982) 'Shortcomings of the psychomedical research of John Money and co-workers into sex differences in behaviour: social and political implications', *Sex Roles* 8: 269–81.

Rolston A.M., Gardner, M., van Leeuwenet, K., Mohnach, L., Keegan, C., Délot, E. (2017) 'Disorders of sex development (DSD): clinical service delivery in the United States', *American Journal of Medical Genetics* 175: 268–78.

Rosario, V.A. (2009) 'Quantum sex: intersex and the molecular deconstruction of sex', *GLQ* 15: 267–84.

Rose, N. (2009) 'Normality and pathology in a biomedical age', *The Sociological Rev* 57: 66–83.

Rubin, D.A. (2017) *Intersex Matters: Biomedical Embodiment, Gender Recognition and Transnational Activism*, New York: State University of New York Press.

Rubin, K. (1998) 'Turner Syndrome and osteoporosis: mechanisms and prognosis', *Pediatrics* 102: 481–5.

Sandberg, D.E., Gardner, M., Callens, N., Mazur, T., the DSD-TRN Psychosocial Workgroup, the DSD-TRN Advocacy Advisory Network, and Accord Alliance (2017) 'Interdisciplinary care in disorders/differences of sex development (DSD): the psychosocial component of the DSD – Translational research network', *American Journal of Medical Genetics* 175: 279–92.

Sanders, C. and Carter, B. (2015) 'A qualitative study of communication between young women with disorders of sex development and health professionals', *Advances in Nursing* 2015: 1–7.

Santos, A.C. (2013) 'Are we there yet? Queer sexual encounters, legal recognition and homonormativity', *Journal of Gender Studies* 22: 54–64.

Sax, L. (2002) 'How common is intersex? A response to Anne Fausto-Sterling', *The Journal of Sex Research* 39: 174–8.

Schweizer, K., Brunner, F., Gedrose, B., Handford, C. and Richter-Appelt, H. (2017) 'Coping with diverse sex development: treatment experiences and psychosocial support during childhood and adolescence and adult well-being', *Journal of Pediatric Psychology* 42: 504–19.

Schweizer, K., Brunner, F., Handford, C. and Richter-Appelt, H. (2014) 'Gender experience and satisfaction with gender allocation in adults with diverse intersex conditions (divergences of sex development, DSD)', *Psychology & Sexuality*, 5: 56–82.

Scottish Government (2018) 'Convention on the elimination of all forms of discrimination against women: position statement', *Scottish Government*, [online] 2 May www.gov.scot/Publications/2018/05/4431/3 [Accessed 15 November 2021].

Senate Legal and Constitutional Affairs Committee (2013) 'Chapter 7: Committee views and recommendations' *Parliament of Australia*, [online] www.aph.gov.au/Parliamentary_Business/Committees/Senate/Legal_and_Constitutional_Affairs/Completed_inquiries/2010-13/antidiscrimination2012/report/c07 [Accessed 15 November 2021].

Sharkey, C.M., Bakula, D.M., Wolfe-Christensen, C., Austin, P., Baskin, L., Bernabé, K.J. et al (2018) 'Parent-rated severity of illness and anxiety among caregivers of children born with a disorder of sex development including ambiguous genitalia', *Hormone Research in Paediatrics* 90: 308–13.

Sharpe, A. (2009a) *Foucault's Monsters and the Challenge of Law*, Oxon: Routledge.

Sharpe, A. (2009b). 'Gender recognition in the UK: a great leap forward', *Social & Legal Studies* 18: 241–5.

Shaw, J.D.M. (2020) 'Confronting jurisdiction with antinomian bodies', *Law, Culture and the Humanities* 1–26.

Shaw, J.D.M. (2021) 'The spatio-legal production of bodies through the legal fiction of death', *Law and Critique* 32: 69–90.

Spurgas, A. (2009) '(Un)queering identity: the biosocial production of intersex/DSD' in M. Holmes (ed) *Critical Intersex*, Oxon: Routledge, pp 97–123.

StopIGM (2019) 'Genital mutilation: how Malta's law fails intersex children' *StopIGM.org*, [online] 15 May https://stopigm.org/genital-mutilation-how-malta-law-fails-intersex-children/ [Accessed 18 November 2021].

Streuli, J.C., Vayena, E., Cavicchia-Balmer, Y. and Huber, J. (2013) 'Shaping parents: impact of contrasting professional counseling on parents' decision making for children with disorders of sex development', *The Journal of Sexual Medicine* 10: 1953–60.

Sudai, M. (2017) 'Changing ethical and legal norms in the management of differences of sex development', *The Lancet Diabetes and Endocrinology* 5: 764–6.

Sudai, M. (2021) 'Sex ambiguity in early modern common law (1629–1787)', *Law and Social Inquiry*: 1–36. doi: 10.1017/lsi.2021.34.

Talmy, S. (2011) 'The interview as collaborative achievement: interaction, identity, and ideology in a speech event', *Applied Linguistics* 32: 25–42.

Tasmanian Law Reform Institution (2020) 'Legal recognition of sex and gender Final Report No 31' *University of Tasmania*, [online] June www.utas.edu.au/__data/assets/pdf_file/0018/1342080/tlri-legal-recognition-of-sex-final-report.pdf [Accessed 15 November 2021].

Taylor Goldhill, F. (2016) 'UK questioned over intersex genital mutilations by UN Committee on the Rights of the Child – Gov Non-Answer + Denial' 72nd Session of the UN Committee on the Rights of the Child (CRC), [online] 23 May, http://stop.genitalmutilation.org/post/UK-Questioned-over-Intersex-Genital-Mutilations-by-UN-Committee-on-the-Rights-of-the-Child [Accessed 2 April 2021].

Tauchert, A. (2002) 'Fuzzy gender: between female-embodiment and intersex', *Journal of Gender Studies* 11(1): 29–38.

Theilen, J. (2020) 'Subversion subverted: developments in German Civil Status Law on the Recognition of Intersex and Non-Binary Persons' in E. Brems, T. Moonen and P. Cannoot (eds) *Protecting trans* rights in the age of gender self-determination*, Cambridge: Intersentia, pp 95–120.

Thomson, M. (2007) *Endowed: Regulating the Male Sexed Body*, New York: Routledge.

Thomson, M. (2022) 'The foetal subject: law, gender & embodiment' in S.H. Vauchez and R. Rubio-Marín (eds) *Cambridge Companion to Gender & Law*, Cambridge: Cambridge University Press, pp 61–97.

Timmermans, S., Yang, A., Gardner, M., Keegan, C.E., Yashar, B.M., Fechner, P.Y. et al (2019) 'Gender destinies: assigning gender in disorders of sex development-intersex clinics', *Sociology of Health & Illness* 41: 1520–34.

Topp, S.S. (2013) 'Against the quiet revolution: the rhetorical construction of intersex individuals as disordered', *Sexualities* 16: 180–94.

Travis, M. (2014) 'Non-normative bodies, rationality and legal personhood', *Medical Law Review* 22: 526–47.

Travis, M. (2015) 'Accommodating intersexuality in European Union anti-discrimination law', *European Law Journal* 21(2): 180–99.

Travis, M. (2019) 'The vulnerability of heterosexuality: consent, gender deception and embodiment', *Social and Legal Studies* 28: 303–26.

Turner, S. (1999) 'Intersex identities: locating new intersections of sex and gender', *Gender and Society* 13(4): 457–79.

UNCRC (2019) 'Concluding observations on the combined third to sixth periodic reports of Malta' CRC/C/MLT/CO/3-6, *UNCRC*, [online] www.ohchr.org/en/documents/concluding-observations/crccmltco3-6-committee-rights-child-concluding-observations [Accessed 16 September 2021].

Vipond, E. (2015) 'Trans rights will not protect us: the limits of equal rights discourse, antidiscrimination laws, and hate crime legislation', *Western Journal of Legal Studies* 6: 1–20.

Vitulli, E. (2010) 'A defining moment in civil rights history? The Employment Non-Discrimination Act, trans-inclusion, and homonormativity', *Sex Res Soc Policy* 7: 155–67.

von Wahl, A. (2019) 'From object to subject: intersex activism and the rise and fall of the gender binary in Germany', *Social Politics* 0: 1–23.

Wang, L. and Poppas, P. (2017) 'Surgical outcomes and complications of reconstructive surgery in the female congenital adrenal hyperplasia patient: what every endocrinologist should know', *The Journal of Steroid Biochemistry and Molecular Biology* 165: 137–44.

Warner, M. (1991) 'Introduction: fear of a queer planet', *Social Text* 29: 3–17.

Warner, M. (1999) *The Trouble With Normal: Sex, Politics, and the Ethics of Queer Life*, New York: The Free Press.

Wilhelm, E. (1909) *Die Rechtliche Stellung Der (Korperlichen) Zwitter De Lege Lata Und De Lege Ferenda*, Halle.

Wilkins, L. (1957) *The Diagnosis and Treatment of Endocrine Disorders in Childhood and Adolescence* (2nd edn) Springfield: Charles, C. Thomas.

Williams, D.I. (1952) 'The diagnosis of intersex', *British Medical Journal*, 14: 1264.

Williams, P. (1980) *Open Secret: The First Question* BBC (First Aired 12 March 1980, 21:35).

Wilson, B.E. and Reiner, W.G. (1998) 'Management of intersex: a shifting paradigm', *Journal of Clinical Ethics* 9: 360–9.

Wolfe-Christensen, C., Wisniewski, A.B., Mullins, A.J., Reyes, K.J., Austin, P., Baskin, L. et al (2017) 'Changes in levels of parental distress after their child with atypical genitalia undergoes genitoplasty', *Journal of Pediatric Urology* 13: 32.e1-32.e6.

Yankovic, F., Cherian, A., Steven, L., Mathur, A. and Cuckow, P. (2013) 'Current practice in feminizing surgery for congenital adrenal hyperplasia: a specialist survey', *Journal of Pediatric Urology* 9: 1103–10.

Young, H.H. (1937) *Genital Abnormalities: Hermaphroditism and Related Adrenal Diseases*, Baltimore: Williams & Wilkins.

Young, I.M. (1990) *Justice and the Politics of Difference*, Oxford: Princeton University Press.

Zillén, K., Garland, J. and Slokenberga, S. (2017) *The Rights of Children in Biomedicine: Challenges Posed by Scientific Advances and Uncertainties*, Strasbourg: Committee on Bioethics of the Council of Europe.

Index

References to endnotes show both the page number and the note number (231n3).